BLACK & DE

THE COMPLETE GUIDE TO
WOOD STORAGE
PROJECTS

Built-in & Freestanding Projects
For All Around the Home

Creative Publishing
international

CHANHASSEN, MINNESOTA
www.creativepub.com

Credits

President/CEO: Ken Fund

For Revised Edition:
Editors: Tom Lemmer, Matthew Paymar
Executive Editor: Bryan Trandem
Assistant Managing Editor: Tracy Stanley
Photo Director: Tim Himsel
Art Director: Jon Simpson
Photographer: Steve Galvin
Scene Shop Carpenter: Randy Austin
Production Manager: Laura Hokkanen

**Creative Publishing
international**

Contents

Ready, Set ... Throw It Out

There's an old adage that if you haven't worn an item of clothing in the past year and can't imagine wearing it in the next year, you probably won't ever wear it again. If this basic concept is true for outdated ties or sweaters, isn't it also true for many other items gathering dust on shelves somewhere in your home?

The message is this: The best storage container may be the trash bin. Or the home of someone who will use an item you've outgrown.

You can simplify your storage issues by sorting through your belongings to determine what you should keep and what you should throw away. You may be relieved to find the situation isn't quite as bad as you feared.

Do yourself a favor and get rid of items that have no purpose. Getting rid of items doesn't mean they're wasted—you can give them away, sell them in a garage sale, or donate them to charity. Remember: One person's trash is another person's treasure.

After you've eliminated unnecessary clutter, sort through the remaining items and figure out where they belong. Get the telephone books out of the pantry and into the home office, move that power drill from the file cabinet to the workshop, transport the spare toilet paper rolls from the laundry to the bathroom.

When you've finished these important steps, look at the projects in this book and decide which of them will be most valuable to you.

Planning New Storage

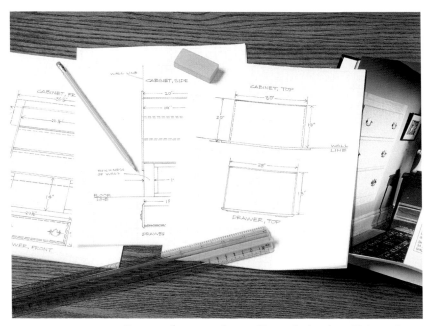

Use graph paper when making scale drawings. Make cutting diagrams as well, to ensure that you use sheet goods and dimensional lumber efficiently.

Before you begin building any storage project, take the time to plan it out properly. Complete the following steps to avoid problems during and after installation.

Visualize the effects the project will have on your living environment. Larger built-in projects that take several days to build may tie up living areas that are used on a daily basis. Consider the impact on your existing decor and furniture as well. To indicate the boundaries of the project, make a cardboard template, or apply masking tape to the floor. You may find that the project will work better in another part of the room, or that a different project will better suit your needs.

Make scale drawings of your project to familiarize yourself with how it goes together. Then make cutting diagrams of sheet goods to help make efficient use of materials. When laying out cutting lines, remember that the blade of the saw will consume up to ⅛" of material.

Consider access problems to specific rooms.

Tight corners, narrow doorways, and shallow stairwells can make it impossible to maneuver large projects into specific spaces. Accurately measure all stairways, turns, and doorways before you begin. If the project won't fit, alter the construction or build it in place, in the room it will occupy.

Locate all plumbing pipes, electrical lines, and heating ducts before you begin projects that require cutting holes in walls. Use a stud finder to locate wall studs and ceiling joists when fastening a project to the wall or ceiling. Don't blindly drill holes in walls: Doing so is risky.

Practice your skills, especially if you'll be using tools that are unfamiliar to you. Follow all manufacturers' directions. Power tools, such as sanders, routers, drills, and saws, operate at high speeds and can be dangerous if not used properly and with the right protection.

Make a cardboard template or tape outline to help you visualize the end result of a project and draw your attention to issues that aren't obvious from a scale drawing.

BASIC TECHNIQUES

Having the right tool for the right job is half the battle when building any project; the other half of the battle is using the right technique. The techniques in this section will be used in many of the projects in this book. If you have difficulty cutting straight lines with a circular saw, build the guide on page 18. Even if you've never used a router before, you'll be cutting dado and rabbet grooves in no time with the jig and the techniques described on page 19. Refer to this section whenever a project includes a technique that's new to you.

This section also includes step-by-step projects for building basic storage components, such as drawers, shelves, and doors. Refer to these projects to make variations to existing storage units you already own, or to the storage projects featured in this book.

Always operate power tools with caution, following the manufacturer's recommendations for ear and eye protection. Wear a particle mask or respirator to avoid inhaling fine sawdust particles, and always work in a well-ventilated area when using products that emit harmful vapors.

IN THIS SECTION:

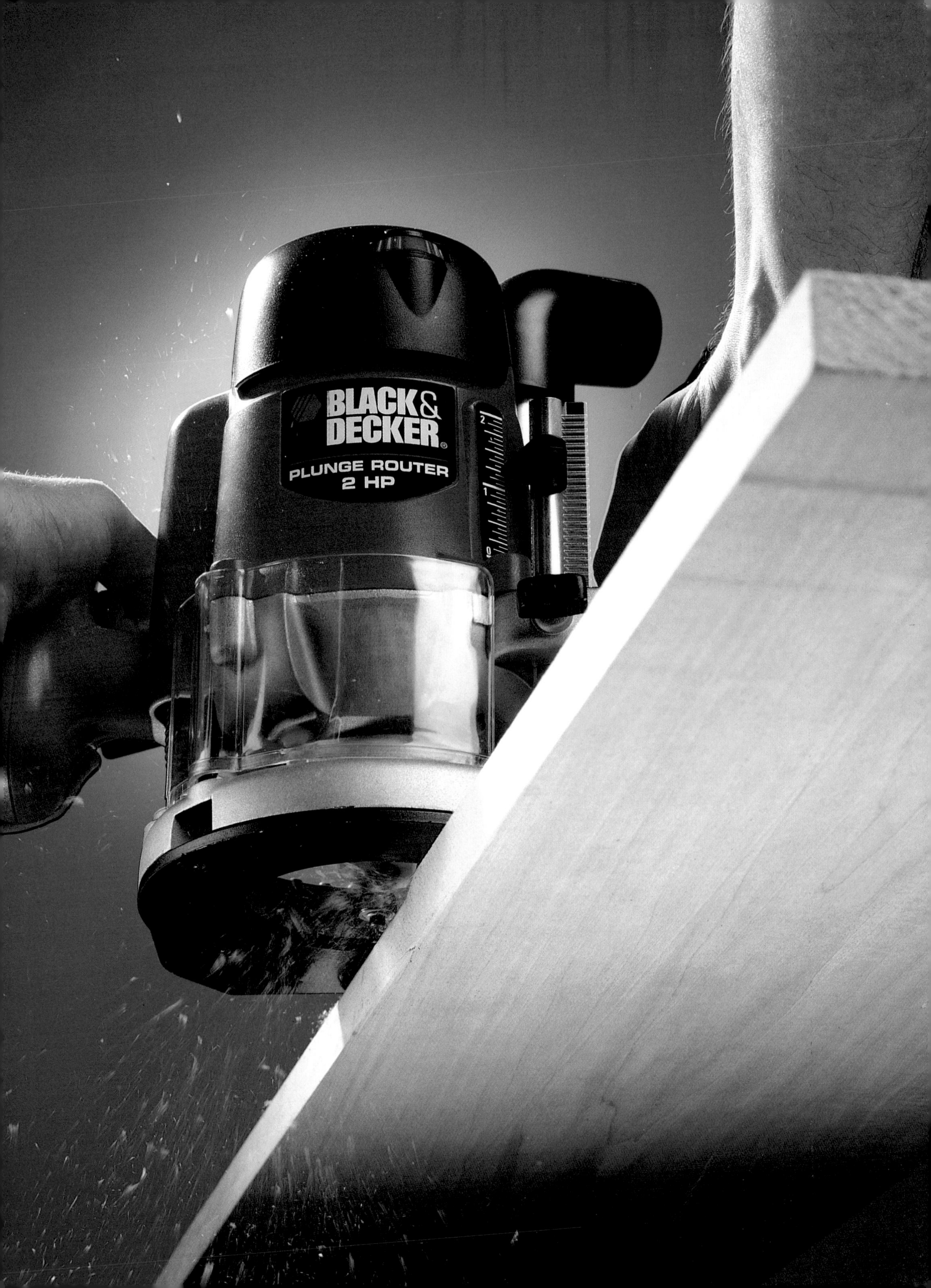
BLACK&DECKER
PLUNGE ROUTER
2 HP

Tools

Every do-it-yourselfer should own a variety of general-purpose tools for maintenance, remodeling, and new construction projects.

Most of the tools used to complete the projects in this book are shown here. If you don't own all of these tools, you shouldn't feel compelled to run out and purchase an entire collection in one day. Most beginning do-it-yourselfers purchase tools as neces-

Tape measure

3-in-1 tool

Torpedo level

Rubber mallet

Hammer

Jig saw

Propane torch

Cordless drill

sary to complete the projects they want to do.

Buy the highest quality tools you can afford. When you buy a low-quality tool you save a few short-term dollars, but you'll probably need to buy the same tool again in a few years. High-quality tools last longer and work better. Whatever the size of your collection, keep your tools well organized in a box or a workstation.

Framing square

Combination square

Pliers

Adjustable wrench

Needlenose pliers

Quick clamp

Channel-type pliers

Utility knife

Tubing cutter

Belt sander

Palm sander

Router

Circular saw

Materials

The projects in this book call for a variety of widely available lumber and hardware products, as shown here. Keep in mind that each project includes a list of suggested construction materials. If you plan on making adaptations to a project, make sure the materials you choose are strong enough to support the loads you plan to store.

Oak plywood

Birch plywood

Pine plywood

THE Fastener Center

Copper fittings

Copper pipe

Electrical conduit

Wood screws

Wire brads

Wallboard screws

Compression fittings

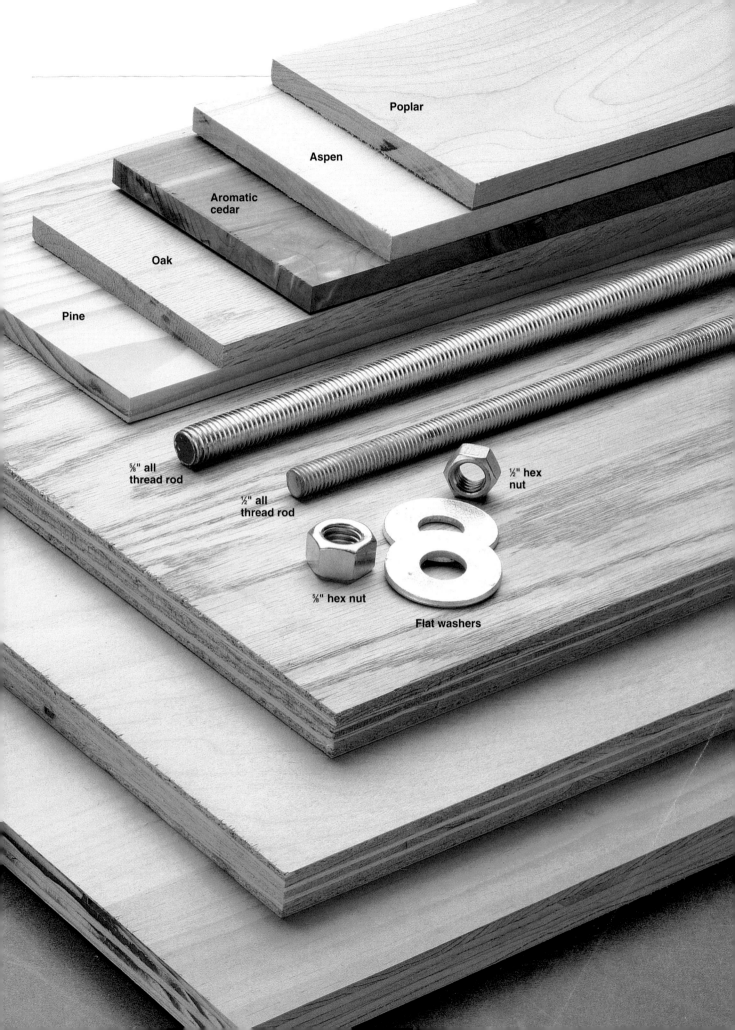

Poplar

Aspen

Aromatic
cedar

Oak

Pine

⅝" all
thread rod

½" all
thread rod

½" hex
nut

⅝" hex nut

Flat washers

Cutting & Soldering Pipe

A soldered pipe joint, also known as a *sweated* joint, is made by heating a copper or brass fitting with a propane torch until the fitting is just hot enough to melt solder. The heat then draws the solder into the gap between the fitting and the copper pipe, forming a strong seal. Because the pipe used in these projects will not carry water, you don't need to worry if the joints aren't perfect.

Using too much heat is the most common mistake made by beginners. To avoid this error, remember that the tip of the torch's inner flame produces the most heat. Direct the flame carefully—solder will flow in the direction heat has traveled. Heat the pipe just until the flux sizzles; remove the flame and touch the solder to the pipe. The heated pipe will quickly melt the solder.

Soldering copper pipe and fittings isn't difficult, but it requires some patience and skill. It's a good idea to practice soldering pieces of scrap before taking on a large project.

Directions: Soldered Copper Joints

Step A: CUT THE PIPE.
1. Measure and mark the pipe. Then place a tubing cutter over the pipe, with the cutting wheel centered over the marked line.
2. Tighten the cutting wheel onto the pipe by rotating the handle, and then turn the tubing cutter one rotation to score a continuous line around the pipe. Next, rotate the cutter in the other direction. After every two rotations, tighten the handle until the pipe separates.
3. Remove the metal burrs from the inside edge of the cut pipe, using the reaming point on the tubing cutter.

Step B: CLEAN THE PIPE & FITTINGS.
To form a good seal with solder, the ends of all pipes and the insides of all fittings must be free of dirt and grease. Sand the outer edge of the pipes with an emery cloth and scour the inside connections of the fittings with a wire brush.

Step C: FLUX & DRY FIT THE PIPES.
1. Apply a thin layer of water-soluble paste flux to the end of each pipe, using a flux brush. The flux

A. Position the tubing cutter, and score a line around the pipe. Rotate the cutter around the pipe until it separates.

B. Clean the inside of the fittings with a wire brush.

C. Brush a thin layer of flux onto the end of each pipe. Assemble the joint, twisting the fitting to spread the flux.

should cover about 1" of the end of the pipe.

2. Insert the pipes into the fitting until they are snug against the fitting socket, and twist the fitting slightly to spread the flux. If a series of pipes and fittings (a "run") is involved, flux and dry-fit the entire run without soldering any of the joints. When you're sure the run is correctly assembled and everything fits, take it apart and prepare to solder the joints.

Step D: HEAT THE FITTINGS.

1. Shield flammable work surfaces from the heat of the torch. Although heat-absorbent pads are available for this purpose, you can use a double layer of 26-gauge sheet metal. The reflective quality of the sheet metal helps joints heat evenly.

2. Unwind 8" to 10" of solder from the spool. To make it easier to maneuver the solder around a joint, bend the first 2" of the solder at a 90° angle.

3. Open the gas valve and light the propane torch. Adjust the valve until the inner portion of the flame is 1" to 2" long.

4. Hold the flame tip against the middle of the fitting for 4 or 5 seconds or until the flux begins to sizzle. Heat the other side of the joint, distributing the heat evenly. Move the heat around the joint in the direction the solder should flow. Touch the solder to the pipe, just below the fitting. If it melts, the joint is hot enough.

Step E: APPLY THE SOLDER & CLEAN THE JOINT.
Quickly apply solder along both seams of the fitting, allowing capillary action to draw the liquefied solder into the fitting. When the joint is filled, solder begins to form droplets on the bottom. A correctly soldered joint shows a thin bead of silver-colored solder around the lip of the fitting. It typically takes about ½" of solder to fill a joint in ½" pipe. If the solder pools around the fitting rather than filling the joint as it cools, reheat the area until the solder liquefies and is drawn in slightly. NOTE: Always turn off the propane torch immediately after you've finished soldering; make sure the gas valve is completely closed.

Step F: WIPE AWAY EXCESS SOLDER & CHECK THE JOINT.
1. Let the joint sit undisturbed until the solder loses its shiny color. Don't touch it before then—the copper will be quite hot.
2. When the joint is cool enough to touch, wipe away the excess flux and solder, using a clean, dry rag. When the joint is completely cool, check for gaps around the edges. If you find gaps, apply more flux to the rim and resolder it.

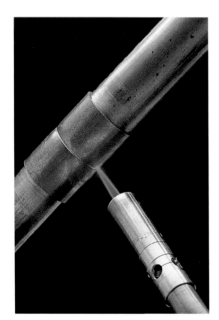

D. *Heat the fitting until the flux begins to sizzle. Concentrate the tip of the torch's flame on the middle of the fitting.*

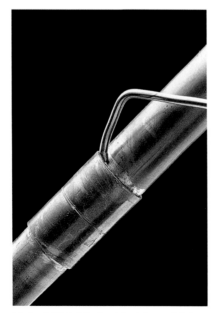

E. *Push ½" to ¾" of solder into each joint, allowing capillary action to draw the liquefied solder into the joint.*

F. *When the joint has cooled, wipe away excess solder with a dry rag. Be careful: Pipes will be hot.*

Tool Techniques

Building your own storage project for any area of your home can be an extremely rewarding experience, especially when the result is a clutter-free environment. But if a project requires the use of a tool you haven't used before, you need an introduction to the tool in order to use it properly and safely.

The following tools and techniques are used throughout this book. Remember to follow the safety precautions outlined in the owner's manual whenever operating a power tool.

Circular saw

The circular saw is a frequently used, general-purpose saw. It can make straight and beveled cuts in a variety of materials. Use a circular saw to make rip or cross cuts in sheet goods, as well as dimensional lumber. To avoid injuring yourself or damaging the saw, always use the proper blade for the material you are cutting.

To operate a circular saw, line up the cutting guide with the waste side of your cutting line, start the saw, and push it through the material, using even pressure. Practice using your circular saw on scrap material before cutting the workpiece; continue practicing until you've learned to recognize exactly where the cut will fall. If you have difficulty making straight cuts, see page 18.

Jig saw

The jig saw is an ideal tool for cutting curves or smaller straight cuts in situations where a circular saw would be impractical.

A wide variety of jig saw blades are available for different types of cuts. Some jig saw blades are designed to make rough or smooth cuts, while others are sized to make tight curves.

Standard blades cut on the up stroke. This upward cutting action sometimes causes splintering on the top side of the workpiece. For this reason, always cut from the back (or unexposed) side of your workpiece. Reverse-tooth jig saw blades are also available. These blades, which cut on the down stroke, provide a cleaner cut on the surface of the material in situations where turning the workpiece over isn't possible.

Before making cuts with a jig saw, clamp your workpiece firmly in place so it overhangs the edge of the worksurface. Otherwise, the vibration of the saw may cause your workpiece to "jump" from the worksurface. Jumping may cause the blade to bounce off the cutting line, or may bend or break the blade.

Maintain constant pressure when making a cut, and release the pressure as you approach the end of the cutting line. To make internal cutouts with a jig saw, drill starter holes near the cutting lines and then finish the cutout with the saw.

Line up the cutting guide *of the circular saw with waste side of the cutting line and push the saw through the material with even pressure.*

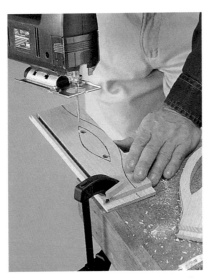

Make contoured internal cutouts *by drilling starter holes and cutting along the lines with a jig saw.*

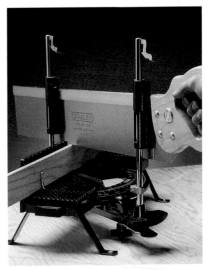

Make angled cuts *in decorative trim moldings with a hand miter box to add a stylish flair to your project.*

Hand miter box

Use a hand miter box equipped with a backsaw to make straight or precisely-angled cuts in molding and decorative trim pieces.

To make cuts with a hand miter box, line the blade of the saw up with the cutting line on your workpiece so the width of the blade is on the waste side of the mark. Hold the workpiece securely in place against the box fence, and start the cut with a back stroke. Keep the blade level with the workpiece on each stroke of the cut.

Belt sander

A belt sander makes short work of sanding tasks and can also be used as a shaping tool.

When operating a belt sander, apply even pressure and always sand with the grain of the workpiece. Do not hold a belt sander in one place for an extended period of time, or you may scorch the surface of the wood.

To use a belt sander as a shaping tool, mount it to your workbench in a bench-top vise with large hand-screws or C-clamps. Then clamp a scrap board to your workbench to use as a platform. Keep the work-piece square and level with the sanding belt. To create identical shapes, clamp the pieces together before shaping them. This technique is known as gang-sanding.

Combination square

The combination square is a multi-purpose measuring tool available with standard ruler lengths of 12" or 16". Combination squares are used to measure and mark cutting lines, check projects for square and level, and mark 45° and 90° angles.

Although precise measurements can be made with a ruler or a tape measure, the combination square speeds up the process and simplifies accurate measuring and marking.

Compass

A compass is a simple, yet indispensible tool, that is often overlooked or forgotten. Throughout this book, however, we suggest using a compass and a grid pattern to create detailed curves and shapes. To do this, you'll need to enlarge and copy the provided grid pattern onto your workpiece, and use the grid to mark accurate centers and endpoints for the shapes. Then, use a compass to create smooth roundovers and curves that connect the points.

Clamp a belt sander and a scrap board to the workbench to create a stationary shaping tool.

Use a combination square to mark a parallel line on the edge of the workpiece.

Use a compass and a square grid pattern to draw cutting lines for curves and shapes on your workpiece.

Making Straight Cuts

One of the most difficult tasks for do-it-your-selfers is cutting straight lines. Whether you need to square off the end of a 2 × 4 or rip an 8-ft. length of plywood, it's all too easy to get off course and ruin your workpiece. Using a straightedge guide greatly simplifies the process of cutting straight lines.

A straightedge guide can be adapted to help you make perfectly straight cuts with a router, circular saw, or jig saw. The best length for your straightedge depends on the workpiece you will be cutting.

Our straightedge guide features a strip of ¼" plywood with a 1 × 2 cleat attached to the top. When using the guide, the base of the cutting tool rides against the cleat. Many woodworkers make straightedge guides in 2-ft., 4-ft., and 8-ft. lengths for convenience. If you plan to use the guide with a router, make sure you trim the plywood with the same bit that you will be using for your project. Make a straightedge guide for each type of router bit you plan to use.

Directions: Straightedge Guide

Step A: PREPARE THE PLYWOOD.
Mark a straight line lengthwise onto a 10"-wide strip of ¼" plywood, about 4" from the edge. Use a 4-ft. carpenter's level or metal ruler to draw the straight line. Cut a 1 × 2 cleat to the length of the 10" plywood piece.

Step B: INSTALL THE CLEAT.
Apply glue to the bottom of the cleat, then position it along the line marked on the plywood. Clamp one end of the cleat to the plywood, adding additional clamps every 12". If necessary, bend the cleat to follow the line. Let the glue dry and remove the clamps.

Step C: CREATE THE SETBACK.
To create the proper setback for a router, circular saw, or jig saw, cut off the excess plywood, using the tool with which you plan to use the guide. Keep the base or foot of the tool firmly against the cleat as you cut.

A. *Use a carpenter's level to mark a straight line on the plywood strip.*

B. *Fasten the cleat to the plywood with glue, and clamp the cleat every 12".*

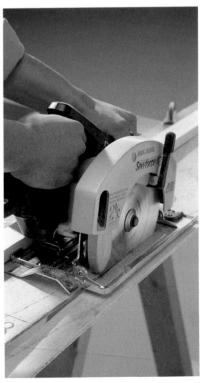

C. *Cut off the excess using a circular saw, router, or jig saw.*

Making Dado & Rabbet Joints

Dadoes and rabbets are two grooved joints often used when building a shelving unit or cabinet. You'll need a router to cut these joints.

Dado joints are used to hold the ends of shelves or the bottom panel of a drawer in place. The groove of a dado joint is routed into the body of a workpiece with a non-piloted, straight bit.

A rabbet joint is similar to a dado, except the groove is routed onto the very edge of a workpiece, so the groove is exposed on one side. Rabbet joints are used when insetting the back or top panel of a cabinet to provide greater lateral support. The groove of a rabbet joint is routed into the edge of the work- piece with a piloted rabbet bit. All rabbet bits have base pilots that guide the bit across the edge of the workpiece.

Use high-quality router bits with carbide blades, especially when routing grooves in harder woods like oak.

Directions: Dado Joints

Step A: MARK DADO LOCATION & SET UP THE ROUTER.
1. Hold the shelf panel perpendicular to the side panel so that the edges are flush, and mark the location of each dado groove with a pencil.
2. Install a straight bit no wider than the width of the planned dado. Make sure the bit diameter is no more than the width of the planned dado. Standard dado depth is half as deep as the thickness of the wood; for a ¾"-thick panel, for example, dadoes should be ⅜" deep. When routing deep dadoes or rabbets in thicker stock, make multiple shallow passes with the router to avoid excessive stress on the router motor or bit.

Step B: SET UP THE STRAIGHTEDGE GUIDES.
Clamp a straightedge guide (page 18) on each side of the planned dado, so the edges of the guides are flush with the marked lines. Check the spacing of the straightedge guides with a piece of scrap wood the same thickness as the planned dado.

Step C: CUT THE DADO.
Rout the dado by making two passes with the router. Make the first pass with the base of the router held

A. *Mark the location of the dado groove with a pencil.*

B. *Clamp straightedge guides on each side of the planned dado, in line with the reference lines from Step A.*

C. *Rout the dado with two passes, holding the router base firmly against the straightedge cleats.*

tightly against one straightedge cleat, then make the second pass in the opposite direction with the router base held against the other cleat.

Step D: REINFORCE THE JOINT.
1. Apply wood glue to the surfaces being joined, then clamp the pieces together at a right angle.
2. Draw a reference line across the back face of the joint to help you align each fastener with the joint. Then, drill pilot holes on the line, spaced 3" to 4" apart.
3. Reinforce each joint with screws or finish nails driven into the pilot holes. When using screws, counterbore the pilot holes with a larger drill bit and cover the holes with wood putty or wood plugs.

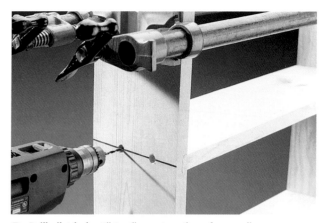

D. *Drill pilot holes 3" to 4" apart on the reference line. Counterbore the pilot holes If you plan on using screws.*

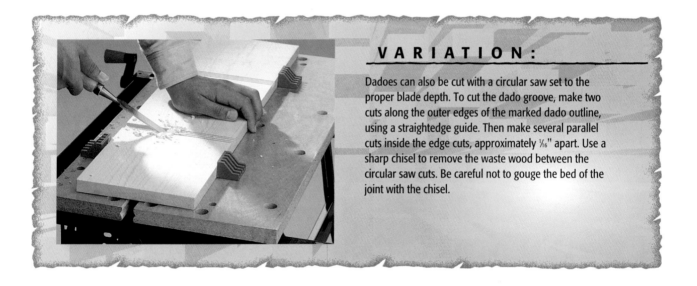

VARIATION:

Dadoes can also be cut with a circular saw set to the proper blade depth. To cut the dado groove, make two cuts along the outer edges of the marked dado outline, using a straightedge guide. Then make several parallel cuts inside the edge cuts, approximately $\frac{1}{16}$" apart. Use a sharp chisel to remove the waste wood between the circular saw cuts. Be careful not to gouge the bed of the joint with the chisel.

Directions: Rabbet Joints

1. Clamp the workpiece firmly in place so that it overhangs the work surface. Use a rabbet bit with the same cutting width as the thickness of the adjoining piece, and set the depth of the cut equal to one-half the thickness of the workpiece.
2. Making sure the bit is not in contact with the workpiece, turn on the router—with the base flat against the workpiece—and rout the rabbet groove, working from left to right.

Rabbet grooves are routed *into the edge of a panel and are used to join two panels into a 90° corner.*

Finishing Touches

Careful finishing work on any project is as important as good construction. An excellent finish will improve the appearance, protect the wood, and hide small errors and imperfections in your project.

Every finishing job consists of three equally important stages: filling gaps and nail holes; sanding and cleaning; and applying a top-coat finish of tinted oil, stain, or paint.

Filling gaps and nail holes with wood putty can be difficult, especially if you are attempting to completely conceal the head of a large fastener. However, there are a wide variety of tinted putties to choose from, making it possible to find an exact match for your stain. Wood plugs made from the same material as the workpiece are easier to conceal than putty, but require additional sanding, sawing, and gluing.

Generally it is easiest to apply finish or paint after the project is assembled, but for projects with deep shelves, consider sanding and finishing the pieces before assembling them. Traditional wood finishes are made from successive coats of sealer, stain, and several coats of varnish or shellac. Newer, one-step finishes also produce a quality finish, and are much quicker and easier to apply.

No matter what products you choose for your finish, carefully read the manufacturer's directions. Always work in a well-ventilated area when working with stain, varnish, or paint.

Use heat-activated veneer tape to cover unfinished edges of plywood or particleboard panels. Bond the tape with a household iron, then rub it with a block of hardwood, and trim the edges with a utility knife. Lightly sand the edges to smooth them.

Specialty tools and materials for finishing work include: 120-grit sanding belt, staining pad, untinted wood filler, clear polyurethane, tack cloth, finish-nail holder, tinted filler sticks, paintbrush with blended bristles, putty knife, and sandpaper in 80-, 120-, and 220-grit sheets.

Painted finishes require a primer coat of sanding sealer to provide a smooth undercoat, followed by one or two coats of latex or oil-based enamel.

Basic Cabinets

Basic cabinets are the backbone for storage in almost every home. These basic cabinets are built with oak plywood, which gives them the look of fine custom-made cabinets, but at a much-reduced cost. The wall cabinet features glass-panel doors, pur-

chased separately, that create an ideal display area for glassware or china. The base cabinet has extra-large drawers that are well suited for storing table linens. However, the drawers, shelves, and doors can be varied to suit just about any purpose.

You can use the methods shown to build a single base cabinet with a wall cabinet above it, or several cabinets side by side for a full wall of storage or display. Use a different type of lumber to build utility cabinets in a basement or garage, or match the existing cabinetry in a kitchen or bathroom.

Keep in mind that both of these cabinets use dado and rabbet grooves as a basic method of joinery. Refer to the diagram for each cabinet for the precise size and location of each groove.

These basic cabinets are easily adapted for any room of the house, providing a wide variety of storage solutions.

TOOLS & MATERIALS*

- Electronic stud finder
- Hammer
- Tape measure
- Router with bits
- Drill with bits
- Right-angle drill guide
- Pegboard scraps
- Clamps
- Level
- Utility screws (¾", 1", 2½", 3½")
- Wood glue
- Finish nails (1", 1½", 2", 3", 4")
- Shims
- Utility knife
- Pin-style shelf supports
- Finishing materials
- Trim or base shoe molding
- Tape

Wall Cabinet
- (1) 2 × 4 × 54" pine
- (1) 1 × 3" × 3 ft. pine
- (3) 1 × 3" × 6 ft. oak
- (1) ¾" × 4 × 8 ft. oak plywood
- (1) ¼" × 4 × 4 ft. oak plywood

Base Cabinet
- (3) 1 × 3" × 8 ft. oak
- (1) 1 × 6" × 6 ft. oak
- (1) ¾" × 4 × 8 ft. oak plywood
- (1) ½" × 4 × 4 ft. oak plywood

* List does not include materials needed for doors and drawers.

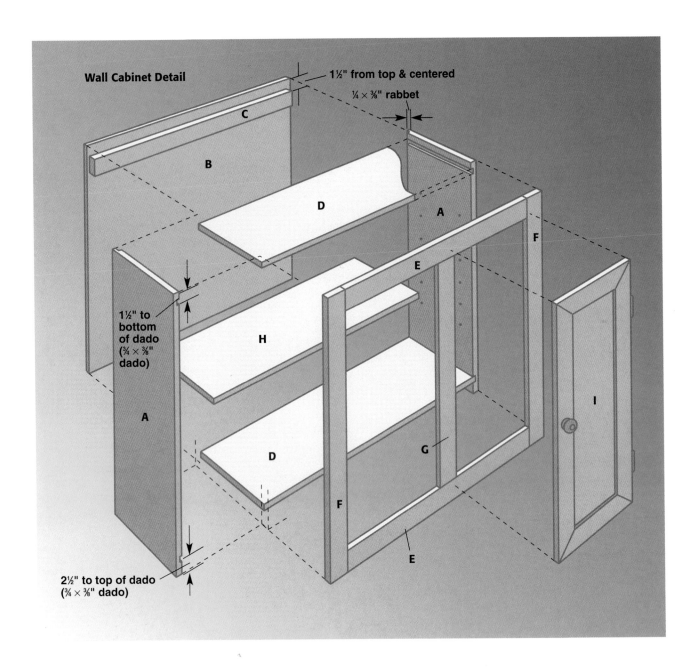

Wall Cabinet Detail

1½" from top & centered

¼ × ⅜" rabbet

C

B

D

A

F

E

1½" to bottom of dado (¾ × ⅜" dado)

H

A

D

G

I

F

E

2½" to top of dado (¾ × ⅜" dado)

Key	Part	Dimension
A	(2) Side panel	¾ × 11¼ × 30" oak plywood
B	(1) Back panel	¼ × 30 × 35¼" oak plywood
C	(1) Nailing strip	¾ × 2½ × 34¼" oak
D	(2) Top, bottom panel	¾ × 11¼ × 34¼" oak plywood
E	(2) Face frame rail	¾ × 2½ × 29¾ oak
F	(2) Long face frame stile	¾ × 2½ × 30" oak
G	(1) Short face frame stile	¾ × 2½ × 25" oak
H	(1) Shelf	¾ × 9¾ × 34¼" oak plywood
I	Wood or glass panel overlay door	See page 40

Directions: Wall Cabinet

The side panels for the wall cabinet are made from ¾" plywood and have ¾"-wide × ⅜"-deep dadoes where the top and bottom panels will fit in place. The side panels also have ¼"-wide rabbet grooves down the back edge—where the back panel will be installed—and two rows of peg holes, 1½" from each side edge, to hold pin-style shelf supports.

A. *Measure and cut the ¾" plywood side panels to size. Then rout the rabbets and dadoes, using a router and a straightedge guide.*

The construction of the wall cabinet includes a 1 × 3 nailing strip mounted to the back panel near the top edge. This strip is used as a mounting plate when installing the cabinet to the wall and gives the frame of the cabinet structural support.

Step A: PREPARE THE SIDE PANELS.
1. Measure and cut the side panels (A) from ¾" plywood, according to the measurements in the Cutting List. Use a circular saw with a plywood blade and a straightedge guide to make each cut.
2. Rout the rabbets and dadoes in each panel, using a router and two straightedge guides (page 18). See the Wall Cabinet Detail on page 23 for the exact size and location of each groove.

Step B: DRILL THE SHELF SUPPORT HOLES.
Drill two parallel rows of ¼" holes for pin-style shelf supports on the inside face of each side panel. Use a right-angle drill guide to ensure the holes are straight, and a scrap of pegboard as a template to ensure that holes line up correctly. Set the drill stop on the right-angle drill guide to a depth of ⅜" to avoid drilling completely through the side panels.

Step C: BUILD THE CABINET FRAME.
1. Measure and cut the ¾" plywood top and bottom panels (D) and back panel (B) to size. Glue and clamp the side panels to the top and bottom panels

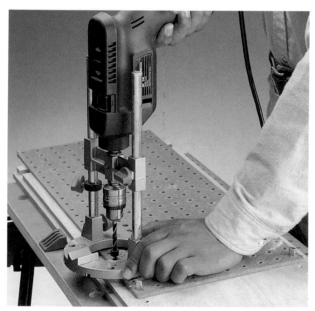

B. *Use a right-angle drill guide and a piece of pegboard to drill the holes in the side panels.*

C. *Reinforce each dado joint with 2" finish nails driven every 3".*

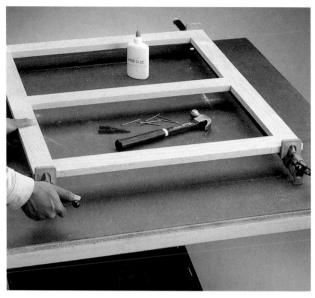

D. *Cut the face frame pieces to size and clamp the rails between the stiles, reinforcing each joint with 4" finish nails.*

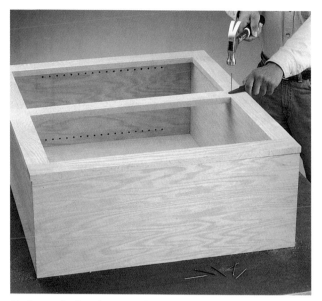

E. *Center the face frame on the cabinet and attach it with glue and 2" finish nails.*

to form dado joints. Reinforce the joints with 2" finish nails driven every 3".

2. Measure and cut a 1 × 3 nailing strip (C) according to the dimensions in the Cutting List and attach it to the back panel using glue and ¾" screws. The nailing strip should be attached 1½" below the top edge and inset ⅜" from either side edge of the back panel.

3. Set the back panel into the rabbet grooves on the back edges of the cabinet, and secure it with 1½" finish nails driven through the back panel and 2" finish nails driven through the side panels, into the nailing strip.

Step D: BUILD THE FACE FRAME.
1. Measure the height and width between the inside surfaces of the cabinet and cut face frame rails and stiles (E, F, G) to length. Cut the rails 4¾" shorter than the width, and the stiles 4" longer than the measured height.
2. Clamp and glue the rails between the stiles, and reinforce the joints by drilling pilot holes and driving 4" finish nails through the stiles into the rails.

Step E: INSTALL THE FACE FRAME.
1. Center the face frame on the cabinet so the overhang on each side is equal, and so the top edge of the bottom rail is flush with the bottom shelf surface.
2. Attach the face frame with glue and 2" finish nails driven through pilot holes.
3. Fill the nail holes and sand and finish the cabinet. See page 21 for information on finishing materials.

F. *Install a temporary ledger strip so the top edge is flush with the reference line.*

Step F: INSTALL A TEMPORARY LEDGER.
1. Mark a level reference line on the wall where the bottom edge of the cabinet will be located. The standard height for mounting cabinets is 54".
2. Mark the wall stud locations below the reference line, and position a temporary 1 × 3 ledger strip so the top edge is flush with the reference line. Attach the strip at the stud locations, with 2½" utility screws.

G. *Set the cabinet on the temporary ledger and brace it in position with a 54"-long 2 x 4.*

Step G: Mount the cabinet.
1. Set the cabinet on the temporary ledger, and brace it in position with a 54"-long 2 × 4. Drill counterbored pilot holes and drive 3½" screws through the nailing strip into the wall studs.
2. Use a level to make sure the cabinet is plumb. If not, loosen the screws slightly and shim behind the cabinet, adjusting it until plumb. Tighten the screws.

Step H: Install the trim moldings.
1. Score the shims with a utility knife and break off the excess. Then remove the temporary ledger and patch the screw holes with wallboard compound.
2. Cut trim moldings to cover any gaps between the cabinet and the wall, and attach the trim with 1" finish nails driven through pilot holes.

Step I: Apply the finishing touches.
1. Build and finish the shelves with pin-style shelf supports (page 38). Then build or purchase overlay doors, and attach them to the face frame (page 41).
2. Sand and finish the cabinets. After the finish dries, attach the doors and door pulls and install the shelf support pins and adjustable shelves.

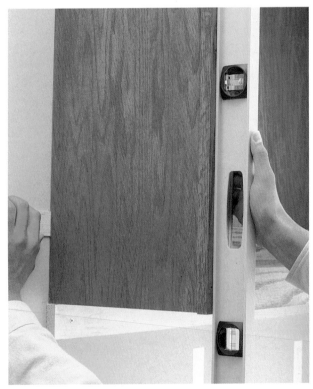

H. *Check to make sure the cabinet is plumb, shimming behind the cabinet if necessary.*

I. *Install overlay doors and door hardware after the finish for the cabinet and doors is dry.*

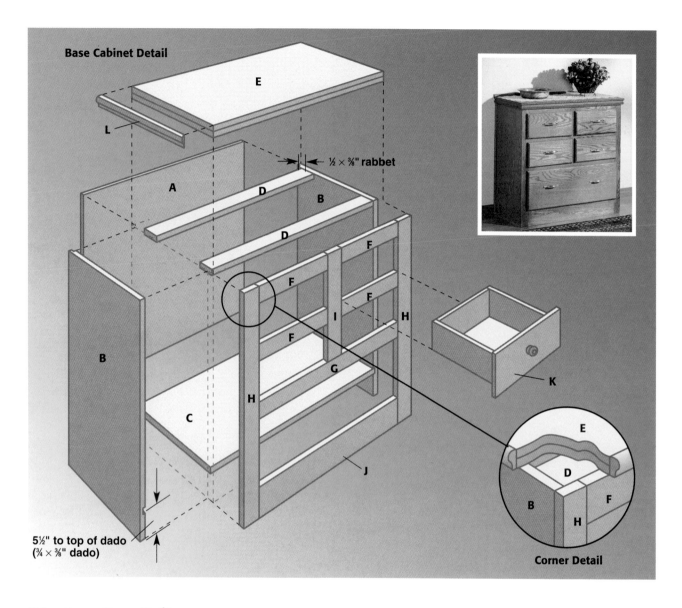

Base Cabinet Detail

½ × ⅜" rabbet

5½" to top of dado
(¾ × ⅜" dado)

Corner Detail

Directions: Base Cabinet

The side panels of the base cabinet are also made from ¾" plywood, but the dado and rabbet grooves differ in size and position from those of the wall cabinet. The side panels have ¾"-wide × ⅜"-deep dadoes to hold the bottom panel in position, and ½"-wide × ⅜"-deep rabbet grooves down the back edge, where the back panel will be installed.

The dado grooves near the bottom edge of the sides are raised slightly higher than on the wall cabinet, so that the bottom drawer will be at a more comfortable height. Due to the elevated height of the bottom drawer, the bottom rail of the face frame is made with a 1 × 6 rather than a 1 × 3.

Key	Part	Dimension
A	(1) Back panel	½ × 34½ × 35¼" oak plywood
B	(2) Side panel	¾ × 17¼ × 34¼" oak plywood
C	(1) Bottom panel	¾ × 16¼ × 35¼" oak plywood
D	(2) Support	¾ × 2½ × 34½" oak
E	(2) Countertop	¾ × 18 × 36¼" oak plywood
F	(4) Short frame rail	¾ × 2½ × 14⅜" oak
G	(1) Long frame rail	¾ × 2½ × 31¼" oak
H	(2) Long frame stile	¾ × 2½ × 34½" oak
I	(1) Short frame stile	¾ × 2½ × 16½" oak
J	Bottom rail	¾ × 5¼ × 31¼" oak
K	Overlay drawers	See page 31
L	Trim molding	Cut to fit

Step A: ASSEMBLE THE CABINET FRAME.
1. Cut the side, bottom, and back panels to size using a circular saw with a plywood blade and a straightedge guide.

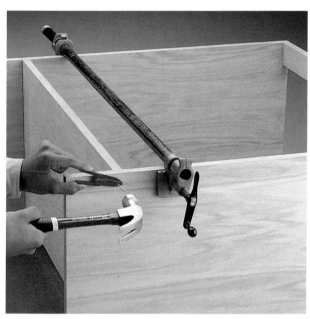

A. *Assemble the side, bottom, and back panels with glue, and reinforce each joint with 2" finish nails.*

2. Use a router and two straightedge guides to make rabbet and dado grooves. See the Base Cabinet Detail on page 27 for the exact size and location of each groove.
3. Assemble the pieces with glue and 2" finish nails, following Step C on page 24.

Step B: INSTALL SUPPORTS & ASSEMBLE THE FACE FRAME.
1. Measure, cut, and install two 1 × 3 supports (D) to fit between the side panels at the top of the cabinet. Attach the supports by driving 2" finish nails through pilot holes in the side panels and into the support rails.
2. Measure and cut the 1 × 3 (F, G, H, I) and 1 × 6 (J) stiles and rails to size. Sand any rough edges smooth with medium-grit sandpaper.
3. Assemble the face frame according to the Base Cabinet Detail on page 27.

Step C: INSTALL THE CABINET BASE AND DRAWER GLIDES.
1. Mark the location of the wall studs in the project area with tape, and set the cabinet in place.
2. Check the cabinet with a level and, if necessary, shim under it to level. Toenail the side panels to the floor at the shim locations, using 2" finish nails.
3. Score the shims, and break off the excess. Then anchor the cabinet by driving 3½" screws through the

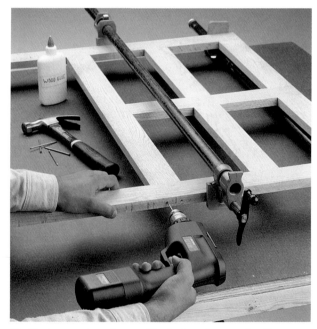

B. *Measure, cut, and assemble the face frame using the dimensions and layout provided in the Base Cabinet Detail on page 27.*

C. *Check the cabinet for level, shimming under it if necessary. When the cabinet is in position, toenail the side panels at the shim locations.*

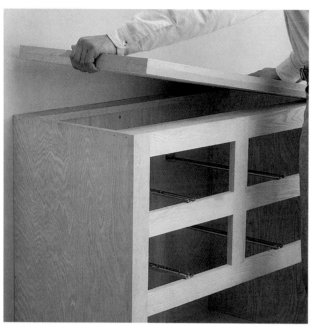

D. *Set the two countertop panels on the cabinet, and anchor them with 2" screws driven up through the supports inside the cabinet.*

E. *Cover the exposed edges of countertop with mitered ornamental molding.*

F. *Finish the cabinet to match the wall cabinet. Install the drawer hardware after the finish has dried sufficiently.*

back panel and into wall studs, just below the top edge of the cabinet. Remove the tape marking the stud locations.

4. Install the tracks for two center-mounted drawer slides on the bottom panel as shown on page 30. Attach the slides for the upper drawers to the face frame rails and the back panel following the manufacturer's directions.

Step D: INSTALL THE TOP.

1. Measure and cut two ¾" plywood countertop panels (E) using a circular saw with a plywood blade and a straightedge guide. Fasten them together with glue and then drive 1" screws up through the bottom layer.

2. Position the countertop on the cabinet, and anchor it with 2" screws driven up through the supports (D) inside the cabinet.

Step E: INSTALL TRIM MOLDINGS & FINISH THE CABINET.

1. Cover the exposed edges of the countertop with mitered ornamental molding. Attach it with glue and 2" finish nails driven through pilot holes.

2. Cover the gaps between the cabinet and the walls and floor with trim molding, attached with 1" finish nails driven through pilot holes.

Step F: BUILD DRAWERS & APPLY FINISHING TOUCHES.

1. Build overlay drawers as directed on page 31. Finish the drawers and the base cabinet to match the wall cabinet.

2. When the finish has dried sufficiently, install the drawer hardware, and install the drawers.

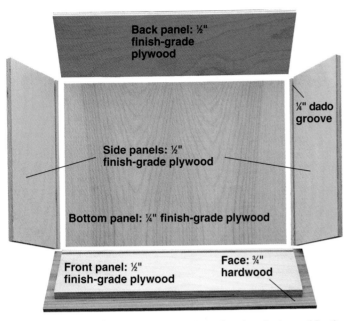

The basic overlay drawer is made using ½" plywood for the front, back, and side panels, and ¼" plywood for the bottom panel. The bottom panel fits into a ¼" dado near the bottom of the front and side panels, and is nailed to the bottom edge of the back panel. The hardwood drawer face is screwed to the drawer front from inside the drawer box.

Basic Drawers

In its simplest form, a drawer is nothing more than a wooden box that slides in and out on a permanent shelf. Adding drawer slide hardware, a hardwood drawer face, and ornamental knobs or pulls makes drawers look more professional.

The drawer shown on the following page is simple to build and will work for any of the projects in this book. The design is called an "overlay" drawer because it features a hardwood drawer face that overhangs the cabinet face frame.

Ready-made hardwood drawer faces are sold by companies specializing in cabinet refacing products. You can also make your own drawer faces by cutting hardwood boards to the proper size and using a router with an edging bit to create a decorative flair.

A center-mounted drawer slide attached to the bottom of the drawer allows the drawer to glide smoothly and acts as a support for drawers installed in open cabinets.

The height, width, and depth of the cabinet, and the opening for the drawer must be carefully measured before the drawer is built, to ensure a good fit.

MEASURING THE CABINET

Part		Dimension
Sides	length	Depth of opening, minus 3"
	height	Height of opening, minus ½"
Front	length	Width of opening, minus 1½"
	height	Height of opening, minus ½"
Back	length	Width of opening, minus 1½"
	height	Height of opening, minus 1"
Bottom	length	Width of opening, minus 1"
	height	Depth of opening, minus 2¾"
Face	length	Width of opening, plus 1"
	height	Height of opening, plus 1"

A. Mount the track for the drawer slide with the rear bracket when installing a drawer in an open cabinet.

Directions: Overlay Drawer

Step A: INSTALL THE DRAWER TRACK.
Install the track for the drawer slide, following the manufacturer's directions. If the slide will be supported by the face frame and the back panel, mount it using the rear bracket included with the slide kit. If the track will rest on a shelf, install it before the cabinet is assembled.

Step B: BUILD THE DRAWER FRAME.
1. Measure the interior dimensions of the face frame and the depth of the cabinet from the back edge of the face frame to the interior surface of the back panel. Then follow the dimensions listed in the table (opposite page) to cut the drawer pieces to size.
2. Outline ¼"-wide dado grooves on the interior faces of the front and side panels. Rout ¼"-deep dado grooves along the marked outlines, using a router with a ¼" straight bit and a straightedge guide (page 19).
3. Clamp and glue the drawer panels together with the front and back panels between the side panels and the top edges of the panels aligned. Reinforce the joints with 2" finish nails driven through the front and back into the side panels.

Step C: ATTACH THE DRAWER BOTTOM.
1. Let the glue dry and remove the clamps. Slide the bottom panel into the dado grooves from the back of the drawer box. Do not apply glue to the dado grooves or the bottom panel.
2. Attach the back edge of the bottom panel to the back panel, using brad nails spaced every 4".

Step D: APPLY THE FINISHING TOUCHES.
1. Finish the drawer face to match your project, and allow the finish to dry.
2. Position the drawer box against the back side of the drawer face, so the face overhangs by ½" on the sides and bottom, and 1" on the top. Attach the face with 1" screws driven from inside the drawer box.
3. Attach the drawer slide insert to the drawer bottom, following the manufacturer's directions.
4. Attach any drawer pulls or knobs as desired, and slide the drawer into the cabinet, making sure the drawer slide and insert are aligned.

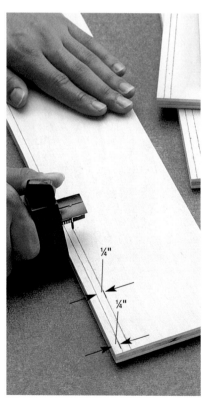

B. *Outline and then rout a dado groove along the bottom edge of the front and side panels.*

C. *Slide the bottom panel into the dado grooves of the drawer assembly.*

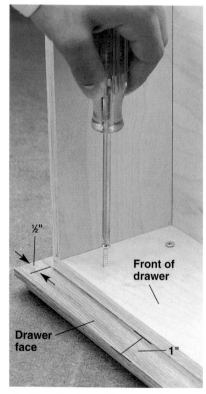

D. *Attach the face of the drawer by driving screws through the front panel into the face.*

Swing-up, Glide-out & Pull-down Shelves

Customize your kitchen storage with swing-up, glide-out and pull-down shelves.

Incorporate heavy-duty, swing-up shelves to bring base-cabinet items like stand mixers to the countertop. Build your own full-extension, glide-out shelves to divide larger spaces into two or more shelves and reduce bending and reaching for wheelchair users and people with back problems.

Choose pull-down shelf accessories to bring upper-cabinet items like spices within reach. When purchasing specialized hardware accessories, check load ratings, locking mechanisms, arc swings and clearance heights to be sure they can support the items you want to store and they will fit in the intended location.

Installing Swing-up Shelves

Swing-up shelves are perfect for storing heavy appliances under the counter. Most swing arms are sold without the shelf surface, which must be purchased separately and cut to fit.

Take accurate measurements of your cabinet's interior dimensions, note any objects that protrude into the interior, and purchase the swing-up unit that is compatible with your cabinetry. Frameless cabinets often have fully concealed hinges that can interfere with swing mechanisms. Framed cabinets have a front perimeter face frame and may have hinges that interfere with lifting hardware.

Refer to the manufacturer's recommendations for the proper length of the shelf to ensure it will fit into the cabinet when the assembly is locked down and the door is closed. Cut the shelf from ¾"-thick plywood, MDF or melamine-coated particleboard. If the shelf is bare wood, finish all sides with a washable paint or varnish. For melamine-coated board, cover the cut edges with melamine tape to prevent water from damaging the wood core.

TOOLS & MATERIALS

- Circular saw
- Tape measure
- Screwdriver
- Shelving,
- 1 × 3 lumber
- #8 machine screws

Directions: Swing-up Shelf

Step A: ATTACH SPACERS TO THE CABINET.
Carefully trigger the locking mechanism on each swing arm and set to fully extended position. Hold each arm against the inside face of the cabinet and make sure arm will clear door hinge and cabinet face frame. If not, use wood spacers to allow the arms to clear the hinges or frames by at least ½". In most cases, 1 × 3 spacers provide enough clearance. Cut spacers to match length of mounting plate.

Step B: MOUNT SWING ARMS TO THE CABINET.
Mark the locations of the swing arm mounting plates onto the inside cabinet faces. Mount the swing arms with screws.

Step C: MEASURE & CUT SHELF
Determine the width of the shelf by measuring across the swing arms between the outer edges of the shelf-mounting flanges. Attach the shelf to the shelf-mounting flanges using #8 machine screws.

Step D: ATTACH SHELF TO LOCKING BARS.
Fasten each locking bar to the bottom shelf face with the provided screws and plastic spacers to en-sure the bars will slide smoothly. Test the locking bars' operation with the shelf in the extended and retracted positions, and make any necessary adjust-ments.

B. *Mark the screw locations for the mounting plates on the spacers, then attach the swing arms*

C. *Determine the width of the shelf by measuring between the outer edges of the swing arm mounting flanges.*

A. *Mount wood spacers, then position each swing arm to make sure it will clear the door hinge and face frame.*

D. *Fasten the locking bars to the bottom of the shelf, using the provided screws and spacers.*

Installing Glide-out Shelves

Glide-out shelves make getting to the back of a base cabinet much easier. This project gives you directions for building the shelves and installing them. Before installing the shelves, carefully measure the items to be stored to truly customize your storage space.

To determine the proper size for the glide-out shelves, measure the inside dimensions of the cabinet and subtract the distance that hinges and face frames protrude into the interior of the cabinet. Then subtract 1" from the width for the two slides and tracks (½" each).

TOOLS & MATERIALS*

- Electronic stud finder
- Jig saw
- Router
- Hammer
- Clamps
- Drill
- Nail set
- Circular saw
- Straightedge
- Sander
- Level
- Screwdriver
- 4d finish nails
- (2) Drawer guides
- Finishing materials
- 1¼" utility screws
- Wood glue

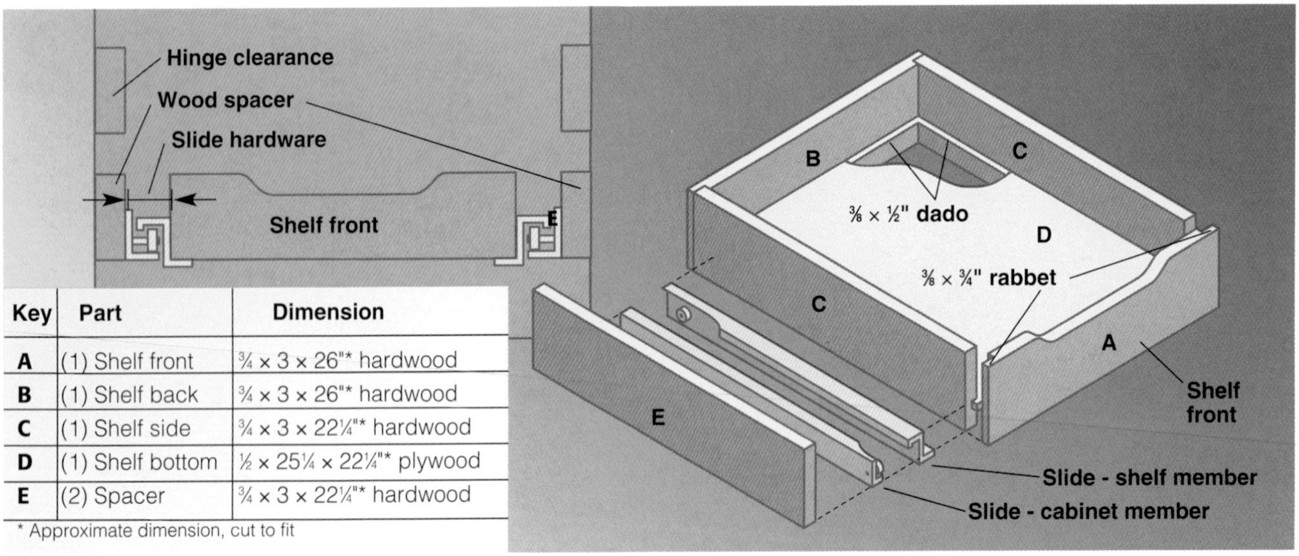

Hinge clearance

Wood spacer

Slide hardware

Shelf front

⅜ × ½" **dado**

⅜ × ¾" **rabbet**

Shelf front

Slide - shelf member

Slide - cabinet member

Key	Part	Dimension
A	(1) Shelf front	¾ × 3 × 26"* hardwood
B	(1) Shelf back	¾ × 3 × 26"* hardwood
C	(1) Shelf side	¾ × 3 × 22¼"* hardwood
D	(1) Shelf bottom	½ × 25¼ × 22¼"* plywood
E	(2) Spacer	¾ × 3 × 22¼"* hardwood

* Approximate dimension, cut to fit

Directions: Build & Install a Glide-out Shelf

Step A: CREATE THE SHELF PIECES.

Rout a ⅜"-deep × ½"-wide dado groove into the front, back, and side panels ½" from the bottom edges. Cut a ⅜"-deep × ¾"-wide rabbet groove across the inside faces of each end of the front and back pieces.

Step B: ASSEMBLE THE SHELVES.

Attach the sides to the shelf fronts using glue and three 4d finish nails. Countersink the nails with a nail set. Slide the bottom panels into the dado grooves, then glue and nail the back pieces in place. Clamp the shelves square, and allow the glue to dry.

Step C: MOUNT THE SHELVES.

Mount the glide-out rails to the bottom edges of the spacer strips, then attach the spacers to the interior walls of the cabinet with 1¼" utility screws. Screw a sliding rail to each side of the shelves, making sure that the bottom edges are flush against the bottom edges of the shelves. Install each shelf by aligning its sliding rails with the glides inside the cabinet and pushing it in completely. The rails will automatically lock into place.

A. *Cut the shelf pieces, then rout the rabbet and dado grooves for assembly.*

B. *Use glue and finish nails to assemble the shelves. Clamp until the glue dries.*

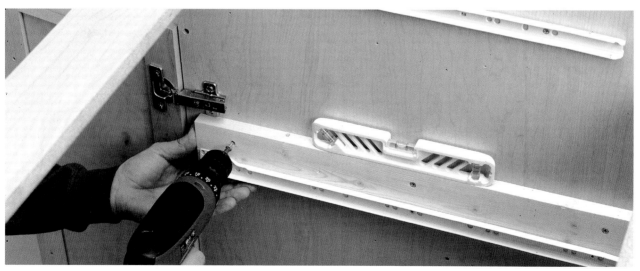

C. *Mount glide-out rails to the bottom of the spacer strips, then attach the spacer strips to the interior walls. Attach the sliding rails to the bottom of the shelves, then install the shelves.*

Installing Pull-down Shelves

A pull-down shelf makes wall cabinets more user friendly by bringing all the contents down to eye level. Because of the space taken up by the mechanism and the shelf boxes, this is not a good project for a narrow cabinet.

Before you begin this project, hold each swing arm assembly against the inside face of the cabinet side and make sure both arms will clear the door hinge and the cabinet face frame. If the arms do not clear, add custom wood spacers of plywood or solid lumber that are at least as large as the swing arm mounting plates

Follow the manufacturer's specifications for the box dimensions, which will be based on the size of your cabinet. If the boxes are bare wood, lightly sand the edges and finish all sides with a highly washable paint or a clear varnish, such as polyurethane. For melamine-coated board, cover the cut edges with melamine tape to keep water from damaging the wood core.

Note: The springs that help raise the arms are strong and may make it difficult to lower empty shelves. When the shelves are loaded, the weight of the items makes it easier to move the shelf.

SHOPPING TIPS
• Specialty hardware catalogs carry pull-down shelf hardware.
• Check that the capacity of the mechanism you are purchasing matches the items you will be storing on the shelf.

TOOLS & MATERIALS

• Tape measure	• Swing-up shelf kit & hardware
• Pencil	• ½" MDF
• Circular saw	• Fasteners & finishing materials for shelf boxes
• Drill	
• Awl	• #8 pan-head screws
• Hacksaw	• Coarse-thread drywall screws
• Allen wrench	• Lumber for custom spacers

A. *Fasten the spacers to the sides of the cabinet, using drywall screws.*

B. *Use the manufacturer's template to mark the locations of the swing-arm mounting plates.*

Directions: Pull-down Shelf

Step A: FASTEN SPACERS.
Determine the general positions of the swing arms, then fasten the spacers to the inside faces of the cabinet sides with coarse-thread drywall screws. The screws should not go completely through the cabinet side.

Step B: MARK SWING ARM LOCATIONS.
Use the template to mark locations of the swing-arm mounting plates. Drill a small pilot hole at each awl mark. Fasten the swing arms to the custom spacers or cabinet sides with #8 pan-head screws (inset).

Step C: BUILD & MOUNT SHELF BOXES.
Build two shelf boxes from ½" MDF, and install be-tween the sides of the shelf unit, using #8 pan-head screws. Because the lower box can be installed in only one position, install it first. Slide the lower handle through the holes in the side pieces.

Step D: MOUNT THE SHELF.
Cut the upper handle to length. Position the box unit in front of the cabinet, rotate the lower arms down, and secure them to the side pieces using the bolts, washers, and nuts provided. Insert the top handle. Lower the upper arms one at a time, and insert the handle end into the arm. Secure the handle with the two set screws in each arm, using an Allen wrench.

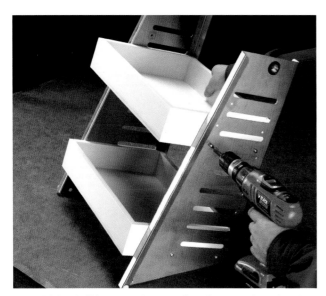

C. *Build the shelf boxes, and mount them between the sides of the shelf unit.*

D. *With the assistance of a helper, secure the shelf unit to the swing arms.*

Basic Adjustable Shelves

Adding adjustable shelves is an easy way to adapt storage units to suit your changing needs. There are many types of adjustable shelving systems available—which type is right for the project depends on the weight and size of the items they will hold.

Pin-style support systems are available in wood, plastic, and metal. Plastic support pins should only be used for light- to medium-weight shelf loads. Metal support pins, like flat brass pins or zinc L-shaped pins, are suitable for larger loads, but should not be used for long-term storage of heavy, fragile items like large televisions or other electronic components.

Metal standards are common because they are easy to install and are available in a variety of colors and sizes. Refer to the manufacturer's recommendations for the specific weight loads the standards can hold.

The strength of a shelf also depends on its span—the distance between vertical risers. In general, the span of a shelf should be no more than 36".

Choose shelving materials appropriate for the loads they must support. Thin glass shelves or parti-cleboard can easily support light loads, like decorative glassware, but only the sturdiest shelves can hold heavy items without bending or breaking. Building shelves from finish-grade plywood, edged with hardwood strips, moldings, or veneer is a good general-purpose choice.

Directions: Pin-style Support Adjustable Shelves

Step A: CUT THE RISERS & DRILL THE HOLES.
1. Cut the risers to size and position them with the outside face toward the worksurface. Then align a pegboard scrap along the inside face of each riser, so the edge of the scrap piece is aligned with the side edge of the riser. Make sure the edge of the pegboard piece is flush with the edges of the risers when drilling the holes, or the shelves will not be level.
2. Mount a drill and ¼" bit in a right-angle drill guide. Set the drill-stop at a ⅜" depth.
3. Use the pegboard holes as a guide to drill two rows of parallel holes in the riser, approximately 1½" from both edges. Make sure the pegboard is station-

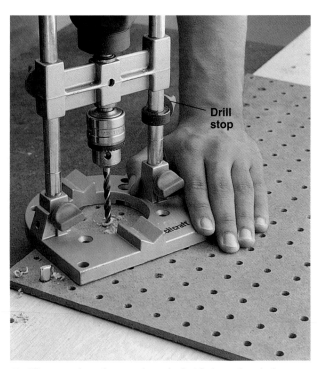

A. *Align a pegboard scrap along the inside face of each riser, flush with the edge. Drill two rows of parallel holes, using the pegboard as a template.*

B. *Build shelves that are ⅛" shorter than the distance between the risers, and install them with four ¼" pin-style shelf supports.*

ary while drilling the holes, or the shelves will wobble after installation.

Step B: BUILD & INSTALL THE SHELVES.
1. After you have completed the assembly of the unit, build and finish shelves that are ⅛" shorter than the distance between the risers.
2. Insert ¼" pin supports (two on each side) into the corresponding holes, and install the finished shelves.

Directions: Metal Standard Adjustable Shelves

Step A: BUILD & INSTALL THE RISERS.
1. Build the risers, making sure the material is deep enough for the type of metal standard you will be installing.
2. Using a marking gauge, mark two parallel dado grooves on the inside face of each riser. The grooves should be at least 1" from the long edges of the side panels. If you do not have a marking gauge, use a combination square and a pencil to make the marks (page 17).

Step B: ROUT THE DADOES & TEST FIT THE STANDARDS.
1. Cut the dadoes to the depth and thickness of the metal standards, using two straightedge guides and a router (page 19).
2. Test-fit the standards to make sure they fit, then remove them.

Step C: BUILD & INSTALL THE SHELVES.
1. Measure the distance between the side panels of the shelving unit. Build and finish shelves ⅛" shorter than this measurement.
2. After the shelving unit has been built and finished, measure the length of the dado grooves on the inside of the unit.
3. Cut the metal standards to length, so they fit into the unit, and attach them using the nails or screws provided by the manufacturer. Position the cut end of each standard at the top of the unit so the slots in the standards are aligned properly. If the standards are uneven, the shelves will not be level.
4. Insert the shelf clips into four level slots on the metal standards. Install the finished shelves, adjusting them as necessary.

A. *Mark the dado grooves at least 1" from the edges on the inside face of each riser, using a marking gauge.*

B. *Test-fit the standards in the dado grooves, then remove them.*

C. *Insert a metal shelf clip into each standard, and place a shelf on top of each set of clips.*

Basic Doors

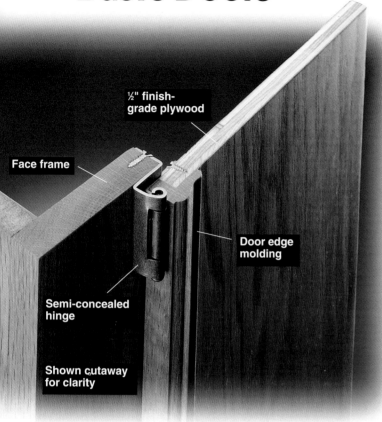

- ½" finish-grade plywood
- Face frame
- Door edge molding
- Semi-concealed hinge
- Shown cutaway for clarity

Adding doors to a cabinet or bookcase often makes a storage unit more attractive and reduces the appearance of clutter. Doors also protect electronics and other sensitive items from dust and direct sunlight.

You can build doors for framed or frameless cabinets out of ½" finish-grade plywood and door-edge molding without using complicated woodworking techniques. These doors can be built in any size necessary and finished to match any project. Better yet, when hung with semi-concealed overlay hinges, they require no complicated routing or mortising techniques.

Traditional frame-style cabinet doors can be hung with a variety of hinge types. In the project demonstrated here, the doors are mounted on a framed cabinet with ⅜" overlay hinges.

If you are mounting doors to a frameless cabinet or bookshelf, use fully-concealed hinges attached to the inside surfaces of the door and cabinet wall (see hinge D below). Panel doors for frameless cabinets should be cut to size so that the door-edge molding sits flush with the top and bottom panels of the cabinet, or flush against the edges of the shelves above and below the doors.

Buying hinges can be confusing. The hinges shown below are commonly found on a variety of cabinets.

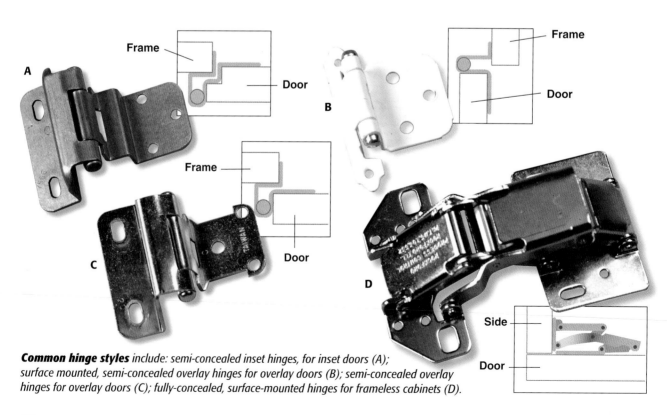

Common hinge styles *include: semi-concealed inset hinges, for inset doors (A); surface mounted, semi-concealed overlay hinges for overlay doors (B); semi-concealed overlay hinges for overlay doors (C); fully-concealed, surface-mounted hinges for frameless cabinets (D).*

Directions: Overlay Doors with Semi-concealed Hinges

Step A: BUILD THE DOORS.
1. Measure the width and height of the opening. If the opening is less than 24" wide, plan to cut a single panel equal to the height and width of the opening. (The molding around the edges of the door will provide the proper overlay height and width.)

If the opening is wider than 24", two doors are necessary. The height of each panel should equal the measured height of the opening. The width of each panel should be one-half the total width of the opening, minus ½".
2. Cut the necessary door panels from ½" finish-grade plywood, using a circular saw with a plywood blade.
3. Measure and cut door-edge molding to frame each door panel, using a power miter saw. Or, use a miter box and backsaw to miter the ends at a 45° angle.
4. Clamp the door-edge molding to the door panels, then drill pilot holes through the side of the molding and into the panels. Attach the molding by driving 1½" finish nails through the pilot holes. Finish the doors to match the project.

Step B: MOUNT THE HINGES & MARK REFERENCE LINES.
1. Mount semi-concealed overlay hinges to the back of the door panels, using the mounting screws supplied by the manufacturer. For doors under 30" tall, place one hinge 2" from the top and another 2" from the bottom of each door. For doors taller than 30", use three evenly spaced hinges.
2. Use masking tape to mark a reference line on the top face frame rail, ½" above the door opening.
3. Position the door over the opening, aligning the top edge of the door with the tape reference line. Then use tape to mark the top hinge location on the face frame.

Step C: INSTALL THE DOOR & HARDWARE.
1. Open the hinges, and position the door against the edge of the face frame so the top hinge is aligned with the tape marking the hinge location.
2. Drill pilot holes, and anchor both hinges to the face frame with the mounting screws. Remove the masking tape and install door pulls, if desired.

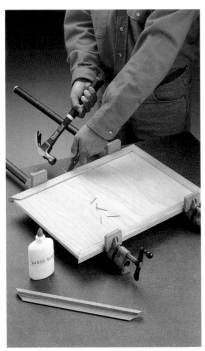

A. *Attach the door-edge molding to the door panel by driving 1½" finish nails through pilot holes.*

B. *Position the door flush with the bottom edge of the reference line and mark the location of the top hinge with masking tape.*

C. *Install the door by driving the mounting screws into the edge of the cabinet frame.*

STORAGE PROJECTS

In this section, you'll find our featured storage projects. For convenience, we've organized them around six basic categories of storage, but you'll quickly realize that many of the projects can be used for a variety of purposes around your home. And although storage is a practical subject, you'll find that many of these projects also add style and decoration to the spaces they occupy.

• **Utility storage** includes a variety of ideas and projects for use throughout the home. These ideas and projects provide solutions for common storage issues.

• **Decorative & display storage** contains projects that will attract attention because they show off items like CDs or fine china. And some of these projects are decorative in their own right.

• **Food & dishware storage** focuses on the challenges of storing kitchen utensils, food and beverages, and dishware. These innovative solutions will help you organize and keep your kitchen countertops clutter-free.

• **Recreation storage** provides solutions for storing athletic and hobby equipment, as well as toys. These projects range from a stackable storage block to a garden center with a bin for potting soil.

• **Clothing storage** includes projects and ideas to help you organize and store all types of clothing in a bedroom, entryway, or basement.

• **Home office storage** is packed with projects to help you organize your home office equipment and supplies, as well as manage your paperwork without losing precious working space.

IN THIS SECTION:

Utility Storage

Utility storage manages practical household items such as yard maintenance equipment, cleaning supplies, recycling, and workshop tools and materials, and provides storage for long-term "inactive" items. The focus tends to be on simply getting clutter off the floors and onto or against the walls or ceiling; presentation isn't as important as keeping everything tidy and readily accessible. Consequently, this type of storage tends to be located in utilitarian areas of the home such as the laundry room, mudroom, garage, shed, or an unfinished basement or attic.

There are thousands of pre-made utility storage units available at stores everywhere. Plastic tubs, wire rack systems, and melamine-coated particleboard units are the most common types. Although there is a large selection of pre-made utility storage units to choose from, pre-made units don't always meet your needs. They aren't always strong enough or big enough, and they don't always fit into the space you have available.

Well-made utility storage units are built with durable materials, and can accommodate a variety of small and oversized items, while making efficient use of space. Ideal for wasted areas behind doors, over a washer and dryer, or in unused corners, utility storage is convenient, cost effective, and, most of all, practical. The projects in this section are useful in many contexts, but do keep in mind the specific items you plan to store when building each project, and adapt accordingly.

Utility Storage Ideas

Shelving lined *with boxes, baskets, bins, and containers keeps even active storage areas tidy.*

Shelving units *mounted under steps or secured between ceiling joists provide perfect storage for reference books, small tools, cleaning supplies, or hobby supplies.*

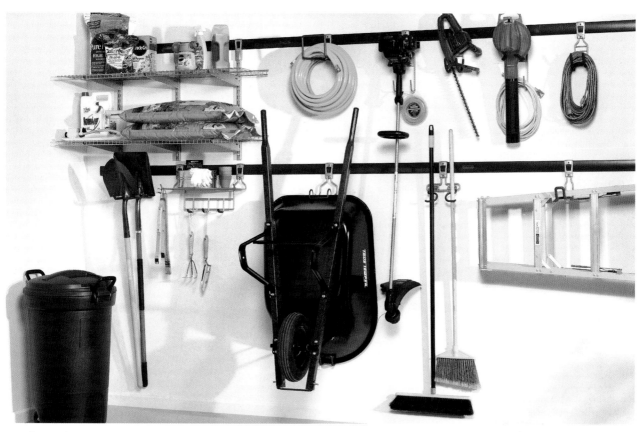

Garden tool organizers *mount to wall studs, and accent a variety of hooks to shelves and tools of narrow sizes.*

Glide-out drawers *with multiple bins make recycling a snap.*

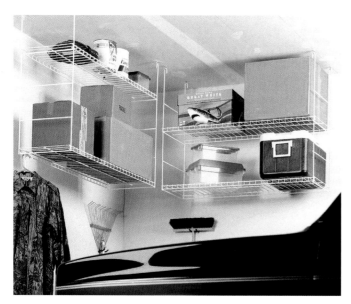

Shelving perfect *for lightweight storage can be suspended from eyehooks drilled into the wood trusses in the ceiling.*

Utility Storage Ideas

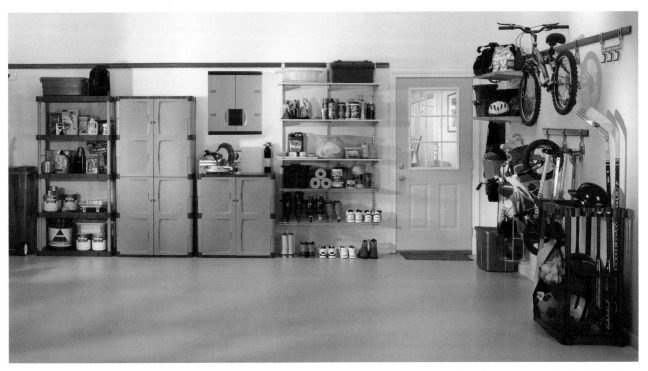

A mixture of freestanding shelves, *cabinets, and track shelving make this garage a paragon of good storage. Note the bracket strips across the top of the walls, used to support storage hooks.*

Rolls of paper *and spools of ribbon fit neatly in a kitchen pantry cabinet and make gift-wrapping a pleasure.*

Deep, pullout shelves *keep tools and supplies in order within a minimum amount of wall space.*

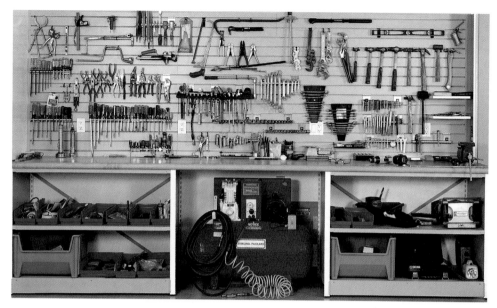

Some storage items make contradictory demands—they need to be right at your fingertips, and out of the way. Wall hooks, clips, and forks attached to thermoplastic sliding tracks are flexible enough to display almost anything, and specific enough to be configured for unique needs.

Fast-mounting track and bracket shelving can hang from an exposed top wall plate without screws or nails and support up to 300 pounds per bracket.

Clutter accumulates at the point of entry in any home; a mudroom can combat that trend by providing designated places to store things as you come in the door.

Bathroom Etagere

The sturdy etagere provides excellent storage space for any bathroom, whether you use it to store towels, toiletries, or cleaning products. The two deep shelves at the top accommodate larger, bulky items like bath towels, while the narrow shelves at the bottom are perfect for toiletries and accessories.

Made of electrical conduit and melamine-covered particleboard, the etagere is inexpensive as well as quick and easy to build. If you shop for materials in the morning, you could be ready to put the shelves to use by afternoon.

Keep in mind that improperly fastening this unit to the wall may compromise this project's usefulness. Make sure the mounting brackets are aligned with the wall studs so the shelf can be securely fastened.

Take advantage of unused space and eliminate countertop clutter with these simple shelves.

TOOLS & MATERIALS

- Drill
- 1" spade bit
- Combination square
- Pipe cutter
- Adjustable wrench
- Pliers
- Stud finder
- 120-grit sandpaper
- (2) ½ × 8" × 2 ft. melamine-covered boards
- (2) ½ × 10" × 2 ft. melamine-covered boards
- (2) ½"-dia. × 10 ft. electrical conduit
- (8) ½"-dia. compression couplings
- (16) 1" to ¾" reduction washers
- (2) ½"-dia. rubber caps
- (2) 1" right-angle brackets
- Wood screws (½", 1½")

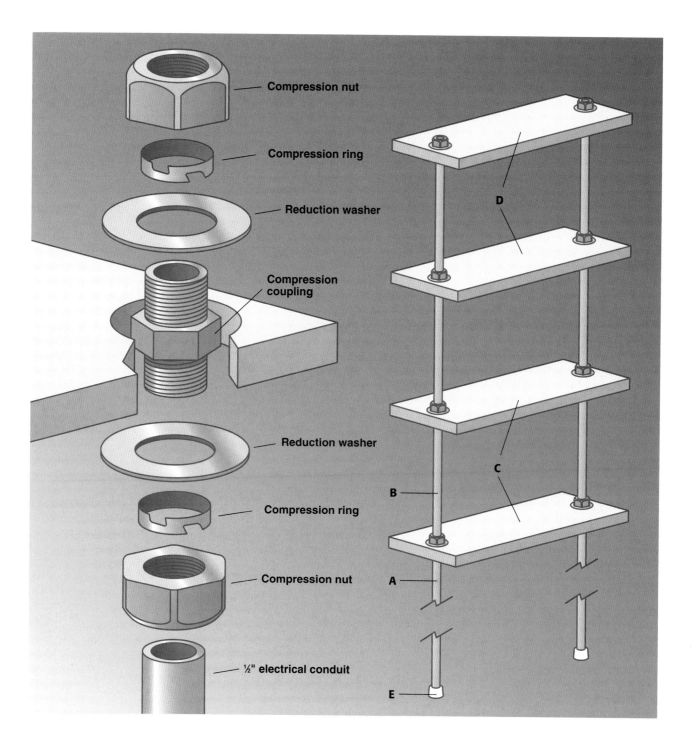

Compression nut

Compression ring

Reduction washer

Compression coupling

Reduction washer

Compression ring

Compression nut

½" electrical conduit

D

C

B

A

E

Key	Part	Dimension
A	(2) Electrical conduit	½"-dia. × 4 ft.
B	(6) Electrical conduit	½"-dia. × 1 ft.
C	(2) Melamine-covered boards	½ × 8" × 2 ft.
D	(2) Melamine-covered boards	½ × 10" × 2 ft.
E	(2) Rubber caps	½"-dia.

Directions: Bathroom Etagere

Step A: PREPARE THE SHELVES.

1. To ensure the holes in each shelf are properly aligned, reference marks are drawn on the face of one narrow shelf panel. Then all the panels are stacked together and the holes are drilled simultaneously. Choose a narrow panel to place on the top of the stack and set a combination square to 1". Draw reference marks 1" from both short ends of the panel. Then set the combination square to 4" and draw two additional reference marks intersecting the first two lines.

2. Stack all the shelf pieces together and clamp them down, so the ends and the back edges of each panel are flush. To avoid breakout on the bottom shelf, apply a piece of electrical tape to the 1" spade bit as a gauge for the drill bit depth. The tip of the drill bit should just puncture the bottom side of the last shelf.

3. Drill a hole on each end of the stack of shelves, stopping when the electrical tape on the bit meets the face of the top shelf and the tip of the bit has just punctured the bottom of the last shelf in the stack.

4. Unclamp the shelves. Flip over the bottom board and complete the holes from the back side.

Step B: PREPARE THE CONDUIT.

1. Sand both 10 ft. lengths of electrical conduit with 120-grit sandpaper. Use a random-orbit sander to reduce the sanding time and create a more even finish.

2. Cut the conduit into six 1 ft. lengths and two 4 ft. lengths, using a pipe cutter. For more information on cutting pipe, see page 14.

Step C: ASSEMBLE THE FITTINGS & SHELVES.

1. Unscrew both ends of each compression coupling and slide the center of each of the couplings into the holes in each shelf. Then sandwich each coupling with reduction washers over the shelves.

2. Place compression rings on the end of the couplings and loosely thread compression nuts over each end of the couplings (see the drawing on page 51).

3. Starting with the bottom shelf, insert the two 4 ft. pieces of conduit into the couplings on the bottom side of the lowest shelf. Then insert two 1-ft. pieces of conduit into the opposing ends of the couplings.

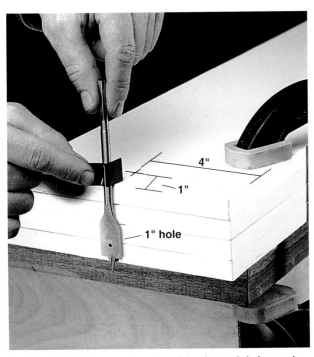

A. Line the drill bit up on the edge of the clamped shelves and apply a piece of electrical tape to the bit as a reference mark.

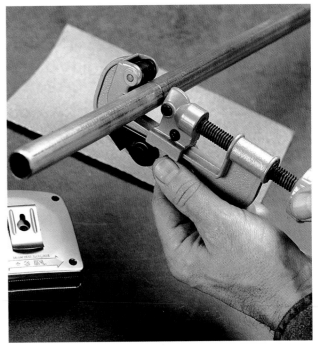

B. Tighten the cutting wheel to the conduit and turn the pipe cutter over the top of the pipe, tightening the cutter every few rotations.

4. Tighten the compression nuts on the top and bottom of the shelf at a uniform rate, until both pieces of conduit are stationary under moderate hand pressure. If either pipe is still loose, the compression nut does not have enough space to tighten the compression ring. If more space is needed, loosen the opposing nut one-half rotation and retighten both nuts until a solid connection is made.

5. Repeat this process, working from the bottom to the top of the unit until all shelves are installed.

Step D: TIGHTEN THE COUPLINGS & INSTALL THE UNIT.
1. Set the entire shelf on a flat surface and tighten the coupling nuts around each shelf, using a large adjustable wrench and a channel-type pliers. The coupling nuts should be tightened at a uniform rate to ensure a good connection.

2. When each joint is tightened, slide the rubber caps on the ends of the 4 ft. lengths, and stand the shelf over your toilet, positioned so the weight of the shelf leans against the wall.

3. Locate two studs in the wall behind your toilet, using a stud finder. Place masking tape on the wall to indicate the stud positions. Then slide the shelf into

position and, holding it in place, make reference marks for the stud locations on the bottom of the lowest shelf and the top of the highest shelf.

4. Lower the etagere to the floor and fasten the brackets to the shelves in the appropriate locations, using ½" wood screws. Stand the etagere up and fasten the brackets to the studs in the wall, using 1½" wood screws.

TIP:

Cover each compression nut with masking tape before assembling the shelf. The masking tape will shield the nuts from scratching during tightening and can be easily removed after assembly.

C. *Tighten the compression couplings until the conduit is stationary under moderate hand pressure.*

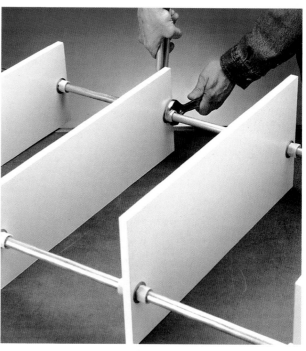

D. *Use channel-type pliers and an adjustable wrench on both coupling nuts simultaneously to avoid loosening the opposite nut.*

Paper Towel Holder

The curved ends and compartment shelf of the paper towel holder make it easy to use and handy for storing smaller items like sandwich bags or hand tools. Ideally suited for any room of your home, you may want to build several units to use in your basement, garage, and laundry area. Built with medium density fiberboard (MDF), the construction of the paper towel holder is solid and will stand up to years of use, even in high-traffic areas. Mount it under a cabinet, on a workbench, or just set it on the table or countertop.

This sturdy dispenser includes a convenient storage shelf to keep frequently used items close at hand.

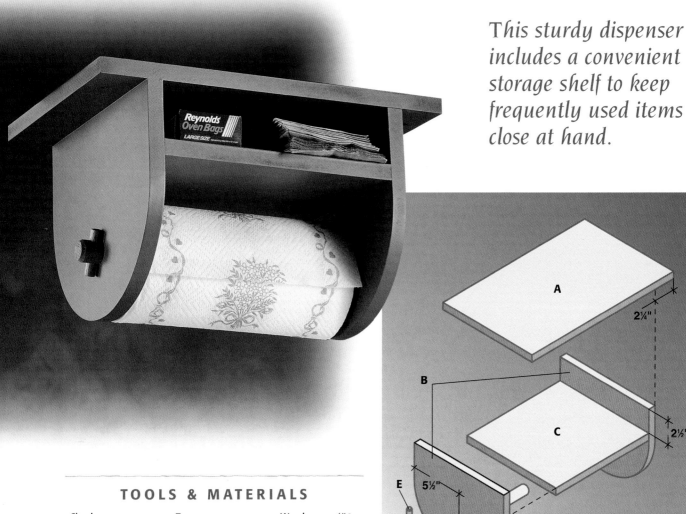

TOOLS & MATERIALS

- Circular saw
- Drill with bits
- Nail set
- Portable drill guide
- Jig saw
- Finish sander
- Belt sander
- Compass

- Tape measure
- (1) ¾ × 2" × 4 ft. medium-density fiberboard
- (1) 1"-dia. × 18" oak dowel
- (1) ½"-dia. × 18" oak dowel
- Wood glue

- Wood screws (#6 × 1½")
- 4d finish nails
- 2 × 8 × 10" scrap wood
- Putty
- Finishing materials

Key	Part	Dimension
A	(1) Top	¾ × 11 × 17½" fiberboard
B	(2) End	¾ × 11 × 9¼" fiberboard
C	(1) Shelf	¾ × 11 × 11½" fiberboard
D	(1) Rod	1"-dia. × 15" oak dowel
E	(1) Stop dowel	½"-dia. × 2" oak dowel

Directions: Paper Towel Holder

Step A: SHAPE THE ENDS & ASSEMBLE THE TOP PIECES.
1. Begin by cutting the end pieces (B) to size. On each end, mark the shelf location and the center-point for the rod holes (see the diagram on page 54).
2. Use a compass set to a 3⅛" radius to draw the semicircle curve on one piece. To ensure that both end pieces are identical, screw them together at the centerpoint of the rod hole. Then cut along the marked line of the curve, using a jig saw. Belt-sand the ends smooth while the pieces are still secured (see Belt Sander, page 17). Unscrew the pieces and drill the rod hole through each end, using a 1⅛"-dia. spade bit.
3. Cut the top (A) and shelf (C) to size, and sand each piece smooth. Drill counterbored pilot holes for attaching the top to the ends. If you will be mounting the holder to a cabinet, drill counterbored pilot holes through the bottom face of the top piece, where the top overhangs the end pieces. Also drill pilot holes through the ends where the shelf will be attached with finish nails. Join the shelf and ends with glue and 4d finish nails. Attach the top with glue and 1½" wood screws.

Step B: DRILL THE STOP DOWEL HOLE.
1. Build a simple V-jig to help you hold the rod firmly in place while drilling the hole for the stop dowel.

Use a circular saw with the blade set at a 45° angle, to make two cuts across the middle of an 18"-long piece of 2 × 8, creating a V-shaped notch. To make your V-jig more stable, mount it to a piece of ¾" plywood.
2. Cut the oak rod (D) and stop dowel (E) to length. Measure and mark a centerpoint ¾" in from one end of the rod.
3. Clamp the rod onto the V-jig and use a portable drill guide to drill the ½" stop dowel hole through the centerpoint. Make sure the drill guide rests flat on the face of the 2 × 8.

Step C: BEVEL THE RODS & APPLY A FINISH.
1. Clamp your belt sander on its side on the work surface, then clamp or nail a scrap piece of wood close to the belt, at an angle of about 45°. Apply a strip of tape ⅛" from each end of the dowel, then rest the dowel against the angled guide and chamfer (bevel) each end of the dowel by rotating it against the spinning belt. Chamfer the stop dowel ends in the same fashion, and glue the dowel into place in the oak rod.
2. Set all nail heads using a nail set, and fill the holes with putty. Sand the entire unit to 150-grit smoothness and apply the paint of your choice. If you are mounting the holder under a cabinet, attach it by driving screws through pilot holes into the top panel.

A. *Use a belt sander clamped on its side to the work surface to gang-sand the end pieces.*

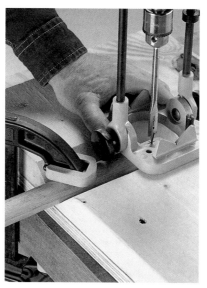

B. *Clamp the rod in the V-jig and support the portable drill guide on the flat sides of the 2 × 8 to create a straight hole.*

C. *Use a mounted belt sander and an angle guide to create precise chamfers.*

Hallway Bookcase

Hallways frequently are underutilized areas of a home. The reason is simple—large furnishings cramp the area. When foot traffic is heavy but space is at a premium, this hallway bookcase makes the most of the situation. Fitting flush against the wall, it allows you to store your books and display your knick-knacks without cluttering the hall or consuming valuable floor space. The bookcase is thinner at the top than at the bottom. This design reduces the chance of tipping and effectively uses precious space. A very simple and inexpensive project to build, this bookcase adds additional storage space to an area that may have been overlooked in the past.

A stable base that tapers to a low-profile top supports storage and display space that fits in the tightest quarters.

TOOLS & MATERIALS

- Circular saw
- Drill with bits
- Finish sander
- Framing square
- Tape measure
- (2) 1 × 10" × 8 ft. pine
- (1) 1 × 8" × 6 ft. pine
- (1) 1 × 6" × 6 ft. pine
- (3) 1 × 4" × 8 ft. pine
- Wood glue
- #8 × 2" wood screws
- Finishing materials

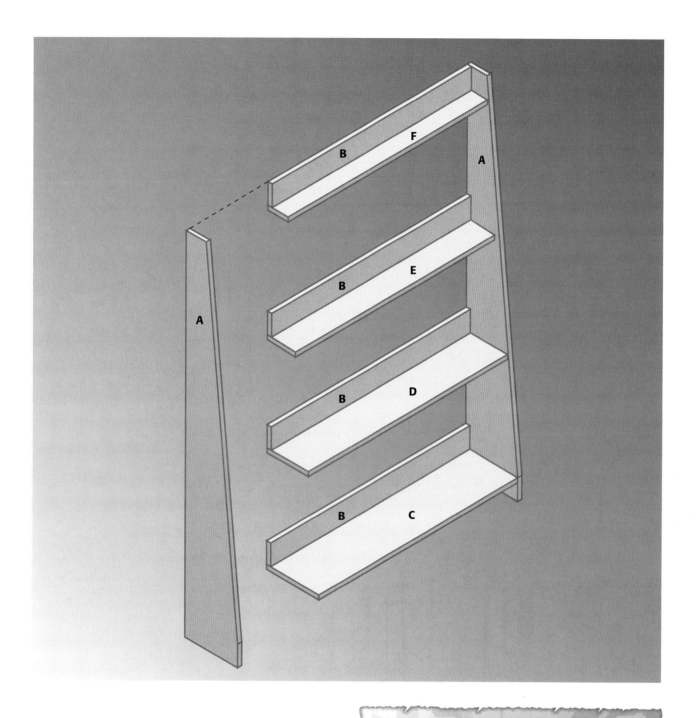

Key	Part	Dimension
A	(2) Standard	¾ × 9¼" × 5 ft. pine
B	(4) Spreader	¾ × 3½ × 34½" pine
C	(1) Shelf	¾ × 9¼ × 34½" pine
D	(1) Shelf	¾ × 7¼ × 34½" pine
E	(1) Shelf	¾ × 5½ × 34½" pine
F	(1) Shelf	¾ × 3½ × 34½" pine

TIP:

Special tapered drill bits make drilling counterbores for screws a snap. Simply select a counterbore bit that matches the shank size of the screws you will use (usually #6 or #8), then drill a pilot hole for each screw with a plain twist bit. Counterbore the pilot holes, using the counterbore bit, set to the correct depth for the wood plugs that will be inserted into the counterbores.

Directions: Hallway Bookcase

Step A: MAKE THE STANDARDS.
The tapered standards are wide at the bottom for stability and narrow at the top to conserve space in a busy hallway.
1. Cut the standards (A) to length from 1 × 10 pine boards. Position the boards against each other on your work surface to make sure they are exactly the same length. On one standard, designate a long edge to be the front.
2. Mark a point on the front edge of the standard, 3½" up from the bottom. Mark another point on the top of the standard, 3½" in from the back edge. Draw a straight line connecting these two points to form a tapered cutting line.
3. Clamp a straightedge to the board, parallel to the cutting line and positioned to guide the foot plate of a circular saw. Then cut the taper using a circular saw, and sand the parts to smooth out any sharp edges or rough surfaces.
4. Use the finished standard as a template to mark the tapered cutting line on the other standard, then cut and sand it to match the first.

Step B: CUT THE SHELF PIECES & MARK SHELF POSITIONS.
1. Cut one spreader (B) to length. To make sure the

boards are cut at the same length, use the first spreader as a guide to mark the length on the remaining spreaders and shelves (C,D,E,F).
2. Cut the remaining shelves and spreaders and smooth out any rough edges with sandpaper.
3. Position the standards face down on your work surface, with the back edges together and the ends even. Use a framing square and a pencil to mark reference lines on each standard, 3½", 20¾", 37½" and 56½" up from the bottoms. These lines mark the top of each shelf. Make sure the reference lines are exactly the same on both standards.

Step C: INSTALL THE SPREADERS.
The spreaders keep books and decorative objects from falling behind the bookcase and out of reach. They also provide structural support. Each spreader should be installed flush with the back edges of the standards, directly above a shelf.
1. Set the standards on their back edges so their outside faces are 36" apart. Position a spreader just above the reference lines for the bottom shelf and drill pilot holes through the standards and into the

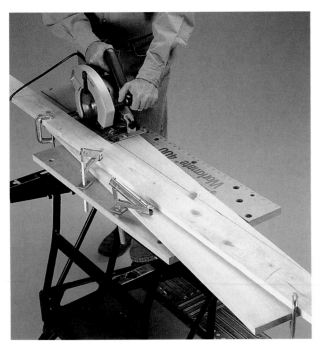

A. *Clamp a straightedge to the standard, and make the taper cut with a circular saw.*

B. *Use a framing square to mark reference lines for shelf placement on the standards.*

ends of the spreader. Counterbore the pilot holes.
2. Attach the bottom spreader with glue and 2" wood screws. Install the remaining spreaders the same way, making sure the top of the top spreader is flush with the tops of the standards.
3. Check the bookcase to make sure it is square by measuring diagonally from one corner to the opposite corner. If the measurements are equal, the bookcase is square. If the project is out-of-square, apply pressure to one side or the other with clamps, pulling it back into square before you fasten the shelves.

Step D: INSTALL THE SHELVES & APPLY A FINISH.
1. Position the bottom shelf between the standards so that the top edge of the shelf is butted up against the bottom edge of the spreader. Make sure the shelf is flush with the reference lines on both sides.
2. Drill pilot holes through the standards, into the shelf ends, and counterbore the pilot holes.
3. Drill pilot holes through the bottom of the shelf, into the bottom edge of the spreader (you don't need to counterbore and plug these holes because the screw heads will not be visible).
4. Apply glue to the ends of the shelf and the bottom edge of the spreader and attach the shelf with 2" wood screws. Countersink the screws under the shelf

slightly so you can apply wood putty before finishing the bookcase.
5. Attach the remaining shelves in the same fashion, working your way to the top of the bookcase.
6. Insert glued, ⅜"-dia. wood plugs into all counterbored screw holes. Fill the remaining holes with wood putty, and sand all the surfaces smooth.
7. Finish-sand the entire project with fine (up to 180- or 220-grit) sandpaper. We finished our bookcase with a light, semitransparent wood stain and two coats of water-based polyurethane to protect and seal the wood.

> **T I P :**
>
> Anchor smaller furnishings to the wall in heavy traffic areas. In many cases, as with this open-back hallway bookcase, the exposed spreaders can be used as strips for screwing the project to the wall. For best results, drive screws into the wall studs through the top spreader and at least one lower spreader. Counterbore the screws, cover the heads with wood plugs, then finish the plugs to match the bookcase.

C. *Fasten the spreaders between the bookcase standards. Make sure the bookcase remains square as you work.*

D. *Attach the shelves, driving wood screws through the standards and into the ends of the shelves.*

Utility Shelves

Utility shelves offer excellent space to organize and store items in a workshop, basement, garage, or attic. Building this unit is a good project for beginning do-it-yourselfers because the construction is relatively simple and the results are produced quickly. We have provided a cutting list for the project as shown, but you can adapt the dimensions of the shelves to suit your needs. In the project shown, corner braces are cut from plywood to support the legs and cross braces. You can also purchase metal connectors to construct the shelf brackets as shown below.

Utility shelves are easy to build and can be adapted to fit just about any space throughout your home or garage.

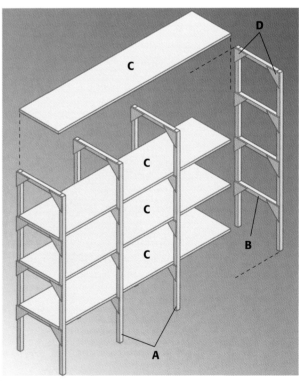

Key	Part	Dimension
A	(8) Leg	1½ × 1½" × 6 ft. pine
B	(16) Cross brace	1½ × 1½" × 2 ft. pine
C	(4) Shelf	¾" × 2 × 8 ft. plywood
D	(32) Corner brace	⅜ × 5 × 5" plywood

TOOLS & MATERIALS

- Tape measure
- Circular saw
- Drill with a ¼" bit
- Carpenter's square
- Jig saw
- (10) 2 × 2" × 8 ft. pine

- (1) 2 × 4" × 8 ft. pine
- (2) ¾" × 4 × 8 ft. plywood
- (1) ⅜" × 2 × 4 ft. plywood
- Wood glue
- Wallboard screws (1", 3")
- Lag screws (1¼")

Directions: *Utility Shelves*

Step A: BUILD THE LADDER BRACKETS.
Cut the legs and cross braces to length from 2 × 2 lumber. The cross braces should be 3" shorter than the desired width of your shelf. Cut the gussets or corner braces from ⅜" plywood, or use metal connectors.

Step B: BUILD AND ATTACH THE LEG ASSEMBLIES.
1. Assemble the legs and cross braces by applying glue to the gussets and driving 1" wallboard screws through the gussets and into the frame pieces. Make sure the gussets are flush with the front or back edge of the leg assemblies and the top edge of the cross support.

2. Installing blocking across exposed wall studs provides a better base to anchor the shelf, and allows you greater flexibility in choosing the width of your shelves. Install blocking in at least two locations on an exposed wall—one near the bottom of the unit and the other near the top. Cut 2 × 4 blocking to the desired width of your shelves and install it across the exposed wall studs, using 3" wallboard screws. Then attach the leg assemblies to wall studs, using 3" wallboard screws.

Step C: MAKE THE SHELVING PANELS.
The thickness of plywood you use for the shelf panels is determined by what you plan to store. For a heavy-duty shelving unit, we suggest ¾" plywood. However, if you will be storing only lighter items, ½" plywood is sufficient.
1. Cut the shelves to the planned length and width, using a circular saw.
2. Slide the shelves over the cross braces of the leg assemblies so the ends of the shelves are flush with the end leg assemblies. Then fasten the shelves in place by driving two 1" wallboard screws through the shelves, into the cross braces at each end of the shelves.

A. *To build ladder brackets, cut the legs and cross braces from 2 × 2 lumber.*

B. *Assemble legs and cross braces with triangular gussets or metal connectors.*

C. *Cut shelves from plywood and slide them into place over the cross braces.*

Under-bed Storage Box

A standard twin-size bed conceals at least 15 cubic feet of storage space beneath the box spring. Put that valuable space to good use with this under-bed storage box. Designed to roll easily in and out from under your bed, it is the perfect spot to store just about anything. And if you use aromatic cedar for the compartment lids, clothing items will be safe from moths and other pests.

Construction of the under-bed storage box is very simple. It is basically a pine frame with a center divider and cleats for the lids and the bottom panels. We mounted bed-box rollers at all four corners so the box can slide easily. Bed-box rollers are special wheels that can be purchased at most hardware stores or woodworker's stores—because they are hard plastic, they will not damage or discolor your carpeting.

TOOLS & MATERIALS

- Circular saw
- Pipe clamps
- Power drill
- Screwdriver
- Power sander
- Tape measure
- (3) 1 × 2" × 8 ft. pine
- (2) 1 × 3" × 8 ft. pine

- (2) 1 × 6" × 8 ft. pine
- (1) ⅜" × 4 × 8 ft. BC plywood
- (1) ¼" × 4 × 8 ft. aromatic cedar
- Bed-box rollers
- Wood screws (#6 × 1⅜" and #6 × 2")
- Wood glue

Put wasted space beneath a bed to work with this simple roll-out storage box.

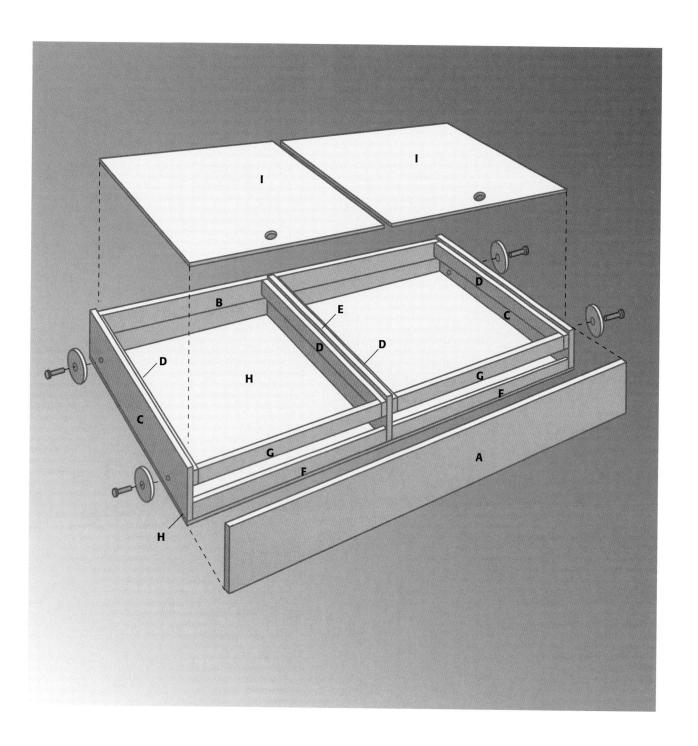

Key	Part	Dimension
A	(1) Box front	¾ × 5½" × 5 ft. pine
B	(2) Box back	¾ × 2½ × 56½" pine
C	(2) Box side	¾ × 5½ × 29¼" pine
D	(4) Lid support	¾ × 1½ × 28½" pine
E	(1) Divider	¾ × 5½ × 28½" pine

Key	Part	Dimension
F	(2) Bottom cleat	¾ × 1½ × 27¾" pine
G	(2) Top cleat	¾ × 1½ × 26¼" pine
H	(1) Bottom panel	⅜ × 29½ × 58" plywood
I	(2) Sliding lid	¼ × 27¾ × 29¼" aromatic cedar

Directions: Under-bed Storage Box

Step A: MAKE THE FRAME.

The frame for the under-bed storage box is a basic box made with butt joints. The front board on the box overhangs the sides by 1" to conceal the front bed-box rollers that are mounted to the sides.

1. Cut the box front (A) and box sides (C) to length from 1 × 6 pine, and cut the box backs (B) from 1 × 3 pine. When laid edge to edge, two 1 × 3s are ½" shorter than one 1 × 6, which will create a recess for mounting the bottom panel. Sand all parts smooth.

2. Draw a reference line on the inside face of the box front, 1" in from each side. Set the box front on a spacer made from ½" plywood. Align the box sides at the inside edges of the reference lines (make sure the box front is ⁵⁄₁₆" higher than the tops of the side).

3. Attach the sides to the front, using glue and #6 × 2" wood screws. Counterbore the screws so the heads can be covered with wood putty. Attach one of the box back 1 × 3s between the sides, flush with the bottom edges, using glue and screws.

4. Attach the other 1 × 3 between the sides, making sure the edges of the two back parts are butted to-gether tightly, and there is a ½" gap between the top of the back and the sides.

Step B: INSTALL THE FRAME DIVIDER & CLEATS.

1. Mark the centerpoints on the inside faces of the box front and box backs. The front centerpoint is 30" from each end. The back centerpoint is 28¼" from each end (measure from the ends of the back, not the outside faces of the box).

2. Cut the divider (E), then position it between the front and the back of the box, with the end of the divider centered on the centerpoints. The top of the divider should be ⁵⁄₁₆" above the top edges of the front and back.

3. Attach the divider with glue and screws driven through the front and back, into the ends of the divider. Cut the lid supports (D), top cleats (G), and bottom cleats (F).

4. Attach the lid supports to the sides of the divider, flush with the tops of the front and back. Use glue and #6 × 1¼" wood screws.

Step C: ATTACH THE CLEATS.

1. Attach the bottom cleats to the inside face of the

A. *Fasten the back between the sides with wood glue and counterbored screws. Keep the bottom flush with spacers.*

B. *Clamp the lid supports in position flush with the top of the box in front and back, then fasten them with wood glue and screws.*

C. *Attach the cleats to the inside face of the box front, trimming them if necessary.*

box front, flush with the bottom edges of the sides.
2. Position the top cleats between the lid supports, against the inside face of the box front. If the cleats are too long, mark and trim them to length. Attach the top cleats to the inside face of the box front, flush with the tops of the lid supports.

Step D: ATTACH THE BOTTOM PANEL.
Cut the bottom panel (H) to size from ⅜"plywood. Turn the frame assembly upside down and apply glue to the bottom edges of the frame components. Fasten the bottom panel into the frame assembly by driving screws through the bottom into the edges of the frame and the divider.

Step E: INSTALL THE LIDS & APPLY FINISHING TOUCHES.
1. Cut the sliding lids (I) to size from ¼"-thick aromatic cedar press board. Mark centerpoints (13⅞" from the sides) 2" in from the front edge of each lid.
2. Drill 1"-dia. holes through the centerpoints to create finger grips for sliding the lids back and forth. Sand the edges of the lids as well as the finger-grip cutouts, to prevent splinters when handling the lids. The lids are designed to simply rest on the lid sup-

ports. Because they are not attached permanently, they can be lifted off for easy access or slid back and forth.
3. Fill all counterbored screw holes with wood putty, then sand the entire unit with fine or medium sandpaper.
4. Install the bed-box rollers on the outside faces of the sides, 3" in from the front and back. The rollers should extend ½" below the bottom edges of the sides. Remove the rollers and axles before finishing. We painted the storage box, then added a coat of polyurethane (except for the cedar lids, which were left unfinished to maintain their fragrance).

Reinstall the rollers after the finish dries. You may choose to mount chest handles or straps (optional) on the front to make it easier to slide the box in and out from under the bed.

D. *Cut the bottom panel to size, then fasten it to the box frame and divider.*

E. *Mount bed-box rollers on the outside faces of the sides so the rollers extend ½" below the box bottom.*

Joist Shelving

If you think you have completely run out of storage space but still have an unfinished ceiling somewhere in the house or garage, think again. This handy little shelf folds directly between unfinished joists, storing utility items until you need them. It is a good place for tools, laundry room supplies, smaller sporting goods, or other items you don't use every day. If you plan on storing liquids on the shelf, make sure the lids are properly fastened before folding up the shelf. The design of the shelf is easy to change to make it stationary or deeper. With a minimum of effort and materials, you can build a perfect place to house your wine collection or to store caulk or paint.

Turn joist cavities into efficient storage cabinets with these inexpensive, easy-to-build folding shelves.

TOOLS & MATERIALS

- Drill with bits
- ½" spade bit
- Circular saw
- Ratchet set
- Combination square
- C-clamps
- Level
- Tape measure
- (1) 1 × 6" × 8 ft. pine
- (1) 1 × 4" × 6 ft. pine
- (1) ½" × 4 × 4 ft. pine plywood

- (2) ½"-dia. × 3" carriage bolts
- (2) ½" lock washers
- (4) ½" flat washers
- (2) ½" hex nuts
- (1) ¾"-thick plywood scrap
- Wood screws (#6 × 1½")
- Wood glue
- (2) ½ × 1½" lag screws

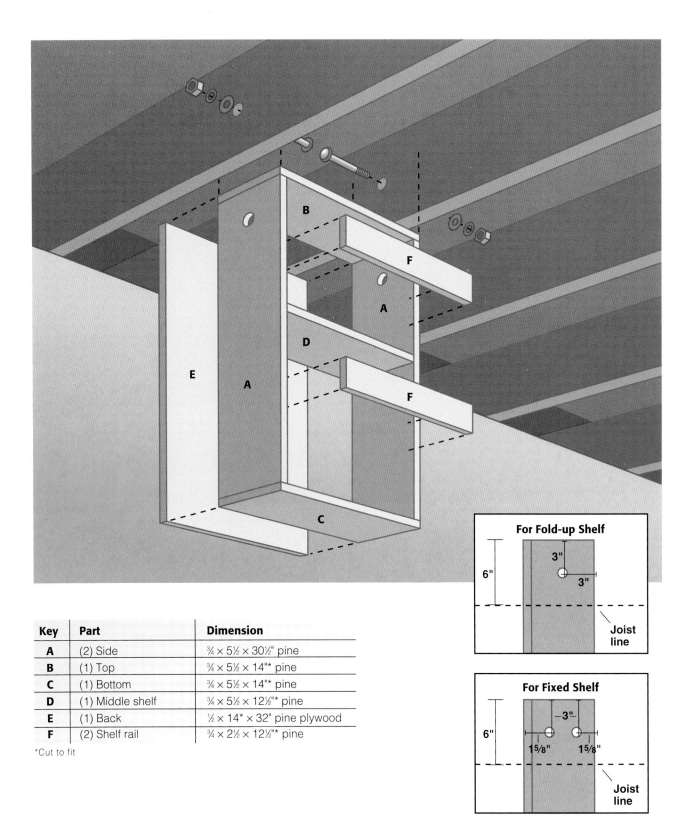

For Fold-up Shelf

6"

3"

3"

Joist line

For Fixed Shelf

6"

3"

1⁵⁄₈"   1⁵⁄₈"

Joist line

Key	Part	Dimension
A	(2) Side	¾ × 5½ × 30½" pine
B	(1) Top	¾ × 5½ × 14"* pine
C	(1) Bottom	¾ × 5½ × 14"* pine
D	(1) Middle shelf	¾ × 5½ × 12½"* pine
E	(1) Back	½ × 14* × 32" pine plywood
F	(2) Shelf rail	¾ × 2½ × 12½"* pine

*Cut to fit

Directions: Joist Shelving

Before you begin cutting the pieces for the frame of the joist shelving, measure the space between the joists where you plan to install the unit. Standard construction should leave a 14½" space between ceiling joists. However, depending on how old the wood is and how your house has settled, the space between your joists could be anywhere from 12" to 16". Make sure you know those dimensions so you can plan the rest of the box construction accordingly.

Step A: MAKE THE BOX.

1. Measure and cut the sides (A), top (B), bottom (C), and middle shelf (D) of the box frame to size from 1 × 6 pine lumber. Sand the edges smooth. Position the sides, top, and bottom panels with their back edges on the work surface, with the perimeter of the box flush at the outer edges.

2. Drill counterbored pilot holes through the bottom and top panels into the side panels. Assemble the frame, using glue and wood screws driven through the ends and into the sides.

3. Using a combination square as a guide, mark a reference line across the interior face of each side panel, 15¼" up from the top of the bottom panel. These lines represent the bottom of the shelf.

4. Slide the middle shelf into position so the bottom edge is flush with the reference lines. Drill counterbored pilot holes through the sides and into the shelf. Attach the shelf using glue and screws.

5. Cut the shelf rails (F) to the proper length and sand the edges smooth. Mark reference lines for the shelf rails 6" up from the top of the bottom panel and 6" up from the top of the middle shelf.

6. Attach the rails so their top edges are flush with the reference lines and the front surface of the rail is flush with the sides. Drill counterbored pilot holes through the sides and into the rails and attach them, using glue and wood screws.

7. Cut the back panel (E) to size and attach it to the back edges of the box frame, using glue and wood screws.

A. *Assemble the frame of the box, using glue and 1½" wood screws.*

B. *Clamp the shelf in place between the joists and drill holes for the carriage bolts.*

C. *Insert a carriage bolt through the outer edge of a joist, then add a washer, lock washer, and hex nut.*

Step B: DRILL HOLES THROUGH THE JOISTS.
1. Refer to the top inset of the diagram on page 67 for specific instructions on the location of the swinging assembly holes.
2. Clamp the unit into position between the joists so it is level and so the top of the shelf is approximately 3" from the subfloor above. When the shelf is in position and clamped tightly, drill a ½" hole on either side of the shelf, through the joists and into the shelf.
Caution: The shelf must be clamped tightly in place; otherwise, it may fall during installation. Do not place weight on the shelf until it is completely installed, or you could risk injury.

Step C: INSTALL THE SWINGING ASSEMBLY.
1. Slide the carriage bolts through the holes from the interior of the shelf, and thread a flat washer, lock washer, and nut onto the carriage bolt until they are snug, using a ratchet set if necessary. Do not overtighten the assembly or the shelf will not rotate.
2. Test the shelf by rotating it up into the ceiling, making sure it glides easily between the joists. With a pencil, make a reference mark on both joists, ap-proximately 2" in from the bottom edge of the shelf in the up position.

Step D: INSTALL THE CLEATS.
1. Cut the scrap piece of ¾" plywood into two pieces approximately ¾ × 1½ × 4".
2. Use two ¼ × 2" lag screws to attach the scrap pieces of plywood to the bottom edges of the joists so that the edges are flush with the inside edges of the joists. The scrap pieces should be tight but still easy to rotate.

VARIATION:

If you want a deeper shelf, use the same construction method, but alter the dimensions. Install this larger box by driving four lag screws through the joists. The shelf will be stationary, but will still utilize space near the ceiling. See the bottom inset diagram on page 67.

D. *Screw plywood cleats into position to act as latches for the shelf.*

To build a deeper, stationary shelf, *build the unit with wider lumber, and drive two ½ × 2" lag bolts through each side of the shelf and into the adjoining joists.*

aundry Supply Cabinet

his laundry supply cabinet can help keep a noto-
iously messy room in check. Although it takes
small amount of floor space, the tall cabinet
s a surprising amount of supplies—including a
ength ironing board. We installed a drop-down
at ironing board level and two stationary shelves
ore folded clothes, as well as laundry detergent,
bleach, dryer sheets—everything you need to get the
job done. On the door we added a handy storage box
that can hold anything from clothespins to spray bottles. A hinged hanger arm will keep freshly pressed
clothing out of the way while you work.

If you plan and cut carefully, you can make all of
the plywood parts for this project from two 4 × 8
sheets of plywood.

*Get maximum use from
a minimum of floor
space with this laundry
supply cabinet. Just
slide it into a corner
and store your laundry
supplies without clutter.*

TOOLS & MATERIALS

- Circular saw
- Drill with bits
- Jig saw
- Finish sander
- Combination square
- Tape measure
- Hand miter box
- (2) $3/4$" × 4 × 8 ft. plywood
- (1) 1 × 8" × 4 ft. pine
- (1) 1 × 6" × 4 ft. pine
- (1) 1 × 4" × 4 ft. pine
- (1) 1 × 2" × 8 ft. pine

- (1) $3/4 × 3/4$" × 8 ft. cove molding
- (1) $3/4 × 3/4$" × 8 ft. base shoe molding
- (1) $3/4 × 1^1/8$" × 8 ft. stop molding
- Wood glue
- Butt hinges ($1^1/2 ×$ 3", $1^1/2 × 1^1/2$")
- 1" brads
- Wood screws (#6 × $1^1/4$", #6 × 2")
- (2) 3" brass mending plates
- (2) Touch latches
- Hook-and-eye clasp
- Finishing materials

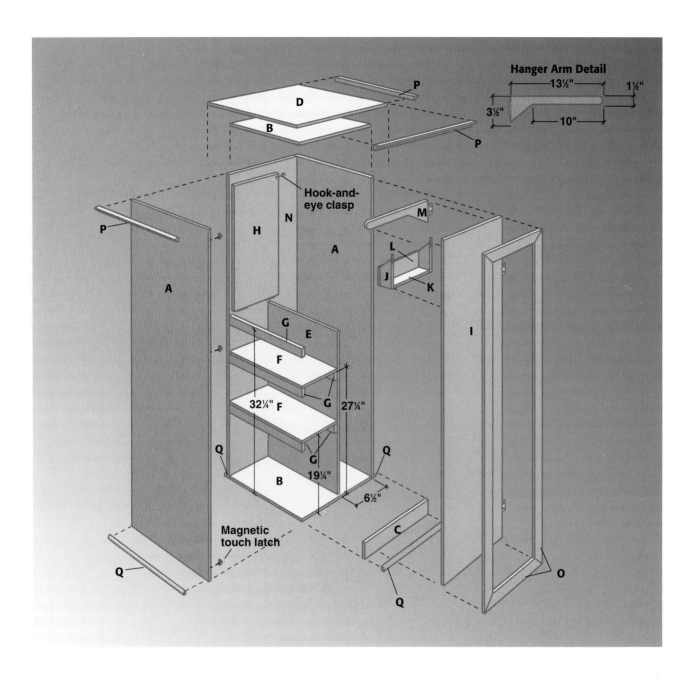

Hanger Arm Detail

Key	Part	Dimension	Key	Part	Dimension
A	(2) Side	¾ × 19 × 65½" plywood	**J**	(2) Box side	¾ × 3½ × 8" pine
B	(2) Top & bottom	¾ × 17½ × 18¼" plywood	**K**	(1) Box bottom	¾ × 3½ × 10½" pine
C	(1) Stringer	¾ × 1 × 17½" plywood	**L**	(1) Box front	¾ × 5½ × 12" pine
D	(1) Cap	¾ × 20½ × 20½" plywood	**M**	(1) Hanger arm	¾ × 3½ × 13½" pine
E	(1) Divider	¾ × 17½ × 32¼" plywood	**N**	(1) Back	¾ × 16½ × 65½" plywood
F	(2) Shelf	¾ × 10¼ × 17½" plywood	**O**	(4) Door frame	¾ × 1⅛ × * molding
G	(5) Cleat	¾ × 1½ × 17" pine	**P**	(3) Top trim	¾ × ¾ × * molding
H	(1) Drop-down shelf	¾ × 12 × 27¾" plywood	**Q**	(3) Base trim	¾ × ¾ × * molding
I	(1) Door	¾ × 17 × 63¼" plywood			

*Cut to fit

Directions: Laundry Supply Cabinet

Step A: ASSEMBLE THE CABINET.
1. Cut the sides (A), top and bottom ends (B), and back (N) to size and sand all the pieces smooth with medium-grit sandpaper.
2. Attach the back panel to the ends, using glue and 2" wood screws driven through the back panel and into the end panels. Then attach the sides to the back and end panels with glue and 2" screws. Make sure the outside edges of the panels are flush before driving the screws.
3. Cut the stringer (C) and cap (D) to size. Center the cap over the top end of the cabinet, and fasten it with glue and counterbored 1¼" wood screws driven up through the end and into the cap.
4. Apply glue to the stringer and position it so that the front face is flush with the cabinet sides. Then drive counterbored 1¼" wood screws through the sides and bottom end to fasten it.

Step B: ATTACH THE DROP-DOWN SHELF.
1. Cut the drop-down shelf (H) to size. On the inside of the cabinet, measure and mark a line on the back, 36¼" from the bottom.
2. Attach the bottom edge of the drop-down shelf at this line, using 1½ × 1½" butt hinges. Make sure there

is a ¼"-wide space between each side of the shelf and the cabinet to allow room for the shelf to drop down.
3. Install a hook-and-eye clasp on the cabinet back and the edge of the drop-down shelf, positioning it to secure the shelf in the upright position.

Step C: MAKE THE DOOR.
1. Cut the door (I) to size from ¾"-thick plywood. Use a straightedge or square to draw guidelines 1" in from the edges on the front face of the door. These guidelines mark the position of the inside edges of the door frame (O).
2. Use a miter box and backsaw to cut the stop molding at 45° angles to fit against these lines. Drill pilot holes, and attach the stop molding to the door, using 1" brads and glue.

Step D: MAKE THE SHELVES.
1. Cut the divider (E), shelves (F), and cleats (G) to size.
2. Draw reference lines for the cleats of the shelves on the left interior face of the cabinet. Measure up 15¼", 28", and 35¼" from the bottom of the cabinet and draw lines using a combination square as a guide.

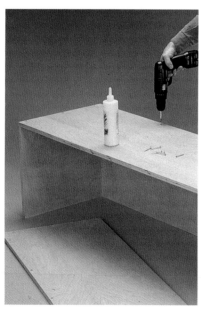

A. *Attach the side panels to the top and bottom ends, and the back panel with glue and wood screws.*

B. *Screw butt hinges into the back panel to secure the drop-down shelf to the cabinet.*

C. *Attach the stop molding to the door, 1" in from the top, bottom, and side edges.*

3. Attach one cleat on each line with glue and 1¼" wood screws driven through the cleats and into the side of the cabinet. Use the same method to attach two cleats to the divider at 15¼" and 28" up from the bottom edge.

4. To insert the divider, mark the bottom and top ends with a line 10¼" from the left side.

5. Slide the divider into the cabinet, so the cleats for each shelf face each other and so the top and bottom edges of the divider line up with the reference lines.

6. Test-fit the shelves to make sure the divider is the proper distance from the side. Drive counterbored 1¼" wood screws through the stringer and into the divider. Attach the shelves to the divider by driving counterbored wood screws through the shelves and into the cleats.

Step E: CUT THE DOOR BOX PIECES.

Cut the box sides (J), front (L), and bottom (K) to size. Measure and mark a point 2½" from one corner along the length of each box side. Using a square, draw a cutting line from the opposite corner to this point, and then cut along the line with a jig saw.

Step F: ADD THE FINISHING TOUCHES.

1. Fasten the box bottom between the box sides with glue and counterbored 1¼" wood screws. Then fasten the box front to the box bottom and sides.

2. Install the box on the door, using brass mending plates. The box should be installed so its bottom edge is approximately 48" from the bottom of the door.

3. Cut the hanger arm (M) to shape, according to the Hanger Arm Detail on page 71. Mount the hanger arm on the inside of the door with a butt hinge, making sure its top edge is 1" down from the top of the door. The hinged end of the hanger should be ¾" in from the door's side edge.

4. Hang the door with hinges mounted to the inside face of the side panel.

5. Use a miter box to cut top trim molding (P) to fit around the base of the cap, and base trim molding (Q) to fit around the bottom of the cabinet. Attach the molding with glue and 1" brad nails.

6. Plug all counterbored holes with putty. Fill all plywood edges, and sand the surface of the entire cabinet with medium (100- or 120-grit) sandpaper to smooth out any rough spots. Finish sand with fine (150- or 180-grit) sandpaper.

7. Prime and paint the cabinet as desired. Attach magnetic touch latches to the cabinet side at the top and bottom of the opening to hold the door closed.

D. *Attach the shelves by driving screws through the shelves into the cleats.*

E. *Draw angled cutting lines onto the box sides, then cut along the lines with a jig saw.*

F. *Use two brass mending plates to attach the box to the inside of the door.*

Dock Box

With its spacious storage compartment and appealing nautical design, this box is a perfect place to stow water sports equipment. You won't have to haul gear to and from the dock anymore. Life preservers, beach toys, ropes, and even small coolers conveniently fit inside this attractive chest, which has ventilation holes to discourage mildew. Sturdy enough for seating, the large top can hold charts, fishing gear or a light snack while you await your next voyage. With a dock box to hold your gear, you can spend your energy carrying more important items—like the fresh catch of the day—up to your cabin.

This spacious dockside hold protects boating supplies, with room to spare.

TOOLS & MATERIALS

- Circular saw
- Drill with bits
- Finish sander
- Hammer
- Tape measure
- Caulk gun
- Clamps
- Straightedge
- (2) 5/8" × 4 × 8 ft. plywood siding
- (7) 1 × 2" × 8 ft. cedar
- (3) 1 × 4" × 8 ft. cedar
- (1) 1 × 6" × 8 ft. cedar
- (3) 2 × 2" × 8 ft. cedar
- Deck screws (1 1/4", 1 5/8")
- 6d finish nails
- 1" wire brads
- Construction adhesive
- Piano hinge (1 1/2" × 30" or 36")
- Hasp
- (2) Lid support chains
- Finishing materials

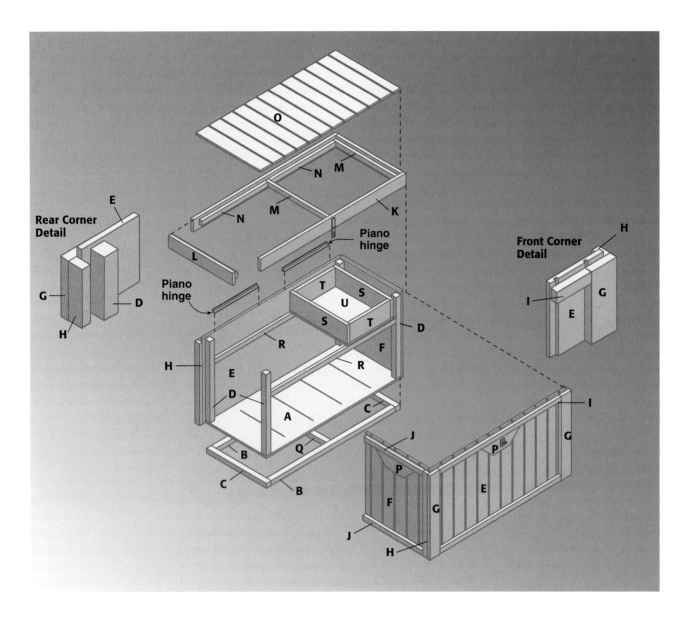

Rear Corner Detail

Front Corner Detail

Piano hinge

Piano hinge

Key	Part	Dimension
A	(1) Bottom	⅝ × 46¼ × 20½" plywood siding
B	(2) Bottom brace	1½ × 1½ × 43¼" cedar
C	(2) End brace	1½ × 1½ × 20½" cedar
D	(4) Corner brace	1½ × 1½ × 24⅜" cedar
E	(2) Large panel	⅝ × 47½ × 27" plywood siding
F	(2) Small panel	⅝ × 27 × 20½" plywood siding
G	(4) Corner trim	⅞ × 1½ × 26½" cedar
H	(4) Corner batten	⅞ × 1½ × 26½" cedar
I	(4) Long trim	⅞ × 1½ × 42¼" cedar
J	(4) End trim	⅞ × 1½ × 18⅝" cedar
K	(2) Lid side	⅞ × 3½ × 49¾" cedar

Key	Part	Dimension
L	(2) Lid end	⅞ × 3½ × 21⅝" cedar
M	(3) Top support	⅞ × 1½ × 21⅝" cedar
N	(4) Ledger	⅞ × 1½ × 22¾" cedar
O	(1) Top panel	⅝ × 21⅝" × 4 ft. plywood siding
P	(4) Handle	⅞ × 3½ × 13½" cedar
Q	(1) Cross brace	1½ × 1½ × 17½" cedar
R	(2) Tray slide	⅞ × 1½ × 43¾" cedar
S	(2) Tray side	⅞ × 5½ × 20½" cedar
T	(2) Tray end	⅞ × 5½ × 14" cedar
U	(1) Tray bottom	⅝ × 15¾ × 20½" plywood siding

Directions: Dock Box

Step A: Make the box bottom.

The bottom of the box is made of grooved plywood siding attached to a rectangular 2 × 2 frame.

1. Cut the bottom (A), bottom braces (B), end braces (C), and cross brace (Q) to size. Apply construction adhesive or moisture-resistant wood glue to the ends of the bottom braces. Clamp the bottom braces between the end braces so the edges are flush. Drill ⅛" pilot holes through each end brace and into the bottom braces. Counterbore the holes ¼" deep, using a counterbore bit. Drive 1⅝" deck screws through the pilot holes to reinforce each joint.

2. Center the cross brace in the frame and attach it with adhesive and 1⅝" deck screws.

3. Attach the box bottom to the box frame, using 1⅝" deck screws.

4. Cut six ventilation slots in the bottom panel by first clamping a straightedge near one edge of the bottom panel. Then place a few pieces of scrap lumber under the panel to avoid cutting your worksurface. Set the cutting depth on your circular saw to about 1" and press the foot of the saw up against the straightedge. Turn on the saw and press down, with the blade in a rocking motion, until you've cut through the bottom panel. The slots should be spaced evenly, 8" to 9" apart.

Step B: Attach the box sides.

1. Cut the corner braces (D), large panels (E), and small panels (F) to size. Align two corner braces under a small panel (grooved side up). Make sure the edges are flush, and that the panel extends ½" beyond the brace on the top and 2⅛" beyond it on the bottom. Fasten the braces with construction adhesive and 6d finish nails.

2. Repeat the procedure for the other small panel.

3. Attach the small panels, with the ½" space at the top, to the end braces, using 6d nails and construction adhesive.

4. Place the large panels in position and drive 6d nails through the panels into the bottom braces and corner braces.

Step C: Make the trim pieces.

1. Cut the corner trim (G) and corner battens (H) to length. Set the assembly on its side. Use construction adhesive and nails to attach the corner battens flush with the bottom, covering the seam between the panels. There should be a ½"-wide gap between the tops of the corner pieces and the top of the box. Then attach the corner trim with 6d finish nails.

A. *For ventilation, cut slots into the bottom panel, using a straightedge as a stop block for the foot of your circular saw.*

B. *Position the corner braces beneath the small panels, and fasten them with construction adhesive and finish nails.*

C. *Attach the corner trim pieces flush with the edges of the corner battens, covering the plywood joints.*

2. Cut the long trim (I) and the end trim (J) to length. Attach the lower trim flush with the bottom, using construction adhesive and 6d finish nails.

3. Attach the upper trim pieces flush with the tops of the corner pieces, using adhesive. Then drive 1¼" deck screws from inside the box into the trim pieces.

Step D: ATTACH THE HANDLES.
The handles (P) are trapezoid-shaped blocks cut from 1 × 4 cedar.

1. Cut four handles to length. Along one long edge, mark each piece 3¾" in from each end. Connect the marks diagonally to the adjacent corners to form cutting lines. Cut along the lines with a circular saw or a miter box.

2. Center a handle against the bottom edge of the top trim piece on each face. Attach each handle with adhesive and 1¼" deck screws.

Step E: MAKE THE TRAY.
The tray rests inside the dock box on slides.

1. Cut the tray slides (R) to length. Mount the slides inside the box, 7" down from the top edge, using adhesive and 1¼" deck screws.

2. Cut the tray sides (S), tray ends (T), and tray bottom (U) to size. Drill pilot holes in the tray ends and counterbore the holes. Then fasten the tray ends between the tray sides with adhesive and 1⅜" deck

screws. Attach the tray bottom with adhesive and 1" wire brads.

Step F: MAKE THE LID.

1. Cut the lid sides (K) and lid ends (L) to length. Use adhesive to fasten them together so the sides cap the end pieces and the edges are flush. Then drive 6d nails through the lid sides and into the ends.

2. Cut the top panel (O), top supports (M), and ledgers (N) to length. Attach two top supports to the inside edges of the frame, ⅜" down from the top edge, using adhesive and 1¼" screws. Then attach the ledgers to the long sides of the lid—one at each corner—using adhesive and 1¼" deck screws. Place the remaining top support into the gap in the middle. Fasten it with 6d nails driven into the ends of the support.

3. Fit the top panel into the lid. Fasten it with 6d nails and adhesive. Sand all exposed edges.

4. Attach the lid to the box with a piano hinge cut in two. Attach a pair of chains between the bottom of the lid and the front of the box to hold the lid upright when open. To lock the box, install a hasp to the handle and lid on the box front.

5. Apply exterior stain or water sealer for protection. Apply exterior caulk to the gap around the top panel and lid frame.

D. *Attach a handle block to each face of the box, flush against the bottom of the top trim piece.*

E. *Counterbore the screw heads so they don't obstruct the movement of the tray on the tray slides.*

F. *Add top supports in the lid frame to strengthen the top panel.*

Outdoor Storage Center

Sturdy cedar construction and a rustic appearance make this storage center an excellent addition to any deck or backyard setting. The top lid flips up for quick and easy access to the upper shelf storage area, while the bottom doors swing open for access to the lower storage compartments. The raised bottom shelf keeps all stored items up off the ground, where they stay safe and dry. Lawn chairs, yard games, grilling supplies, fishing and boating equipment, and much more can be kept out of sight and protected from the weather. If security is a concern, simply add a locking hasp and a padlock to the top lid to keep your property safe and secure. If you have a lot of traffic in and out of the top compartment, add lid support hardware to prop the lid open.

Create additional storage space for backyard games and equipment with this efficient outdoor storage center.

TOOLS & MATERIALS

- Circular saw
- Drill with bits
- Jig saw
- (2) ⅝" × 4 × 8 ft. textured cedar plywood siding
- (2) ¾" × 2 × 4 ft. BC fir plywood handy panels
- (2) 1 × 2" × 8 ft. cedar
- (5) 1 × 3" × 8 ft. rough-sawn cedar
- (2) 1 × 4" × 8 ft. rough-sawn cedar
- (1) 2 × 2" × 8 ft. pine
- (2) 1 × 2" × 8 ft. pine
- Moisture resistant glue
- (4) Butt hinges
- (2) Strap hinges
- Deck screws (1¼, 2½")
- (2) Door catches or a 1"-dia. × 12" dowel and a ¼"-dia. × 4" carriage bolt
- Finishing materials

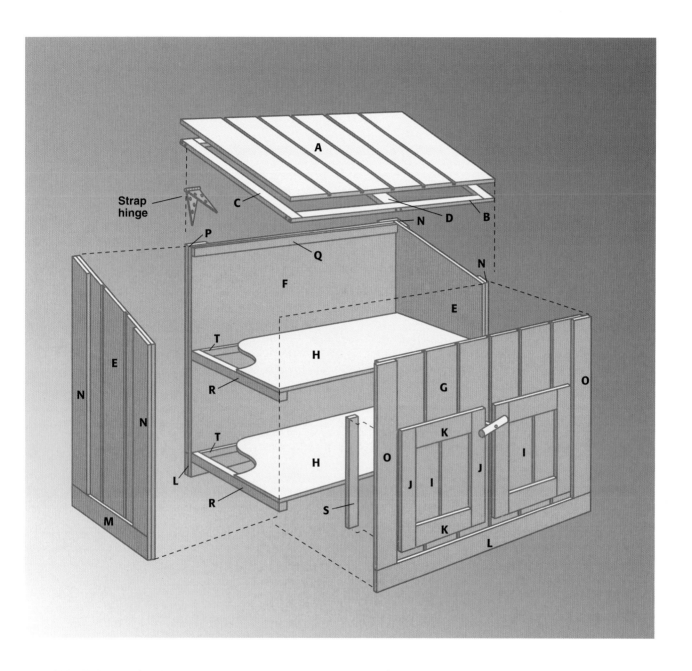

Strap hinge

Key	Part	Dimension
A	(1) Lid	⅝ × 24 × 48" plywood siding
B	(2) Lid edge	¾ × 1½ × 45" cedar
C	(2) Lid end	¾ × 1½" × 2 ft. cedar
D	(1) Lid stringer	¾ × 2½ × 21" cedar
E	(2) End panel	⅝ × 22 × 42" plywood siding
F	(1) Back panel	⅝ × 44¾ × 42" plywood siding
G	(1) Front panel	⅝ × 44¾ × 37½" plywood siding
H	(2) Shelf	¾ × 20¾ × 44¾" fir plywood
I	(2) Door panel	⅝ × 15¾ × 17¾" plywood siding
J	(4) Door stile	¾ × 3½ × 2¼" cedar

Key	Part	Dimension
K	(4) Door rail	¾ × 3½ × 12¼" cedar
L	(2) Kickboard	¾ × 2½ × 47½" cedar
M	(2) End plate	¾ × 2½ × 22" cedar
N	(4) End trim	¾ × 2½ × 39½" cedar
O	(2) Front trim	¾ × 2½ × 35" cedar
P	(2) Back trim	¾ × 2½ × 39½" cedar
Q	(1) Hinge cleat	¾ × 1½ × 44¾" pine
R	(4) Shelf cleat	1½ × 1½ × 20¾" pine
S	(2) Back cleat	1½ × 1½ × 41¾" pine
T	(2) Door cleat	¾ × 1½ × 18" pine

Directions: Outdoor Storage Center

Step A: MAKE THE LID ASSEMBLY.
1. Use a circular saw and a straightedge to cut the lid (A), lid edges (B), lid ends (C), and lid stringer (D) to size.
2. Lay the lid ends and edges on their faces, smooth side up. Attach the ends flush with the outsides of the edges, using glue and 2½" deck screws. Attach the stringer midway between the ends.
3. Apply glue to the top faces of the lid ends, stringer, and lid edges. Set the lid on the frame assembly and screw it in place with 1½" deck screws.

Step B: MAKE THE PANELS.
1. Cut the back panel (F) and front panel (G) to size. On the inside face of the front panel, measure from the bottom and draw straight lines at 5" and 23". Measure in 4" and 20" from each side and draw lines. These lines mark the cutout for the door openings.
2. Drill a ⅜"-dia. starter hole at one corner in each door opening. Cut out the door openings with a jig saw and sand the edges smooth.
3. Cut the end panels (E) to size. On the front edge of each panel, measure down 4½" and place a mark. Draw a line connecting each mark with the top corner

on the back edge of the panel, creating cross-cutting lines for the back-to-front tapers. Crosscut along the lines, with a circular saw.

Step C: ASSEMBLE THE PANELS.
1. Stand the back panel on its bottom edge and butt it between the end panels, flush with the back edges.
2. Fasten the back panel between the end panels with glue and 1¼" deck screws.

Step D: ATTACH THE SHELVES.
1. Cut the shelves (H) to size. Measure up 25" from the bottoms of the end panels and draw reference marks for positioning the top shelf. Cut the shelf cleats (R) and back cleats (S) to length. Attach the cleats just below the reference lines with glue. Drive 1¼" deck screws through the end panels and back panels and into the cleats.
2. Fasten the shelf to the cleats with 1¼" deck screws. Drive 1¼" deck screws through the back panel and into the shelf.
3. Mark reference lines for the bottom shelf, 4" from the bottoms of the end panels. Install the bottom shelf in the same manner as the top shelf.
4. Fasten the front panel (G) between the end panels with glue and 2½" deck screws.

A. *Cut and fasten the lid to the framework with the grooves in the panel running from back to front.*

B. *Drill a ⅜"-dia. starter hole at a corner of each door opening and cut out the opening.*

Step E: ATTACH THE TRIM, DOORS, & LID & APPLY A FINISH.

1. Cut the kickboards (L), end plates (M), end trim (N), front trim (O), and back trim (P) to length. Sand the ends smooth. Attach the end plates at the bases of the end panels. Drill ⅛" pilot holes in the end plates, then counterbore them ¼" deep. Drive 1¼" deck screws through the end plate and into the end panels. Then attach the front and back kickboards to the bases of the front and back panels.

2. Hold the end trim pieces against the end panels at both the front and back edges. Trace the profile of the tapered end panels onto the trim pieces. The trim pieces at the front edges should be flush with the front panel. Cut along the lines, using a circular saw, and attach the end trim pieces to the end panels with 1¼" deck screws. Attach the front and back trim to the front and back panels, covering the trim edges.

3. Cut the door stiles (J) and door rails (K) to length. Attach them to the cutout door panels (I), forming a frame that extends 1¼" past the edges of the door panel on all sides.

4. Cut the door cleats (T) to length. Screw them to the inside faces of the front panel directly behind the hinge locations at the outside edges of the openings. Mount two butt hinges on the outside edge of each door, using 1¼" deck screws.

5. Install a door catch for each door or use a 1" dowel bolted to the front panel as a turnbuckle.

6. Cut the hinge cleat (Q) and attach it to the inside face of the back panel, flush with the top edge.

7. Put the lid and strap hinges in place, with the upper hinge plates positioned between the back trim and lid ends. Drill pilot holes on the back trim for the lower hinge plate and mark the hinge pin location on the back edge of the lid end. Remove the lid and use the location marks to attach the upper hinge plate with 1¼" deck screws. Put the lid in place and attach the lower hinge plates in the same way.

8. Sand the edges of the box smooth and apply a layer of clear wood sealer or the finish of your choice.

C. *Attach the end panels to the back panel, keeping the back panel flush with the back edges of the end panels.*

D. *Place the shelf on top of the cleats and fasten with glue and screws.*

E. *Attach the end trim to the end panel, keeping the front edge of the trim flush with the edge of the front panel.*

Recycling Center

Finding adequate storage for recyclables in a kitchen or pantry can be a challenge. Gaping paper bags of discarded aluminum, newspaper, glass, and plastic are an unsightly nuisance. Our recycling center eliminates the nuisance and makes recycling easy. It holds up to four bags of recyclables, keeping the materials in one place and out of sight. Arches create four feet on the bottom of the cabinet and a bold detail on the front edges. The two spacious bins pivot forward on a dowel for easy deposit and removal of recyclables, and the broad top of the cabinet serves as a handy, low shelf.

Recycling is no longer a chore when this convenient recycling center is a fixture in your home.

TOOLS & MATERIALS

- Circular saw
- Drill with bits
- Jig saw
- Finish sander
- Belt sander
- Bar clamps
- Tape measure
- Combination square
- (1) ¾" × 4 × 8 ft. birch plywood
- (1) 1¼" dia. × 3 ft. birch dowel
- (3) ¼ × 3 × 3" scrap wood or hardboard
- Wood screws (#4 × ⅜", #6 × 1½", and #8 × 2")
- 4d finish nails
- (2) 10" metal chains
- (2) Screw hooks
- (2) Drawer pulls
- Paste wax
- Wood glue
- Finishing materials
- Compass

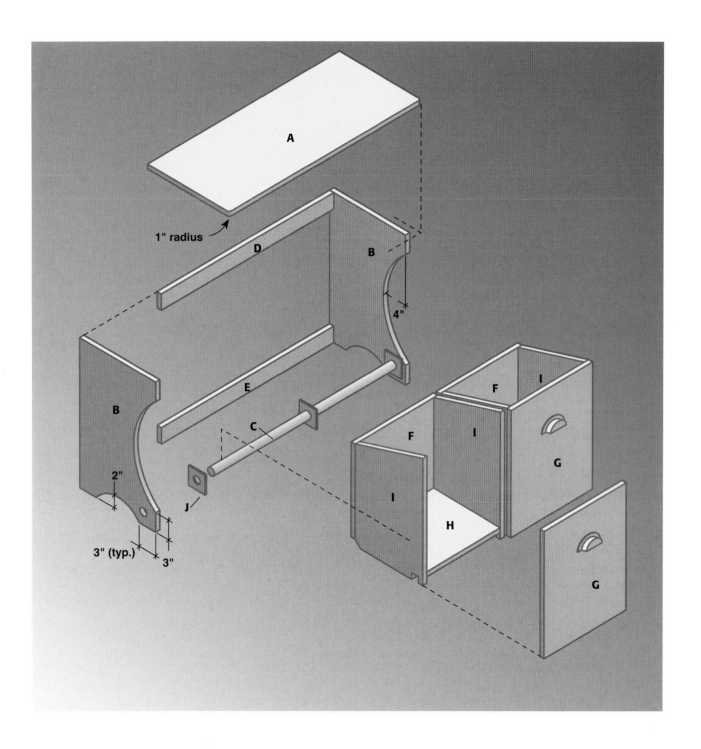

1" radius

D

B

4"

A

E

C

B

2"

J

3" (typ.)

3"

F

I

F

I

G

I

H

G

Key	Part	Dimension
A	(1) Top	¾ × 14¾ × 34¾" plywood
B	(2) End	¾ × 13¾ × 23" plywood
C	(1) Dowel	1¼"-dia. × 34" dowel
D	(1) Top stretcher	¾ × 2½ × 31" plywood
E	(1) Bottom stretcher	¾ × 2½ × 31" plywood

Key	Part	Dimension
F	(2) Bin back	¾ × 15 × 16½" plywood
G	(2) Bin front	¾ × 15 × 19½" plywood
H	(2) Bin bottom	¾ × 12¼ × 13½" plywood
I	(4) Bin side	¾ × 12¼ × 19½" plywood
J	(3) Spacer	¼ × 3 × 3" scrap wood

Directions: Recycling Center

For all #6 wood screws used in this project, drill ⁵⁄₆₄" pilot holes. Counterbore the holes ⅛" deep, using a ⅜" counterbore bit.

Step A: MAKE THE TOP & ENDS.
1. Cut the top (A) and ends (B) to size. Sand the edges smooth with medium-grit sandpaper.
2. To create rounded front corners on the top, mark reference points 1" in from the side and front edges at each front corner. Set a compass to 1", and draw the roundovers, holding the compass point on the intersecting point of the reference marks. Sand the

TIP:
When checking a cabinet for square, measure diagonally from corner to corner. If the measurements are equal, the cabinet is square. If not, apply pressure to one side or the other with your hand or clamps until the cabinet is square.

corners down to the curved lines, using a belt sander.
3. An easy way to draw the front arches on the end pieces is to use a thin, flexible piece of metal, plastic, or wood as a tracing guide. Along the front edge of each piece, make marks 3" in from each corner. Make a mark on the side face of each piece, 4" in from the center point of the front edge. Tack finish nails at these three points. Then hook the flexible guide behind the center nail, and flex each end, setting them in front of the edge nails so the guide bows in to create a smooth curve. Trace the arches with a pencil, and remove the guide and nails.
4. Draw the curves for the bottom edges, using the same technique. Along the bottom edges, make reference marks 3" in from the bottom corners and 2" up from the center point of the bottom edge. Tack finish nails at the marks, set the guide and trace the arches.
5. Make the cuts for the bottom and front arches with a jig saw. Sand the cuts smooth with medium-grit sandpaper.
6. Mark the location for the dowel hole on each end piece, 2¼" in and 2" up from the bottom front corner. Set the end pieces, inside faces down, onto a backer

A. *Drill pilot holes for the anchor screws through the bottom edges and into the dowel holes.*

B. *Apply glue and drive screws through the ends and into the stretchers. Use bar clamps to ensure square joints.*

board to prevent splintering during drilling. Drill the dowel holes, using a 1¼" spade bit.

7. The dowel will be pinned in the holes on each end by an anchor screw. Drill pilot holes for the anchor screws, using a ³⁄₃₂" bit. Align the drill bit with the center of the dowel hole, and drill through the bottom edge of the end piece and into the dowel hole.

Step B: ATTACH THE STRETCHERS.
1. Cut the dowel (C), top stretcher (D), and bottom stretcher (E) to size. Sand all of the parts smooth.
2. Apply glue to the ends of the stretchers and position them between the end pieces so they are flush at the back edges and corners. Clamp the parts together and measure diagonally between opposite corners to make sure the assembly is square (see Tip on page 84). Adjust the clamps, if necessary, to square the workpiece, then drive 1½" wood screws through the end pieces and into the ends of the stretchers.

Step C: ASSEMBLE THE TOP & ENDS.
1. Set the cabinet on its back. Lay the top piece flat on your worksurface, bottom-side-up. Butt the back

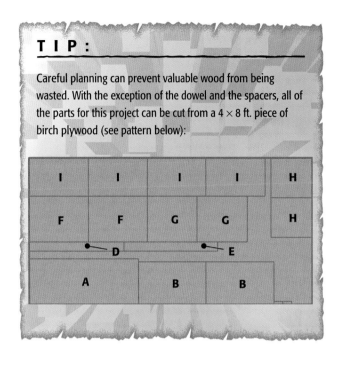

C. *Draw reference lines on the top to use for positioning when attaching the top to the sides.*

D. *Anchor the dowel by driving screws through predrilled holes and into the dowel.*

edge of the top against the top stretcher so it over-hangs the cabinet equally on both sides. Mark the bottom face of the top piece to indicate where it will rest on the cabinet ends.

2. Set the cabinet upright and position the top, aligning the reference lines with the outside faces of the ends. The back edge of the top should be flush with the back of the top stretcher. Attach the top with glue, and drive 1½" wood screws through the top and into the edges of the ends and the top stretcher.

Step D: INSERT THE DOWEL.
Place spacers along the dowel to separate the bins, ensuring smooth operation.

1. Make the three spacers (J) by cutting 3" squares from ¼" scrap wood or tempered hardboard. Tempered hardboard is a good choice because it has hard, smooth surfaces that create little friction.

2. Mark the center points of the spacers, and drill holes with a 1¼" spade bit to accommodate the dowel.

3. Apply paste wax to the dowel for lubrication. Slide the dowel through one end. Then install the spacers, and slide the dowel through the hole in the other end. Position the dowel so it protrudes an equal distance from each end. Anchor the dowel in position by driving #8 × 2" wood screws through the pilot holes on the bottom edges of the ends and into the dowel.

Step E: MAKE THE BIN SIDES.
The bin sides have a notch near the bottom front edge so they can rock safely on the dowel. There are bevels on the top edges and at the bottom rear corners to provide clearance.

1. Cut the bin sides (I) to size. Sand the pieces smooth.

2. Use a jig saw to cut a 1¼"-wide, 1"-high notch, located ¾" from the bottom front corner of each bin side (see drawing below).

3. To make the short bevel on the bottom, measure and draw marks along the bottom and back edges, 1" from the bottom rear corner. Draw a diagonal cut line between these two marks, and cut off the corner with a jig saw.

Bin Side Detail

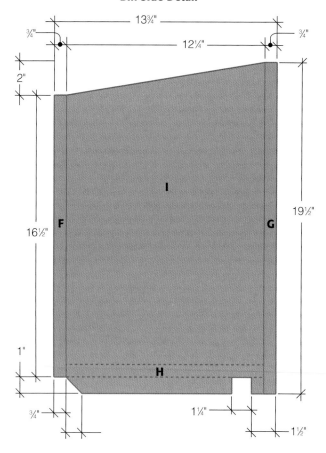

E. *Clamp the bin sides to your work surface, and use a jig saw to cut the notches and bevels.*

4. To make the long bevel on the top edge, measure down 2" from the top back corner, and draw a mark. With a straightedge, draw a diagonal cut line from the mark to the upper front corner, and cut along the line with a jig saw. Sand all of the cuts smooth.

Step F: ASSEMBLE THE BINS & APPLY FINISHING TOUCHES.
1. Cut the bin backs (F), fronts (G), and bottoms (H) to size. Sand the pieces smooth.
2. Position a bin front over the ends of two sides so their tops and outside edges are flush. Attach the front to the sides with glue, and drive 1½" wood screws through the bin front and into the edges of the bin sides.
3. Position a bin bottom between the sides so it is recessed 1" and is flush with the top of the dowel notches. Attach the sides to the bottom with glue and 1½" wood screws.
4. Set the bin back over the edges of the bin sides, keeping the top edges flush. Attach the back with glue, and drive 1½" wood screws through the back and into the edges of the bin sides and bottom. Repeat this process to assemble the other bin.
5. Center and attach the screw hooks on the top edge of the bin backs. Attach 10" chains with #4 × ⅜" wood screws to the underside of the top, 8" from the front edge and 8" from the inside faces of the ends.
6. Place the bins in the cabinet, with spacers between them and on both sides. For smoother movement, sand the notches as necessary.
7. Fill all screw holes with wood putty. Finish-sand the cabinet and bins with fine-grit sandpaper. For a finish, choose an enamel with a medium gloss or eggshell finish to make cleaning easy.
8. When the finish is dry, install a metal drawer pull on the front of each bin.

NOTE: To prevent the bins from falling forward when adding or removing recyclables, our design uses chain and screw hooks to attach the bins to the top panel. The chains can easily be detached when the recycling center needs cleaning.

F. *Position the bin bottom flush with the dowel notch, and attach it with glue and screws.*

T I P :

Ensure a smooth finish by working in a well-ventilated, dust-free area. Airborne dust can ruin a painted finish. Avoid painting a project in an area where woodworking tools have recently operated, and wipe down sanded surfaces with a clean rag to remove all dust.

Hardware Organizer

For most homeowners, weekend projects seem to include several trips to the hardware store to buy a handful of screws, a pair of hinges, a few finish nails, or other common pieces of hardware forgotten in the initial shopping trip. You can eliminate most of those annoying trips by stocking up on a basic assortment of hardware. And with this roomy hardware organizer, you can store your supplies where they are easy to find when the need arises.

With the portable trays at the top of the organizer, you can load up all the hardware you need for a project and bring it right to the job site. The tray dividers fit lengthwise into the trays, and feature cutouts that work as handles. The trays are sized differently, so make sure you are using the right pieces when assembling each tray.

Keep a supply of hardware essentials well organized and close at hand in this portable storage center.

TOOLS & MATERIALS

- Circular saw
- Drill with bits and bit extender
- Jig saw
- Finish sander
- Straightedge
- Portable drill guide
- Tape measure
- (1) ¾" × 4 × 8 ft. plywood
- (1) 2 × 6" × 6 ft. pine

- (1) 1"-dia. × 2 ft. dowel
- Wood glue
- Utility hinges (1½ × 1½")
- Wood screws (#6 × 2")
- Knob
- Bullet catch
- Rubber bumpers
- Finishing materials
- (1) 1 × 4 × 8 ft. pine
- (1) 1 × 3 × 8 ft. pine

TIP:

Common hardware to keep in ready supply (buy an assortment of sizes and styles):
- Wood screws
- Deck screws
- Common nails, finish nails, galvanized nails
- Assorted brads & tacks
- Hinges
- Bolts, nuts, washers
- Staples
- Door & drawer hardware
- Angled brackets & mending plates

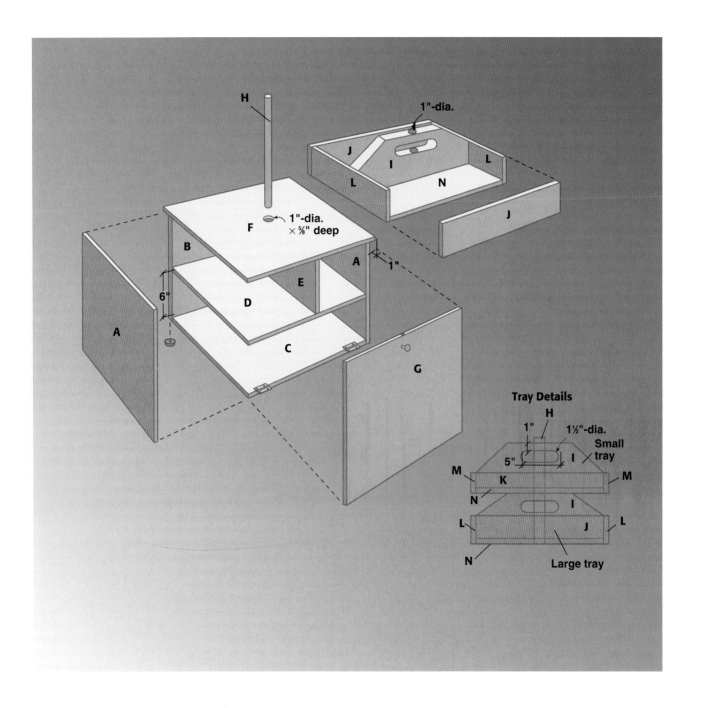

1"-dia.

1"-dia. × ⅝" deep

6"

1"

Tray Details

1" 1½"-dia. Small tray

5"

Large tray

Key	Part	Dimension
A	(2) Side	¾ × 13½ × 16" plywood
B	(1) Back	¾ × 13½ × 17¾" plywood
C	(1) Bottom	¾ × 15¼ × 17¾" plywood
D	(1) Shelf	¾ × 15¼ × 17¾" plywood
E	(1) Cabinet divider	¾ × 6 × 15¼" plywood
F	(1) Top	¾ × 17 × 19¼" plywood
G	(1) Door	¾ × 12⅝ × 19¼" plywood

Key	Part	Dimension
H	(1) Dowel	1"-dia. × 14" hardwood
I	(2) Tray divider	1½ × 5½ × 16½" pine
J	(2) Tray side	¾ × 3½ × 18" pine
K	(2) Tray side	¾ × 2½ × 18" pine
L	(2) Tray end	¾ × 3½ × 14" pine
M	(2) Tray end	¾ × 2½ × 14" pine
N	(2) Tray bottom	¾ × 14 × 16½" plywood

Directions: *Hardware Organizer*

Step A: MAKE THE CABINET.
Cut the sides (A), back (B), and bottom (C) to size from ¾"-thick plywood. Finish-sand all the pieces, and fasten the side panels to the back panel with glue and countersunk 2" wood screws. Make sure the top and bottom edges of each panel are flush. Fasten the bottom panel to the side and back panels with glue and countersunk wood screws.

Step B: MAKE THE SHELF, DIVIDER & TOP.
1. Cut the shelf (D), cabinet divider (E), and top (F) to size and finish-sand the pieces. Center the divider from front to back on the top face of the shelf. Drill pilot holes, counterboring them slightly so the screw heads later can be concealed with wood putty. Fasten the divider to the shelf, using glue and 2" wood screws.
2. Fasten the divider/shelf assembly to the sides and back of the cabinet, with the shelf 6" above the bottom edges of the side. Position the top onto the sides and back with a 1" overhang at the front and side edges.
3. Attach the top to the sides, back, and divider with glue and counterbored wood screws.

Step C: INSERT THE DOWEL.
1. Measure and mark points 1" back from the front top corners. Use a straightedge to draw lines from these points to the opposite back corners of the top. The intersecting point of these lines is the centerpoint of the hole for the dowel. Drill a 1"-dia. × ⅝"-deep hole at this point.
2. Cut a 1"-dia. hardwood dowel (H) to 14" in length. Apply glue to one end of the dowel and insert it into the hole.

Step D: MAKE THE DOOR & PREPARE TRAY DIVIDERS.
1. Cut the door (G) to size from ¾" plywood and drill a centered, 1½"-dia. × 1"-deep hole in the top edge of the door for the bullet catch (check the directions on the package to confirm the required dimensions for the hole).
2. Drill a corresponding ¼"-dia. × ¼"-deep hole into the underside of the top (where you will install the bullet catch after the project has been painted). Then install evenly spaced 1½" utility hinges on the door and the edge of the bottom panel. Sand the entire assembly with medium-grit sandpaper to smooth

A. *Attach the sides to the back, using glue and counterbored #6 × 2" wood screws.*

B. *Drive wood screws through the back and sides to attach the shelf and divider.*

out the rough edges, then install a small knob on the door.

3. Cut the tray dividers (I) to length from 2 × 6 pine. Mark a centerpoint on the top edge of each divider. Then fit a drill with a bit extender and a 1"-dia. spade bit, and drill a 1"-dia. hole all the way through the 2 × 6 at the centerpoints. Use a portable drill guide to ensure straight holes.

4. To lay out cutting lines for the handle cutouts in both dividers, mark a reference line parallel to and 1" down from each top edge. Draw a 1½"-wide × 5"-long cutout below each reference line, centered from end to end (see Tray Details, page 89). Make the radius cuts on each end of the handle slots with a 1½"-dia. drill bit or hole saw. Finish the handle cutout with a jig saw, and sand any sharp edges smooth.

Step E: MAKE THE TRAYS & APPLY FINISHING TOUCHES.
1. Mark points on the face of the large tray divider, at the ends and 3¼" up from the bottom edge. Then mark additional points 4¼" in from each end on the top edge of the divider. Connect these points, and cut along the reference line with a jig saw.
2. Cut the large sides (J), large ends (L), and one tray bottom (N). Finish-sand all the rough edges. Center the divider on the tray bottom, and attach it with

glue and counterbored wood screws, driven up through the bottom into the divider.
3. Extend the hole in the divider through the bottom of the tray. Attach the ends to the tray bottom with glue and screws, driven through the ends, into the tray bottom. Then attach the side pieces to the ends and bottom panel with glue and screws.
4. Mark points on the face of the small tray divider, 1¾" up from the bottom. Mark points 4¼" in from each end on the top edge of the divider. Connect the points and cut along the line with a jig saw.
5. Cut the small sides (K), small ends (M), and other tray bottom (N). Assemble them using the same techniques used for the large tray.
6. Finish-sand the project, then apply primer and paint. Install the bullet catch in the door. Attach rubber bumpers to the underside of the cabinet bottom and slide the trays onto the dowel.

C. *Apply glue to the dowel and insert it into the hole on the top of the cabinet.*

D. *Drill a 1"-dia. hole through the handles, using a piece of scrap as a backing board.*

E. *Lay out the handle shapes separately, using a straightedge, and cut them with a jig saw.*

Decorative & Display Storage

Decorative and display projects are among the most rewarding home storage projects to tackle because they are more personal than other storage concerns. Rather than just trying to get clutter out of your way, each project in this section is designed to show off the things you love. This includes your entertainment center, artwork, photographs, china, books, and other favorite collectables. Well-designed decorative and display storage is not only useful, it enhances the character of your house.

The hallway bookcase can encourage people to linger and to appreciate the narrow passageway rather than rush through it on the way to somewhere else. The bin and shelving unit displays towels and other bathroom items, combating clutter on a vanity. You can store all of your electronic devices and much more in the handsome entertainment center. Get your china out of the basement or kitchen cabinets and display it proudly with the china cabinet. These are just a few of the storage solutions available in this section.

The dimensions of each project were created for a specific space and with particular storage items in mind, but you can customize each project for your particular needs. A little planning will help you use your available space most efficiently, and make each project more useful.

Decorative & Display Storage Ideas

Modern open design *bookcases make a room feel larger by not cutting off sight lines like traditional shelving. Placed near a stairway, they double as a safety rail.*

Shelving doesn't have to be level. *This playful, non-linear shelf is perfect for a child's stuffed animals but could be an attractive addition to any room.*

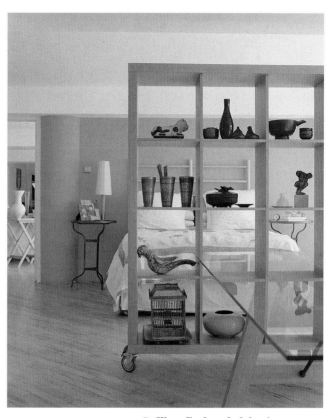

Glass shelving *placed in an unused window makes a dramatic backlit display cabinet.*

Rolling display shelving *is an elegant way to partition a room, and places your artwork, photographs, books, and other favorite collectables exactly where you want them.*

Freestanding modular shelving *can do more than fade into the background; they can become part of the display.*

Decorative & Display Storage Ideas

Stackable cubes *come in a variety of finishes to match different room styles; they are especially useful in apartments.*

Criss-crossing ribbon across a bulletin board, wall, or door creates a flexible system to display photographs and notes.

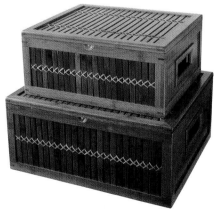

Woven steel baskets designed for gym and pool lockers could be great to organize periodicals, kids' toys, stationery, cloth napkins, CD's, or jars of tea.

Antique boxes or suitcases, or trunks can be great display items themselves, while keeping over-sized books, art supplies, or extra blankets within easy reach.

Bin & Shelving Unit

This versatile wall accessory offers clever storage space for rolled hand towels, soaps, and other small items. The unit can be custom-designed to fit the available wall space and depth for any room. In areas with less wall space, a shorter unit may be built by making only two V-sections. Or, add more V-sections for a larger wall space. For even more versatility, the V-sections may be mounted in a stair-step fashion.

Store smaller items in the bins of this shelving unit, reducing clutter on your countertop or vanity.

TOOLS & MATERIALS

- Circular saw
- Jig saw
- Clamps
- Drill with bits
- #8 adjustable counterbore bit
- Hammer
- Small hand saw
- 1 × 6" × 4 ft. pine

- 1 × 8" × 4 ft. pine
- ⅜"-dia. dowel
- Cotton swabs
- Wallboard screws (#8 × 1⅝")
- Wood glue
- Finishing materials
- Sandpaper
- Stud finder

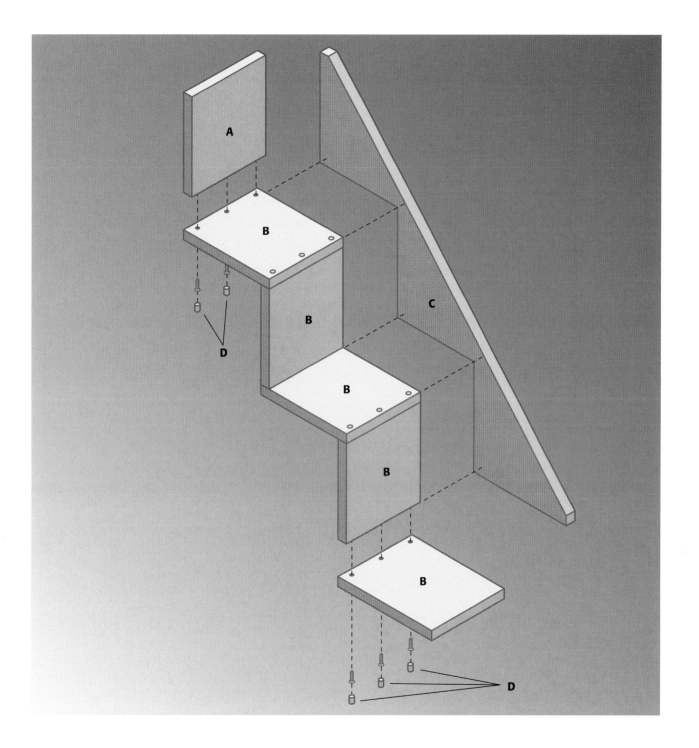

Key	Part	Dimension
A	(1) Shelf panel	¾ × 5½ × 8¼" lumber
B	(5) Shelf panel	¾ × 5½ × 7½" lumber
C	(1) Backer board	¾ × 7¼" × 3 ft. lumber
D	(15) Dowel pieces	⅜"-dia × ½" dowel

Directions: Bin & Shelving Unit

Step A: CUT SHELF PANELS & ASSEMBLE A V-SECTION.
1. Cut the longer shelf panel (A) and all five additional shelf panels (B) to size using a circular saw and a straightedge guide. Sand any rough edges smooth using 150-grit sandpaper.
2. Position the panels on the table as they will be assembled, checking the fit and layout of each panel. Make sure the longer shelf panel (A) is farthest to the left of the assembly.
3. Clamp the longer shelf panel (A) to one of the regular shelf panels (B) at a right angle so that the edges are flush against the worksurface.
4. Adjust a #8 counterbore bit to a total depth of 2". Drill three equally spaced counterbored pilot holes through the longer shelf, ⅜" from the lower edge. Each hole should have a ¼" counterbore. Drive 1⅝" wallboard screws into each hole of the clamped assembly.

Step B: ATTACH THE REMAINING SHELF PANELS.
Attach each remaining shelf panel at a right angle, repeating the construction methods described in Step A. Clamp each new shelf to the workpiece so that the new shelf is flush against the worksurface,

with the side edges of each new panel flush with the side edges of the workpiece.

Step C: PREPARE THE BACKER BOARD.
1. Lay the completed shelf assembly on the backer board, so that the top point of each V-section is flush with the backer board's top edge.
2. Trace the outline of the V-sections on the backer board and cut along the lower cutting lines using a jig saw.
3. Draw lines on the front of the backer board showing the locations of the wallboard screws in the V-section assembly.
4. Mark the position for three screws along each side of the V-sections, avoiding the lines made for the wallboard screws inside the V-sections. Then drill holes through the backer board at the placement marks, using a ⅛" drill bit.

Step D: INSTALL THE BACKER BOARD.
1. Place unit on the table, with the front edge facing down. Turn the backer board over, and position it on top of the workpiece, aligning the edges.
2. Keeping the unit aligned with the backer board, drill a pilot hole in the placement mark closest to the center of the middle V-section with the adjustable

A. *Clamp shelf A to shelf B and drill three equally spaced counterbored pilot holes through shelf A and into shelf B.*

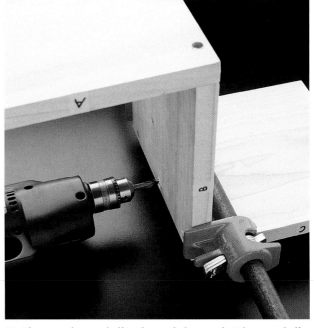

B. *Clamp each new shelf to the workpiece so that the new shelf is flush against the work surface.*

counterbore bit. Only drill deep enough with the bit to create a countersink for the head of the screw.

3. Drive a wallboard screw into the countersunk pilot hole and recheck the alignment of the two pieces.

4. Drill and countersink the remaining pilot holes and drive wallboard screws through the holes and into the V-sections, starting with the ends of the unit and working your way back toward the center.

Step E: Apply the finishing touches.

1. Cut a ⅜" dowel into ½" lengths to use as wood plugs for the counterbored holes. Bevel one end of each plug by sanding or filing it slightly.

2. Place a small amount of wood glue in the counterbored holes using a cotton swab. Insert a wood plug into each hole, beveled end first, and tap it in place with a hammer or a rubber mallet. Wipe away any excess glue using a dampened cloth. Allow the glue to dry overnight.

3. Sand the outer edges of the backer board and edges of the shelves. Cut off the excess of the plugs after the glue has dried using a small hand saw. The plugs should only extend slightly from the surface. Take care not to scratch the wood surface when trimming the plugs.

4. Sand the plugs flush with the surface, using 80-grit sandpaper on a sanding block. Sand the entire unit until smooth, using fine-grit sandpaper.

5. Paint the unit or apply the stain of your choice and a clear acrylic finish. Let the unit dry according to the manufacturer's instructions.

6. To mount the shelving unit, locate studs in the wall to use as mounting points. If no studs are available, make sure to use the proper type of wall fastener.

V A R I A T I O N :

Using the same assembly steps, make a diagonal shelving unit as shown on page 98. Increase the "step up" effect by cutting the shelf panels to graduated lengths. Cut the lowest shelf at 8¼" long, the second shelf at 7½" long, the next two at 6½", and the last two at 5½" long. Then hang the shelf on the wall diagonally. The graduated shelves allow you to place heavier, larger objects on the lower shelves and lighter more decorative pieces above.

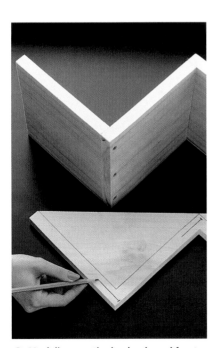

C. *Mark lines on the backer board front, indicating where the V-sections are screwed together. Then mark reference lines for three screws along each section.*

D. *Position the backer board over the workpiece, aligning the edges, and drive screws through countersunk pilot holes, starting with the hole closest to the center.*

E. *Tap the wood plugs into the counterbored holes. Allow the glue to dry, and trim the wood plugs using a small hand saw.*

Corner Display Stand

The open back on this corner display stand lets you add a lot of display space to any room without adding a lot of weight to the decor. Its roomy shelves are perfect for flower vases, fine china, picture frames, and other knick-knacks and collectibles.

But this corner display stand is much more than a practical space-saver. The gentle arches on the front and the slatted back design blend into just about any contemporary decorating style. If you're looking for furnishings with a more formal appearance, substitute oak boards and oak plywood, then apply a warm-toned wood stain.

This light and airy unit brings hard-working display shelving to even a small corner.

TOOLS & MATERIALS

- Circular saw
- Drill with bits
- Jig saw
- Finish sander
- Combination square
- Clamps
- Miter box
- Nail set
- Tape measure
- (7) 1 × 4" × 8 ft. pine

- (1) ¾" × 4 × 8 ft. plywood
- (1) ¾ × ¾" × 6 ft. cove molding
- Wood glue
- Wood screws (#4 × ⅜", #6 × 1¼", #6 × 2")
- 1¼" brads
- Finishing materials

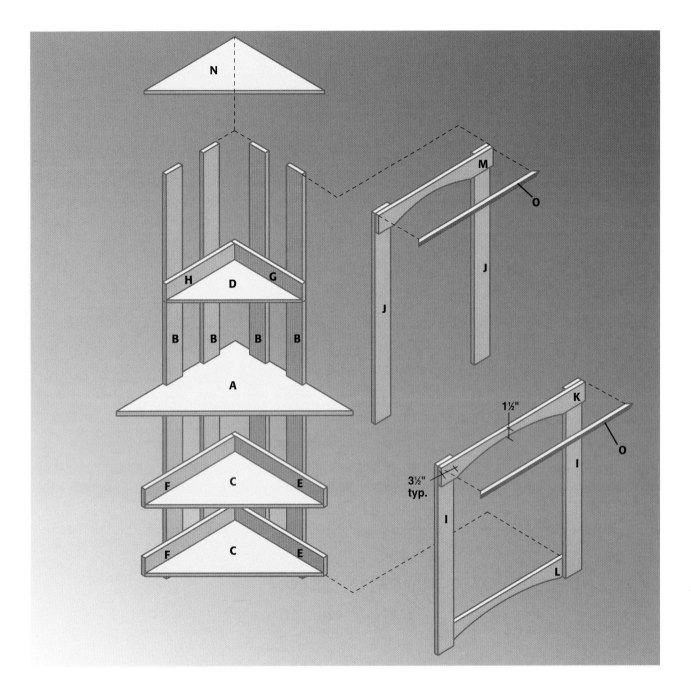

Key	Part	Dimension
A	(1) Center shelf	¾ × 26 × 26" plywood
B	(4) Standard	¾ × 3½ × 75¼" pine
C	(2) Bottom shelf	¾ × 19½ × 19½" plywood
D	(1) Top shelf	¾ × 15 × 15" plywood
E	(2) Bottom rail	¾ × 3½ × 20¼" pine
F	(2) Bottom rail	¾ × 3½ × 19½" pine
G	(1) Top rail	¾ × 3½ × 15¾" pine
H	(1) Top rail	¾ × 3½ × 15" pine

Key	Part	Dimension
I	(2) Lower stile	¾ × 3½ × 35¼" pine
J	(2) Upper stile	¾ × 3½ × 39¼" pine
K	(1) Lower front rail	¾ × 3½ × 32" pine
L	(1) Lower front rail	¾ × 3½ × 30¼" pine
M	(1) Upper front rail	¾ × 3½ × 25¼" pine
N	(1) Top	¾ × 21¼ × 21¼" plywood
O	(2) Trim	¾ × ¾ × 35"* cove molding

*Cut to fit

Directions: *Corner Display Stand*

Step A: MAKE THE SHELVES.

1. To make the center shelf (A), cut a 26⅛" plywood square in half diagonally using a circular saw with a straightedge guide. The result is two triangles with 26"-long sides (the extra ⅛" allows for the thickness of the saw blade).
2. Use a square to lay out ¾ × 3½"-long notches for the standards on the shelf sides, starting 4" and 12¼" in from both 90° corners. Cut out the notches with a jig saw and sand any rough spots smooth.
3. To make the bottom shelves, cut a 19⅝"-square plywood piece in half diagonally, making two 90° angle triangles with 19½" sides. Cut the top shelf (D) to size from a 15⅛" square, making a 90° triangle with two 15" sides.
4. Cut the bottom rails (E, F) and the top rails (G, H) to length from 1 × 4 pine.
5. Attach one longer rail (E) and one shorter rail (F) to the back edges of each bottom shelf with glue and 2" wood screws driven through countersunk pilot holes. The rails should be flush with the ends of the shelf and form a tight butt joint. Attach the longer top rail (G) and shorter top rail (H) to the back edges of the top shelf, in the same fashion.

Step B: ATTACH THE STANDARDS.

1. Cut the standards (B) to length. Sand the legs smooth, and clamp them together so that the top and bottom edges are flush.
2. Using a combination square, draw reference lines across the standards 3½", 16", 35¼", and 52" from the bottom ends. Then draw reference lines on each shelf rail, 3¾" and 11½" from the back corner, to mark the positions for the inside edges of the standards.
3. Clamp the shelves to the standards so the reference lines are aligned, and attach them with glue and 2" wood screws, driven through pilot holes in the backs of the standards, into the shelves. Drill the pilot holes carefully so you do not miss the shelf and puncture the face of the rail.

Step C: CUT THE FACE FRAME ARCHES.

The face frames consist of vertical stiles and horizontal rails. The rails feature decorative arches.
1. Cut the lower stiles (I), upper stiles (J), lower front rails (K, L), and upper front rail (M) to length.
2. Make the cutting lines for the top and bottom arches with a thin, flexible straightedge as a marking guide. Find the centerpoint of each rail, and mark points 13" out from the center.
3. Tack a 1¼" brad at these points, as close to the

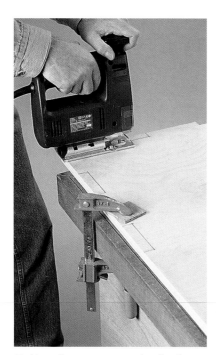

A. *Use a jig saw to cut notches for the standards in the back edges of the center shelf.*

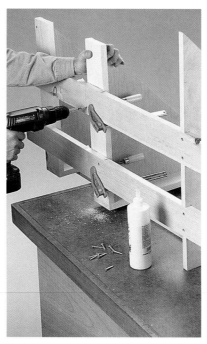

B. *Drive screws through the standards and into the shelf rails.*

C. *Use a flexible marking guide to draw the arches on the front rails.*

bottom edge as possible. Also tack a brad at the centerpoint, 2" up from the bottom edge. Hook the marking guide over the middle brad, and flex each end of the guide to the marked points.

4. Trace the curve on each rail, and cut along the curved lines with a jig saw.

Step D: BUILD THE FACE FRAMES.
1. Center the shorter of the two lower front rails (L) across the back of the lower stiles. The edge of the rail with the arch should be flush with the ends of the stiles.
2. Clamp the rail to the stiles. Then clamp the longer of the lower front rails (K) to the front of the tops of the stiles, so the straight edges are flush.
3. Attach both lower front rails to the lower stiles with four 1¼" screws driven at each joint.

Step E: ATTACH THE LOWER FACE FRAME.
1. With the stand upright, slip the lower face frame in position. The bottom rail should fit beneath the lowest shelf, and the top rail should fit beneath the center shelf. Center the face frame from side to side so any overhang is equal.
2. Clamp the face frame to the stand, and attach it with 2" screws driven through the stiles and into the

edges of the shelves. Then drive screws through the top of the shelf, into the end of each rail.

Step F: ADD THE UPPER FACE FRAME & FINISH THE STAND.
1. Position the upper face frame so the bottoms of the stiles rest on the center shelf, and the stiles overhang the corners of the top shelf by equal amounts.
2. Tack the face frame in place by driving one 2" wood screw through each stile and into the front edge of the top shelf. Then drive screws up through the underside of the center shelf and into the bottom ends of the stiles.
3. Cut the top (N) to size, and attach it to the tops of the standards and the top rail of the upper face frame with glue and 2" screws. The back sides of the top should be flush with the outside faces of the standards.
4. To make the trim pieces (O), cut strips of ¾" cove molding to fit along the front edges of the center shelf and top shelf. Miter-cut the ends to follow the edge of each shelf. Attach the trim pieces with 1¼" brads driven into pilot holes.
5. Set all nail heads, then cover the nail and screw heads with wood putty.
6. Sand the entire project, and apply the finish of your choice.

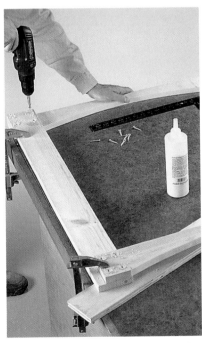

D. *Assemble the arched front rails and the stiles into face frames.*

E. *Drive screws through the center shelf and into the face frame.*

F. *Drive wood screws up through the center shelf to secure the upper stiles.*

Threaded-rod CD Shelf

If you have CDs scattered throughout your home, you probably could free up storage space and eliminate some clutter by grouping them in a single location. This efficient, streamlined unit was designed to hold over 480 compact discs.

The shelves are adjustable to accommodate other items, such as videotapes or DVD cases. Plus, the whole unit spins on a lazy Susan base, giving you quick and easy access to every item on every shelf.

With enough space for over 480 CDs, this shelf can effectively store and attractively display your entire music collection.

TOOLS & MATERIALS

- Circular saw with a plywood cutting blade
- Combination square
- Drill with ⅝" spade bit and ¾" Forstner bit
- Household iron
- Utility knife
- Level
- (1) ¾" × 4 × 8 ft. birch plywood

- (4) ½" × 3 ft. all-thread rod
- (1) 12" lazy Susan
- (44) ½" hex nuts
- (36) ⁷⁄₁₆" flat washers
- 36 ft. birch veneer tape (¾")
- ½" sheet metal screws
- Finishing materials
- Wood glue

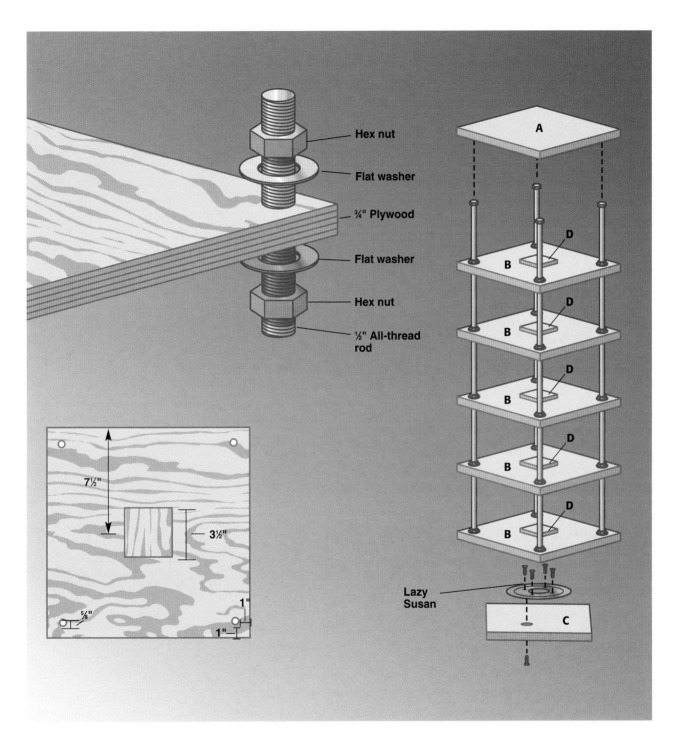

Hex nut

Flat washer

¾" Plywood

Flat washer

Hex nut

½" All-thread rod

A

D

B

D

B

D

B

D

B

D

Lazy Susan

C

7½"

3½"

⅝"

1"

1"

Key	Part	Dimension
A	(1) Top panel	¾ × 15 × 15" birch plywood
B	(5) Shelf	¾ × 15 × 15" birch plywood
C	(1) Base panel	¾ × 12 × 12" birch plywood
D	(5) Divider square	¾ × 3½ × 3½" birch plywood

Directions: Threaded-rod CD Shelf

Step A: MAKE THE SHELVES, TOP & BASE.
1. Using a pencil, tape measure, and straightedge, measure and lay out the top panel (A) on a sheet of finish-grade ¾" plywood.
2. Use a utility knife and straightedge to score the top layer of veneer along each cutting line. This will help you avoid splintering the surface of the plywood while cutting.
3. Cut the top panel to size with a straightedge guide and a circular saw with a plywood-cutting blade. Then cut the shelves (B) and base panel (C) to size, repeating the process used to cut the top panel. Sand the edges of each piece smooth with medium-grit sandpaper.
4. Set the length of a combination square to 1" and use the end of the ruler as a guide to make two reference marks on each corner of the top surface of one shelf, creating an "X" mark 1" in from both edges of every corner. Make the same reference marks on the bottom face of the top panel.
5. Stack the shelves together so that all the edges of the panels are flush and so the reference marks are visible on the top of the stack. Then place a backer board on the bottom of the stack and clamp the shelves to a worksurface so the edge of the stack overhangs the worksurface edge.

6. Drill holes through the shelves on the "X" marks, using a ⅝" spade bit. (The backer board prevents the bottom layer of veneer from splintering.)
7. Use a ¾" forstner bit to drill a hole at each reference mark on the bottom face of the top panel. Drill the holes deep enough to partially recess a hex nut, but be careful not to drill completely through the panel.

Step B: INSTALL THE DIVIDER SQUARES.
1. Using a pencil and straightedge, mark reference lines on the top face of each shelf from diagonally opposite corners, creating an "X" over the center of each shelf panel.
2. Cut the divider squares (D) to size and sand the edges smooth. Then apply glue to the bottom of a divider and line up the corners of the divider with the reference lines on a shelf. Press the divider directly onto the center of the face of the shelf, adjusting it so the corners of the divider square line up with the reference lines.
3. Tack the divider square in place, using two 1¼" brads. Repeat this process for each shelf.

Step C: FINISH THE PIECES & MOUNT THE LAZY SUSAN.
1. Cut strips of self-adhesive birch veneer tape to fit

A. *Clamp the shelves and a backer board together, with their edges flush. Drill a hole at each reference mark.*

B. *Install the divider squares, using wood glue and 1¼" brads.*

C. *Fasten the lazy Susan to the base panel. Drill a hole in the bottom of the base to access the mounting holes inside the revolving ring.*

the edges of the shelves, top panel, and base panel. Use a household iron set at low-to-medium heat to press the veneer onto the edges. After the adhesive cools, trim away any excess tape, using a utility knife.
2. Sand all the panels with fine-grit sandpaper and apply the finish of your choice. Let the finish dry.
3. When the finish is dry, install the lazy Susan in the center of the 12" base panel, following the manufacturer's instructions. You may need to drill an access hole in the base to attach the lazy Susan to the bottom shelf. Use ½" self-tapping sheet metal screws to fasten the lazy Susan to the top of the base panel.

Step D: ASSEMBLE THE RODS & SET THE SHELF HEIGHT.
1. Thread two hex nuts and a washer approximately 2" from the end of each threaded rod.
2. Insert the end of a rod into a hole in the bottom shelf of the rack so the shelf rests on the washer. Fasten the shelf in place by threading another washer and hex nut onto the bottom of the rod, below the shelf. Repeat this step with all four pieces of rod.
3. Raise the top hex nut up to a height of 6" from the top face of the bottom shelf and slide a washer down each rod to rest on the raised hex nuts.

Step E: ASSEMBLE THE SHELVES & INSTALL THE TOP.
1. Slide the second shelf down the rods so that it rests on the washers from the previous step. Then slide another set of washers down on top of the shelf and secure each corner by adding another hex nut.
2. Repeat this assembly until all shelves are in place and a hex nut is positioned at the top of each rod.
3. Position the top panel onto the four hex nuts on top of the threaded rods. Check to make sure the top panel and all the shelves are level, using a torpedo level. Adjust the hex nuts as necessary.
4. Remove the top and set it on a work surface with the holes facing up. Apply a thin layer of epoxy to each hole, then set the entire assembly upside down with the hex nuts set into the epoxy. Let the epoxy cure as the manufacturer recommends.

TIP:

Consider purchasing a veneer edge trimmer to cut down on the amount of finishing time needed for the panels. Edge trimmers create a smooth uniform edge on the veneer edging, and are much easier to use than a utility knife. Although you may not use it often, an edge trimmer is an inexpensive way to produce a project with a more professional appearance in less time.

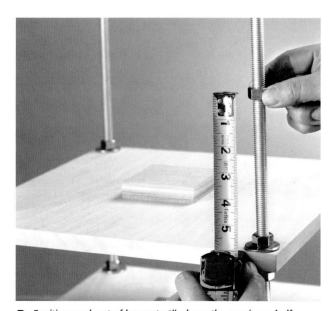

D. *Position each set of hex nuts 6" above the previous shelf.*

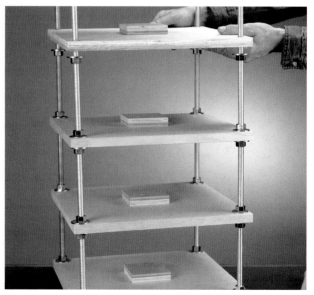

E. *Slide the shelves down to rest on the washers below. Be careful not to chip the veneer surfaces.*

Threaded-rod Table

The all-thread table employs the same construction as the CD shelf, but it's designed to be used as an entertainment center. Or, by adding a keyboard drawer and changing the shelf spacing, you can convert the table to a desk.

Depending on the configuration you put together, you can store a stereo receiver, dual-cassette player, CD player, horizontal-style PC, TV, VCR, and cable box on this table. However, as you plan how you will use your table, keep in mind that some equipment—such as stereo speakers—emit magnetic fields that can damage video screens and computer data devices. Refer to the owner's manual for each component's proper placement before you make final design decisions.

TOOLS & MATERIALS

- Circular saw
- Utility knife
- Drill with ⅛" forstner bit
- (4) ½" × 30" all-thread rod
- (28) ½" hex nuts
- (24) ⁷⁄₁₆" flat washers
- (4) ½" rubber caps
- 30" birch veneer tape (¾")
- Finishing materials
- Computer keyboard drawer (optional)

Key	Part	Dimension
A	(3) Shelf	¾ × 18" × 2 ft. birch plywood
B	(1) Top panel	¾ × 20 × 30" birch plywood

Directions: Threaded-rod Table

Step A: PREPARE THE SHELVES & TABLE TOP.
1. Mark cutting lines on the plywood, laying out the shelves (A) and the top panel (B), using a straightedge. Score the plywood with a utility knife as described on page 108.
2. Cut the pieces to size, using a straightedge guide and a circular saw with a plywood blade.
3. Set the length of a combination square to 1⅛" and use the end of the ruler as a guide to make two reference marks on the top surface of each shelf corner. This will create an "X" 1⅛" in from both edges of every corner, marking the holes for the legs.
4. Stack the shelves so the edges are flush and the reference marks are visible on the top of the stack. Clamp the shelves to a backer board and lay them on a flat work surface, with the edge of the stack hanging over the edge of the worksurface.
5. Drill holes through the shelves at the "X" marks, using a ¾" spade bit or a ¾" forstner bit.
6. Using the ruler of a combination square as a guide, draw two lines across the bottom surface of the top panel, 3" in from each short edge. Place a shelf on top of the panel, lining up the edges of the shelf with the reference lines. Make sure the front edges of the panels are flush with one another.
7. Use a pencil to trace the holes of the shelf onto the bottom of the top panel. Drill the holes in the top panel, centering a 1⅛" forstner bit in each reference circle. Drill out only enough material to recess a portion of a hex nut. Be careful not to drill completely through the top panel.

Step B: FINISH THE PANELS.
1. Apply birch veneer tape to all edges of the top and shelves, using a household iron. Trim away any excess tape with a utility knife or an edge trimmer.
2. Sand all the panels smooth and finish them as desired. Let the finish dry.
3. If you've chosen to add a keyboard drawer, draw two reference lines on the bottom surface of the top panel, 4" in from each short edge. Install the drawer brackets, according to the manufacturer's directions, and flush with the reference lines. Make sure the end of each bracket is at least ½" away from the holes for the table legs. Install the sliding drawer on the brackets, according to the manufacturer's instructions.

Step C: ASSEMBLE THE TABLE.
1. Assemble the table and install the top panel as directed in Steps D and E on page 109. Adjust the shelf height to fit your individual components.
2. Slide a rubber cap on the end of each leg to protect your flooring from damage.

A. *Mark reference lines and drill a hole at each corner of each shelf.*

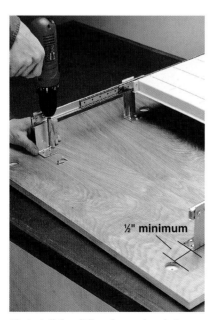
B. *Install the sliding drawer brackets on the bottom of the top panel.*

½" minimum

C. *Thread nuts and washers onto the rod to position the shelves as desired.*

China Cabinet

This modern-looking china cabinet features a unique, efficient design that showcases and stores all types of china and dishware with elegance. The bottom half of the cabinet is a simple cupboard for storing everyday serving trays, napkins, silverware, and miscellaneous household items. The upper half is an open rack for displaying your favorite porcelain statues, china, vases, and collectibles.

Among the more interesting features of this china cabinet are the 1" dowel columns that support the shelves in the open area. The asymmetrical design allows you to store and display a wider range of items than if the cabinet were equally divided from side to side. And the overall slenderness of the cabinet means you can fit it into just about any room, tucked into a corner or featured prominently along the center of a wall.

Plates and other items that are displayed in the open area of the cabinet can be accentuated with plateholders. Or, you can do as we did and build a few custom-sized plate holders from scraps of molding. Just cut the molding into strips, about the same width as the plates, and inset the strips at ¼" intervals in a plain wood frame.

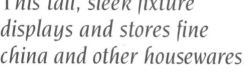

This tall, sleek fixture displays and stores fine china and other housewares.

TOOLS & MATERIALS

- Circular saw
- Compass
- Household iron
- Utility knife
- Drill with bits
- Jig saw
- Combination square
- Finish sander
- Belt sander
- Pipe clamps
- (2) ¾" × 4 × 8 ft. birch plywood
- (2) 1"-dia. × 3 ft. dowel

- (1) ½ × ½" × 6 ft. quarter-round molding
- Wood glue
- Wood screws (#6 × 1¼", #6 × 2")
- Birch veneer edge tape (50 ft.)
- ⅜"-dia. birch wood plugs
- (4) 1¼" brass butt hinges
- 1¼" brads
- (2) Magnetic door catches,
- (2) 2½" brass door pulls
- Finishing materials

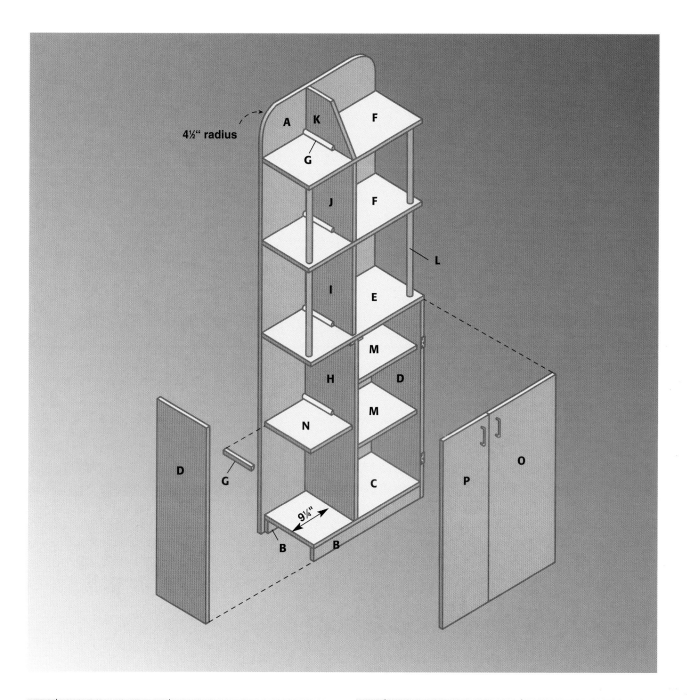

4½" radius

9¼"

Key	Part	Dimension
A	(1) Back	¾ × 24 × 75" plywood
B	(2) Bottom rail	¾ × 2¼ × 22½" plywood
C	(1) Cupboard bottom	¾ × 10½ × 22½" plywood
D	(2) Cupboard side	¾ × 10½ × 35¼" plywood
E	(1) Cupboard top	¾ × 10½" × 2 ft. plywood
F	(2) Rack shelf	¾ × 10" × 2 ft. plywood
G	(6) Cleat	½ × ½ × 6" quarter round molding
H	(1) Cupboard divider	¾ × 10½ × 32¼" plywood

Key	Part	Dimension
I	(1) Rack divider	¾ × 10 × 15⅛" plywood
J	(1) Rack divider	¾ × 10 × 14¾" plywood
K	(1) Rack divider	¾ × 10 × 7½" plywood
L	(2) Column	1"-dia. × 30⅝" dowel
M	(2) Cupboard shelf	¾ × 13¼ × 10" plywood
N	(1) Cupboard shelf	¾ × 8½ × 10" plywood
O	(1) Large door	¾ × 14⅜ × 33¾" plywood
P	(1) Small door	¾ × 9½ × 33¾" plywood

Directions: China Cabinet

Step A: MAKE THE BACK PANEL & CUPBOARD.

1. Cut the back (A) to size and sand the edges smooth. Use a compass to draw a semicircle with a 4½" radius at each top corner of the back panel. Cut the curves with a jig saw and sand the edges smooth.

2. Use a household iron to apply birch veneer tape to the side and top edges of the back panel. Trim the excess tape with a utility knife and sand the edges smooth.

3. Measure in 9¼" from the left edge of the back panel, and make reference marks at 52¾" and 67½" up from the bottom edge. These reference marks are used as guides for installing the rack shelves.

4. Cut the bottom rails (B) and the cupboard bottom (C) to size. Apply edge tape to the front edge of the cupboard bottom, and position the bottom rails beneath the cupboard bottom, flush with the edges.

5. Drill counterbored pilot holes through the cupboard bottom, into the tops of the rails, and attach the pieces with glue and 2" wood screws.

6. Cut the cupboard sides (D) to size, and apply edge tape to the front edges. Position the cupboard bottom between the cupboard sides so the front edges are flush and drill counterbored pilot holes through the side panels, into the edges of the cupboard bottom. Then apply glue to the joints and drive wood screws into the pilot holes to reinforce the joints.

7. Cut the cupboard top (E) to size, and apply edge tape to the front and side edges. Position the cupboard top flush with the edges of the sides. Use glue and screws to attach it to the tops of the sides.

Step B: ASSEMBLE THE SHELVES & RACK.

1. Cut the cupboard divider (H) and cupboard shelves (M, N) to size. Apply veneer tape to the front edges of all the shelves.

2. Draw reference lines on the cupboard bottom and cupboard top, 9¼" in from the left cupboard side, for proper positioning of the divider. These lines should align with the marks made earlier on the back panel.

3. Set the divider between the cupboard top and bottom, so the left face is aligned with the reference lines. Attach it with glue and wood screws driven through the top and bottom panels, into the divider.

4. Draw reference lines on the interior face of the right side panel and on the right side of the divider, 12" and 24" up from the cupboard bottom. Use these lines to position the larger cupboard shelves (M).

5. Draw reference lines for the smaller cupboard shelf (N) on the interior of the left side panel and left face of the divider, 16" up from the cupboard bottom.

6. Apply glue to the side edges of all three shelves and position them between the cupboard sides and the divider, with the bottom edges of each shelf flush on the reference lines.

7. Fasten the shelves with 2" wood screws, driven through the sides and the divider, into the shelves.

8. Glue ⅜"-dia. birch wood plugs into all the exposed counterbores in the cupboard. When the glue has

A. *Attach the cupboard bottom by driving screws through the cupboard sides and into the edges.*

B. *Attach the shelves and divider to the sides. Then carefully sand the wood plugs to level.*

dried, sand the plugs down to the surface of the plywood, being careful not to scar the wood. Then attach the back panel to the cupboard with glue and 2" wood screws driven into the side, bottom, and top cupboard panels. Make sure the edges of the back panel are flush with the side panels of the cupboard.

9. Cut the rack dividers (I, J, K) and shelves (F) to size. To make the angled cut in the upper divider (K), mark a point on one long edge, 5¼" from the end. Draw a straight line from that point to the bottom corner on the opposite end. Cut along the line, using a circular saw. Sand the edges of the pieces smooth.

10. Attach veneer tape to the front edges of the dividers, and to the front and side edges of the shelves. With the taped edges of the shelves facing you, use a combination square to draw reference lines 9¼" in from the edges on the left side of each panel.

11. Drill two 1"-dia. holes for the columns in the lower rack shelf. Use a combination square to find the center of each hole (1¾" in from the front edge and 1¼" in from the side edge of the shelf).

Step C: INSTALL THE RACK.
1. Use glue and 2" screws, driven through counterbored pilot holes in the back panel, to install the shelves and dividers of the rack. Alternate between shelves and dividers during installation. Start by fastening the lower rack divider (I) flush with the reference marks.

2. Cut cleats from quarter-round molding (G) to size, and use glue and 1¼" brads to attach the cleats to each side of the divider, flush against the back panel.

Apply glue to the top edge of the lower divider; and position the shelf with the 1"-dia. holes on top of the divider, so the holes are in front.

3. Attach the shelf to the divider with wood screws, driven through the back, into the shelf, and through the shelf, into the lower divider. Then cut the columns (L) to length and sand the edges smooth.

4. Apply glue to the bottom of each column, and slide each through a hole in the shelf. Use a square to make sure they are straight, then drive a 1¼" wood screw up through the cabinet top, into each column.

5. Position the middle rack divider (J) on the shelf and fasten it with glue, screws, and cleats. Attach the upper shelf to the middle divider and back panel with glue and screws. Then, drive 1¼" screws through the shelf and into the tops of the columns.

6. Apply glue to the back and bottom edges of the upper divider, and attach it with cleats and 2" wood screws driven through the back panel.

Step D: INSTALL THE DOORS & APPLY FINISHING TOUCHES.
1. Cut and sand the doors (O, P), and apply veneer tape to every edge of each door. Give the project a final sanding, and wipe it clean with a rag dipped in mineral spirits. Apply the finish of your choice.

2. Attach 1¼" brass butt hinges to the doors, 3½" down from the top edges and ½" up from the bottom edges. Fasten the doors to the cupboard sides, flush with the cabinet top. Then install magnetic door catches.

3. Attach door pulls to the outside faces of the doors, 1½" from the top edges, and 1½" in from the side edges.

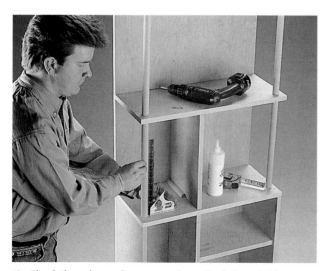

C. *Check the columns for square, then attach them to the cabinet top.*

D. *Hang the doors, using brass butt hinges.*

Entry Valet

This entry valet is designed to provide handy storage in one of the busiest areas of your home: the entryway. It is equipped with a spacious pivoting bin at the top—for mittens, gloves, or hats—and a scarf storage box with a hinged lid below which also functions as a shelf.

Because the entry is the first part of your home that most visitors see, it is especially important that entry furnishings be attractive as well as functional. For that reason, we used simple construction, reminiscent of popular Shaker styling, and added decorative contours that give the valet a touch of Colonial style as well.

The friendly face of this valet hides the fact that it's a functional storage unit, with a drop-down bin and a covered scarf box.

TOOLS & MATERIALS

- Circular saw
- Drill with bits
- Jig saw
- Finish sander
- C-clamps
- Portable drill stand
- Wooden mallet
- Tape measure
- (1) 1 × 12" × 6 ft. pine
- (2) 1 × 10" × 8 ft. pine
- (1) 1 × 6" × 6 ft. pine
- (1) 1 × 4" × 6 ft. pine
- (1) 1 × 3" × 6 ft. pine
- (1) ¾ × ¾" × 6 ft. pine stop molding
- (1) ¼" × 4 × 4 ft. plywood
- Wood screws (#6 × 1¼" and 2")
- Wood screws (#8 × ½")
- 16-ga. × 1¼" brads
- (10) 1½" brass corner braces
- ⅜"-dia. wood plugs
- Wood glue
- Finishing materials
- 1" wire nails
- Butt hinges

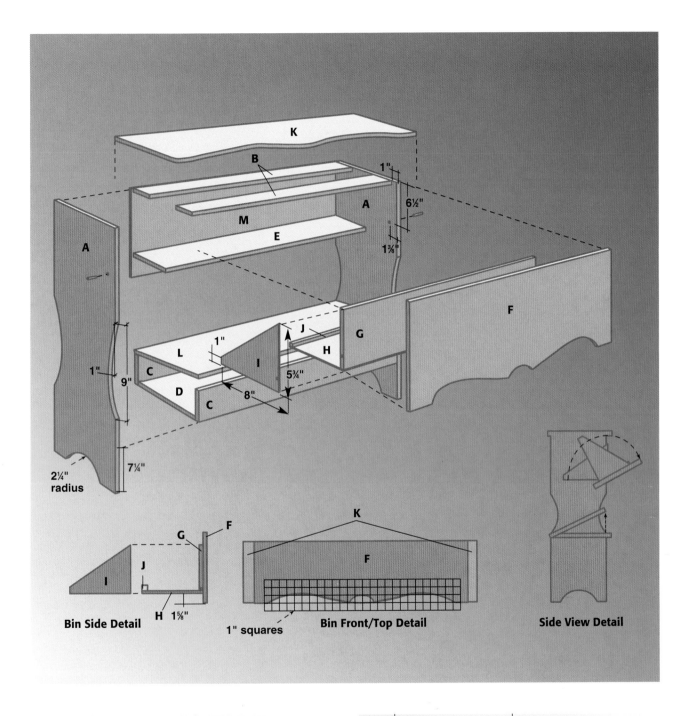

Bin Side Detail

1" squares

Bin Front/Top Detail

Side View Detail

Key	Part	Dimension
A	(2) End	¾ × 9¼ × 33¼" pine
B	(2) Top stretcher	¾ × 2½ × 28½" pine
C	(2) Box side	¾ × 3½ × 28½" pine
D	(1) Box bottom	¾ × 7¾ × 28½" pine
E	(1) Bin stop	¾ × 5½ × 28½" pine
F	(1) False front	¾ × 9¼ × 28¼" pine
G	(1) Bin front	¾ × 5½ × 27⅝" pine

Key	Part	Dimension
H	(1) Bin bottom	¼ × 8 × 27⅝" plywood
I	(2) Bin side	¼ × 5¾ × 8" plywood
J	(1) Bin back lip	¾ × ¾ × 27⅜" stop molding
K	(1) Top	¾ × 11¼ × 32" pine
L	(1) Lid	¾ × 9½ × 28¼" pine
M	(1) Valet back	¼ × 8⅜ × 29½" plywood

Directions: Entry Valet

Step A: CUT & CONTOUR THE END PIECES.
1. Cut the end panels (A) to length.
2. To make the side cutouts, mark points at each side edge, 17⅜" from the bottom edges. At these points, measure in 1" from the side edge to mark the deepest point of the cutout. Mark points 4½" above and below each mark at the side edges to mark the endpoints of the cutout. Flex a ruler between the endpoints as a guide, then draw curved lines from one endpoint to the other, passing through the centerpoint. Make the cutouts with a jig saw and sand the edges smooth.
3. To make the bottom cutouts, mark the center of each end panel on the bottom edge. Set a compass to 2¼" radius, and set the tip on the centerpoint. Draw a semicircular cutting line at the bottom of each panel. Make the cutouts and sand the edges smooth.

Step B: ASSEMBLE THE FRAMEWORK.
1. Cut the scarf box sides (C), box bottom (D), top stretchers (B), and bin stop (E) to size.
2. Position the box pieces for assembly, and drill ⁵⁄₆₄" pilot holes through the box sides and into the edges of the box bottom. Counterbore the holes ¼" deep, using a ⅜" counterbore bit. Attach the pieces with glue and three or four evenly spaced 1¼" wood screws.
3. Attach the box assembly to the inside faces of the end panels so the box sides are flush with the front

and back edges of the end panels. The box bottom should be 7¼" above the bottoms of the end panels.
4. Position the top stretchers between the end panels, face up. One stretcher should be flush with the back and top edges of the end panels, and the other should be flush with the tops, but recessed 1" from the front edges (see the diagram on page 117). Drill pilot holes through the end panels and into the stretchers. Counterbore the holes and attach the stretchers to the panels, using glue and 1¼" wood screws.
5. Install the bin stop between the end panels so its top face is 7⅞" down from the tops of the panels, and its back is flush with the back edges.

Step C: BUILD THE BIN.
1. Cut the bin front (G) and the bin bottom (H) to size. Attach the bin bottom to the bin front with glue and 1" wire nails driven up through the bottom and into the front piece.
2. Cut the triangular bin sides (I) to size (see the diagram on page 117). Attach the sides to the bottom/front assembly with glue and 1" wire nails.
3. Cut the stop molding to length for the bin back lip (J). Glue the lip to the top face of the bin bottom, centered between the bin sides.

Step D: CUT & ATTACH THE FALSE FRONT FOR THE BIN.
1. Cut the false front (F) to length. Plot a grid with 1"

A. *Use a compass to draw 2¼"-radius semicircles on the bottoms of the end pieces.*

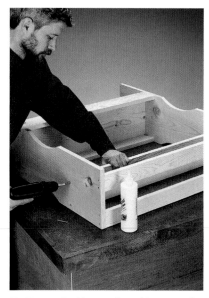

B. *Fasten the bin stop board between the end panels to complete the assembly of the framework.*

C. *Fasten the bin sides with glue and wire nails.*

squares on the face of it. Use the pattern on page 117 as a guide to draw the shape onto the false front. Make the cutout with a jig saw, and sand the edges smooth.

2. Draw a reference line on the inside face of the false front, 1⅝" down from the top edge. Attach the false front to the bin front so the top of the bin is flush with the reference line. Apply glue to the joint and drive 1¼" wood screws through the bin and into the false front.

Step E: INSTALL THE BIN & APPLY FINISHING TOUCHES.
1. Set the bin on the bin stop board so it is flush against the front top stretcher and the bin stop. Use spacer blocks and C-clamps to hold the bin in place. Mount a portable drill stand to your portable drill, and drill a ⅜"-dia. × 1⅜"-deep hole through each end panel and into the sides of the bin. The centerpoints of the holes should be 6½" down from the tops of the end panels, and 1⅜" in from the front edges. Remove the C-clamps and the bin.

2. Cut the valet top (K) to size. Make the decorative cutout on the front edge using the same pattern and techniques used for the bin false front, omitting the small scallop in the center.

3. Drill pilot holes through the valet top and into the end panels. Counterbore the holes. Attach the top with glue and 1¼" wood screws, positioning the top so it overhangs the outside faces of the end panels

by 1" and the front edges of the panels by 1¼".
4. Cut the scarf box lid (L) to size from the 1 × 12 lumber.

5. Fill the screw holes in the end panels, box sides, and top with ⅜" wood plugs. Sand the plugs flush with the surface with 80-grit sandpaper and a sanding block. Then finish-sand all the pieces and apply the finish of your choice.

6. Attach the lid to the box with 2" butt hinges at the back of the lid. Attach one leaf of the hinges to the bottom face of the lid and the other leaf to the back face of the rear box side.

7. Cut two 1½" pieces from the ⅜"-dia. dowel. The dowels will serve as pivot points for the bin. Squirt a small amount of wood glue into the dowel holes and position the bin. Drive the dowels into the holes, using a wood block to prevent splitting. After the glue sets, sand the dowels flush and refinish the dowel areas.

8. Cut the valet back (M) to size. Position it so its top edge butts against the bottom of the valet top. Center it side to side. Drive 1" wire nails through the valet back and into the back edges of the top stretcher, bin stop, and end panels.

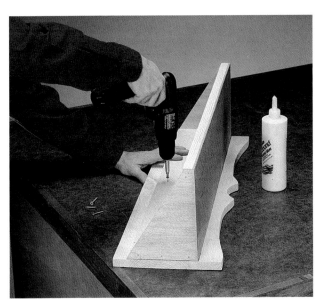

D. *Drive wood screws through the inside of the bin and into the back of the false front.*

E. *Clamp the bin to the framework. Then, drill dowel holes through the sides and into the bin.*

Sideboard

The sideboard is an attractive, multipurpose fixture that can be used for anything that requires shelf or counter space, from food to files. The sideboard is a traditional home fixture, adding low-profile storage to just about any area of the home. Positioned against a wall or behind a desk, the sideboard is out of the way, yet is perfect for storing games, photo albums, and other items you want to keep close at hand.

We made the sideboard out of oak and oak plywood. The construction is simple and sturdy. Two long interior shelves span the length of the project, giving you a surprising amount of storage space for such a small unit. The top shelf is concealed by two plywood doors, while the bottom shelf is left open for easy access to stored items. Cove molding fastened around the edges of the top and the curved profiles of the legs add a touch of style to this simple project.

This elegant sideboard has plenty of room to hold everything from a meal with all the trimmings to stacks of important files.

TOOLS & MATERIALS

- (1) ¾" × 4 × 8 ft. oak plywood
- (2) 1 × 4" × 8 ft. oak
- (2) ¾ × ¾" × 8 ft. oak cove molding
- Utility knife
- Self-adhesive edge tape
- Drill with bits
- Jig saw
- Power screwdriver
- Wood glue

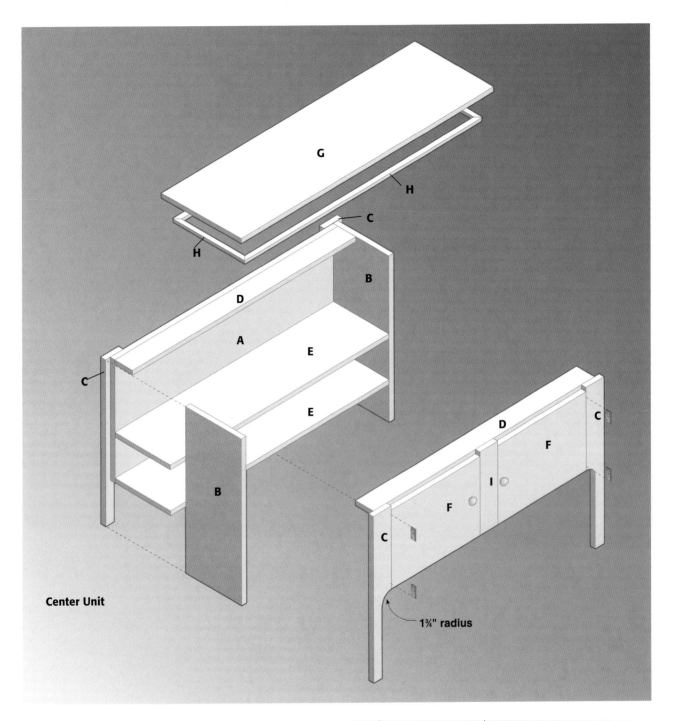

Center Unit

1¾" radius

Key	Part	Dimension
A	(1) Back panel	¾ × 20" × 44" plywood
B	(2) End panel	¾ × 11 × 29¾" plywood
C	(4) Leg	¾ × 3½ × 29¾" oak
D	(2) Cleat	¾ × 2½ × 44" plywood
E	(2) Shelf	¾ × 10 × 44" plywood

Key	Part	Dimension
F	(2) Door	¾ × 13⅛" × 17⅜ plywood
G	(1) Top panel	¾ × 15½ × 50" plywood
H	(4) Top trim	¾ × ¾ × *" Cove molding
I	(1) Stile	¾ × 3½ × 14" oak plywood

*Cut to fit

Directions: Sideboard

Step A: MAKE THE CARCASE.

For all screws used in this project, drill ³⁄₃₂" pilot holes. Counterbore the holes ¼" deep, using a ⅜" counterbore bit.

1. Cut the back panel (A), end panels (B), and shelves (E) to size. Sand the shelf edges.

2. Use a household iron to apply self-adhesive edge tape to one long edge of each shelf. Trim the edges with a utility knife. Sand all parts smooth.

3. Set the back flat on your worksurface. Position one face of an end panel against each short edge of the back panel, making sure the top edges are flush. Attach the panels with glue and drive 2" wood screws through the end panels and into the back. Be sure to keep the outside face of the back panel flush with the back edges of the end panels.

4. Position the bottom shelf between the end panels,

making sure the edge with the veneer tape faces away from the back panel. The bottom face of the shelf should be flush with the bottom edge of the back. Attach the bottom shelf with glue and drive 2" wood screws through the end panels and back panels and into the shelf.

5. Set the carcase (or cabinet frame) upright. Position 5¼"-wide spacer blocks on the bottom shelf. Set the top shelf on the spacer blocks. Attach the top shelf with glue and 2" wood screws (photo A).

6. Cut the cleats (D) to size, and sand them smooth.

7. Use glue and 2" wood screws to fasten one cleat between the end panels so one long edge is flush with the front edges of the end panels.

8. Attach the remaining cleat to the end and back panels so one long edge is butted against the back panel. Both cleats should be flush with the tops of the carcase.

Step B: MAKE THE LEGS.

The sideboard legs have curves that taper them to 1¾" in width.

1. Cut the legs (C) to length.

2. Designate a top and bottom of each leg. Draw a centerline from top to bottom on each leg. Then, draw reference lines across the legs, 14" and 15¾" up from the bottom. Set a compass to draw a 1¾"-radius semicircle. Set the point of the compass on the lower reference line, as close as possible to one long edge. Draw the semicircle to complete the curved portion of the cutting line.

3. Clamp the legs to your worksurface, and use a jig saw to cut them to shape, starting at the bottom and following the centerline and semicircle all the way to the end of the top reference line (photo B). Sand the cutouts smooth.

A. *Use 5¼" spacer blocks set on the bottom shelf to position the top shelf for fastening.*

B. *Cut the curved tapers in the legs with a jig saw.*

C. *Fasten the legs to the front edges of the end panels. Make sure the outside edges of the legs overhang the end panels by ¼".*

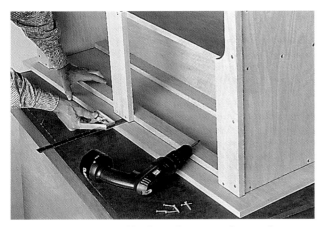

D. *Measure the front and back overhang to make sure the carcase is centered on the top panel.*

E. *Miter-cut cove molding to cover the joint between the top panel and the carcase.*

Step C: ATTACH THE LEGS AND STILE.
1. Position two legs against the front edges of the end panels, with the cutout edges facing in. Make sure the legs are flush with the end panels at the top and bottom edges, and that they overhang the outside faces of the end panels by ¼". Attach the legs to the edges of the end panels with glue and 2" wood screws (photo C).
2. Cut the stile (I) to length.
3. Center the stile between the legs so it spans the gap between the cleat and top shelf. Make sure the bottom edge of the stile is flush with the bottom of the top shelf. Attach it with glue and 2" wood screws.
4. Turn the project over. Fasten the remaining legs to the back and ends. Maintain the ¼" overhang of the end panels, and keep the top edges flush.

Step D: INSTALL THE TOP PANEL.
1. Cut the top panel (G) to size.
2. Apply edge tape to all four edges of the top. Sand the surfaces smooth.
3. Lay the top on your worksurface with its better face down. Center the carcase over the top. The top should extend 1½" beyond the front and back of the legs, and 2¼" beyond the outside faces of the end panels (photo D). Drive 1" wood screws through the cleats and into the top.
4. Cut the top trim (H) to fit around the underside of the top, miter-cutting the ends at 45° angles so they fit together at the corners.
5. Drill ⅟₁₆" pilot holes through the trim pieces to prevent splitting. Apply glue and drive 1¼" brads through the top trim and into the top panel. Set the brads with a nail set (photo E).

F. *Attach each door to a leg, using 1½ × 3" butt hinges.*

Step E: ATTACH THE DOORS.
1. Cut the doors (F) to size.
2. Apply edge tape to all four edges of each door.
3. Attach 1½ × 3" brass butt hinges to one short edge of each door, starting 2" in from the top and bottom. Mount the doors on the carcase by attaching the hinges to the legs (photo F). Make sure the bottom edges of the doors are flush with the bottom of the top shelf.

Step F: APPLY FINISHING TOUCHES.
1. Fill all nail holes with stainable wood putty. Glue oak plugs into all screw holes. Finish-sand all of the surfaces. Remove the door hinges and apply the finish of your choice.
2. Reattach the doors after the finish has dried. Fasten 1"-dia. brass knobs to the door fronts, and mount roller catches on the doors and stile, 5" down from the top of the stile. Tack furniture glides to the bottom ends of the legs.

Entertainment Center

This handsome and unique entertainment center provides ample storage for all your home electronics, yet is relatively compact—5 ft. high and less than 7 ft. wide. The three-unit design features a 20"-deep center unit, spacious enough to hold a large television set, and two 16"-deep end units, ideal for storing stereo speakers, compact discs, DVDs, videotapes, and books.

Because the project is built in three units, it is easy to adapt. For example, you might choose to expand the project by building additional end units to occupy a long wall. Or, for a small room you might choose to build only the center unit. You can also change the width of the center unit to match the size of your television.

This entertainment center provides an attractive and convenient place to store electronics, books, and games.

TOOLS & MATERIALS

- Circular saw
- Straightedge guide
- Router with bits
- Hammer
- Drill with bits
- Power screwdriver
- Right-angle drill guide
  - Pegboard scraps
  - Miter saw
  - Jig saw
  - Bar clamps
  - Utility knife
  - Colored chalk
- Masking tape
- Finish nails (1", 1¼", 2")
- Wood glue
- 1" wire nails
- Shims
- Utility screws (1")
- ¼" wire brads
- Electrical accessories
- Drawer and door hardware
- Finishing materials

- Base shoe molding
- (1) ¼" × 4 × 8 ft. oak plywood
- Pin-style shelf supports
- Nail set
- Power sander

Center unit*
- (2) ¾" × 4 × 8 ft. oak plywood
- (1) ½" × 4 × 8 ft. oak plywood
- (1) ¾ × ¾" × 6 ft. door edge molding
- (3) 1 × 3" × 8 ft. oak
- (1) ¾ × 1½" × 6 ft. ornamental molding
- Wire organizer track

End unit*
- (1) ¾" × 4 × 8 ft. oak plywood
- (1) ¾" × 2 × 4 ft. oak plywood
- (1) ½" × 4 × 8 ft. oak plywood
- (1) ¾ × ¾" × 6 ft. door edge molding
- (1) ¾ × 1½" × 6 ft. ornamental molding
- (2) 1 × 3" × 8 ft. oak

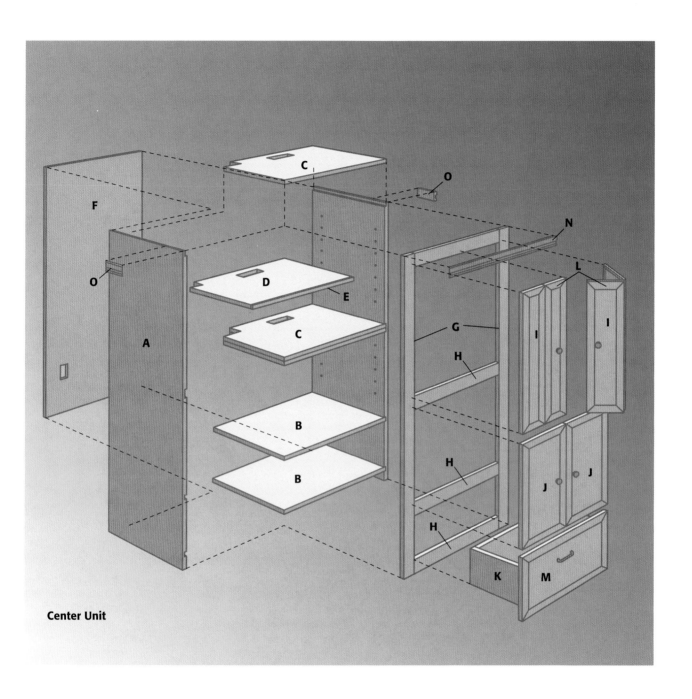

Center Unit

Key	Part	Dimension
A	(2) Side panel	¾ × 20" × 5 ft. oak plywood
B	(2) Bottom panel	¾ × 20 × 31¼" oak plywood
C	(3) Perm. shelf	¾ × 20 × 31¼" oak plywood
D	(2) Adj. shelf	¾ × 19½ × 30¼" oak plywood
E	(2) Shelf edge	¾ × ¾ × 30" door edge molding
F	(1) Back panel	½ × 32" × 5 ft. oak plywood
G	(3) Face frame stile	¾ × 2½ × 5 ft.* oak
H	(4) Face frame rail	¾ × 2½ × 26"* oak

Key	Part	Dimension
I	(4) Folding panel	½ × 6 × 23½" oak plywood
J	(2) Door panel	½ × 13 × 17½" oak plywood
K	Overlay drawer	See page 30
L	Door edge molding	See page 40
M	(1) Drawer face	½ × 9 × 27 " oak plywood
N	(1) Front top trim	¾ × 1½ × 31"* ornamental molding
O	(1) Side top trim	¾ × 1½ × 4"* ornamental molding

*Cut to fit

125

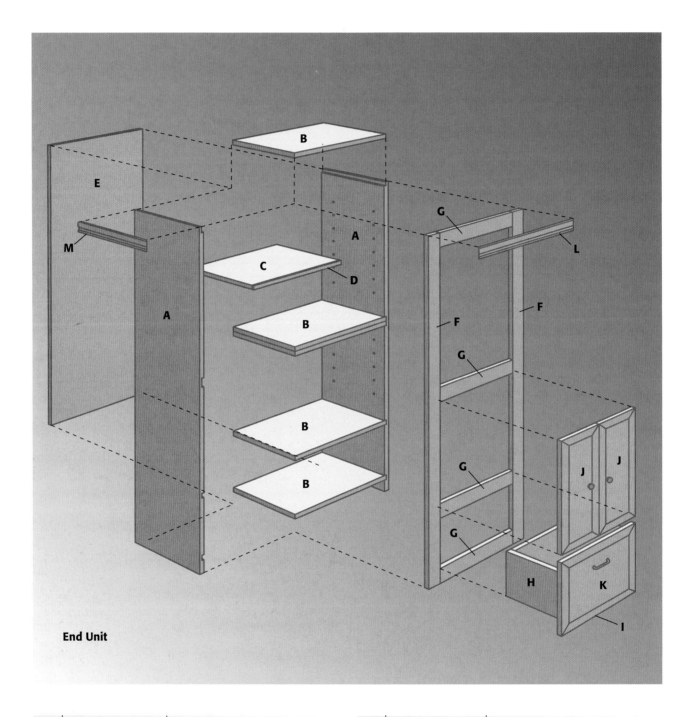

End Unit

Key	Part	Dimension
A	(2) Side panel	¾ × 16 × 60" oak plywood
B	(5) Fixed shelf	¾ × 16 × 23¼" oak plywood
C	(2) Adjustable shelf	¾ × 15½ × 22½" oak plywood
D	(2) Shelf edge	¾ × ¾ × 22¼" door edge molding
E	(1) Back panel	½" × 2 × 5 ft. oak plywood
F	(2) Face frame stile	¾ × 2½ × 5 ft. oak
G	(4) Face frame rail	¾ × 2½ × 19" oak

Key	Part	Dimension
H	Overlay drawer	See page 31
I	Overlay door edge	See page 41
J	(2) Door face	½ × 9 × 17½" oak plywood
K	(1) Drawer face	½ × 9 × 19" oak plywood
L	Front top trim	¾ × 1½" × 2 ft.* ornamental molding
M	Side top trim	¾ × 1½" × 16"* ornamental molding

*Cut to fit

Directions: *Entertainment Center*

Before you begin the construction of the entertainment center, assess the space where you plan to use the unit. Keep in mind how the the unit will impact the room. Because the entertainment center is a large project, it is important to design it so that it doesn't overcrowd the room. A little extra planning helps make sure it will be a useful means of storage for years to come.

Step A: PREPARE PROJECT LOCATION & CUT SIDE PANELS.
1. Remove the baseboards and other moldings in the planned location of the entertainment center. Then make an outline of the entertainment center on the floor, using masking tape. If the entertainment center will block access to a receptacle, make note of the receptacle's location and plan to cut out the back panel of the entertainment center to provide access to the receptacle.
2. Measure and cut the ¾" plywood side panels (A) for the center unit to size, using a circular saw and a straightedge guide (page 18).

Step B: ROUT THE RABBETS & DADOES.
Dadoes and rabbets will hold the top and bottom panels and the permanent shelves in place. Rout the rabbets and dadoes (page 19) in the side panels at the locations shown in the Project Details below. Use a router and two straightedge guides.

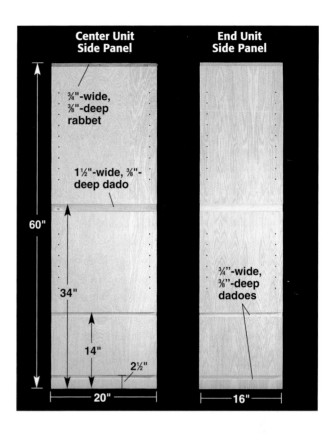

Center Unit Side Panel

¾"-wide, ⅜"-deep rabbet

1½"-wide, ⅜"-deep dado

60"

34"

14"

2½"

20"

End Unit Side Panel

¾"-wide, ⅜"-deep dadoes

16"

A. *Use masking tape to mark the planned location of the entertainment center.*

B. *Cut rabbets and dadoes in the side panels.*

C. *Drill two vertical rows of ¼" holes along the inside face of each side panel to hold pin-style shelf supports.*

Step C: DRILL THE PEG HOLES & PREPARE THE SHELVES.
1. Drill two vertical rows of ¼" holes along the inside face of each side panel to hold pin-style shelf supports for the adjustable shelves. For more information on pin-style shelf supports see page 38. Use a right-angle drill guide, and a pegboard scrap as a template to ensure the holes are aligned correctly. The holes should be drilled 2" from each edge of both panels.
2. Cut the permanent shelves (C) and adjustable shelves (D) to size. The permanent shelves in the center unit have notches cut in the back corner to ac-

commodate a vertical wire organizer track, and cutouts sized to hold ventilation screens. Use a jig saw to cut the corner notches for the wire organizer, and to make cutouts for the ventilation screens. See the project details on page 125 for more details.

Step D: PREPARE THE SHELVES.
1. Join two of the notched permanent shelves together with glue and 1¼" finish nails to form one double-layer shelf for the middle of the center unit. This shelf is double-layered to provide enough support for a large television. Make sure all edges of both shelves are flush before joining them together.
2. Measure and cut door edge molding (E) to cover the exposed front edges of the adjustable shelves. To attach the moldings, apply glue to the shelves and clamp the moldings to the shelves. Then drill pilot holes and drive 1¼" finish nails through the molding and into the shelves. Set the nails with a nail set.

Step E: PREPARE THE BOTTOM PANELS.
The bottom panels (B) of the entertainment center make up the housing for the overlay drawer. Cut the ¾" plywood bottom panels to size and sand the edges smooth with medium-grit sandpaper. Then attach the

Notch for wire organizer

Permanent shelf:
20" × 31¼"

Cutout for ventilation screen

Adjustable shelf:
19½ × 30¼"

Shelf-edge molding

D. *Join two of the notched permanent shelves together with glue and 1¼" finish nails to form one double-layer shelf.*

E. *Attach the track for a center-mounted drawer slide at the center of one of the bottom panels.*

Side panel   Top of cabinet

F. *Glue and clamp the bottom panels and permanent shelves between the side panels and reinforce the joints with finish nails.*

track for a center-mounted drawer slide at the center of one of the bottom panels according to the directions on page 35.

Step F: ASSEMBLE THE CABINET FRAME.
1. Apply glue to the side edges of the bottom panels and permanent shelves, then clamp them between the side panels, forming the dado and rabbet joints. Check to make sure the front edge of each panel is flush with both side panels. Then reinforce each joint with 2" finish nails driven 4" to 6" apart, and set the nails with a nail set.
2. Measure and cut the ½" plywood back panel (F) to size. Using a pencil and combination square, make a reference line on the interior face of the back panel, 1" from the edge, along the side where the notches will be located. Then tack a 30" wire organizer track flush with the reference line. This spacing should allow the wire organizer track to fit directly into the notches cut in each shelf panel.

Step G: INSTALL THE BACK PANEL.
1. Position the back panel over the back of the center unit so the edges are flush around the perimeter of the cabinet. Attach the panel by driving wire nails at

4" intervals into the side panels and shelves.
2. If the cabinet will cover a wall receptacle, make a cutout in the back panel, slightly larger than the cover plate, to make the receptacle accessible. To make the cutout, rub colored chalk on the face of the receptacle. Then, place the cabinet in position and push it flush against the receptacle. Pull the cabinet away from the wall and check to make sure a colored outline of the receptacle is visible on the back of the cabinet.
3. Draw the outline of the faceplate over the chalk markings using the faceplate to trace the lines on the back panel of the cabinet. Then, drill a starter hole inside the outline and use a jig saw to cut along the outline. After cutting the hole, sand the edges of the cut line smooth with medium-grit sandpaper.

Step H: PLUMB THE CABINET.
Position the center unit against the wall—inside the floor outline. Use a level to make sure the cabinet is level and plumb. If necessary, use shims under the sides. Score the shims with a utility knife, and snap off the excess so the ends are flush with the base of the cabinet.

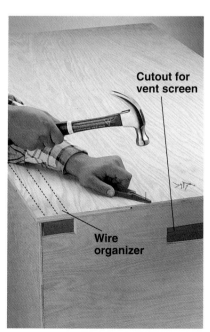

Cutout for vent screen

Wire organizer

G. *Position the back panel over the back of the center unit so edges are flush.*

H. *Shim under the sides of the center unit, if necessary, until it is level and plumb.*

I. *Build each end unit by cutting the pieces to size and following steps A to F.*

Step I: BUILD THE END UNITS.

1. Measure, cut, and prepare the side panels (A), fixed shelves (B), and back panel (E) for each end unit. See the project details on page 127 for precise placement of the dado and rabbet grooves.

2. Assemble the pieces, following Steps A through F for the center cabinet. The end units are built with the same construction methods as the center unit, with the exception of the holes for wiring and ventilation in each shelf. Customize each end unit to meet your specific storage needs.

Step J: INSTALL THE END UNITS.

1. Position the end units next to the center unit. If necessary, shim under the side panels to align the tops of the end units with the center unit.

2. Join each end unit to the center unit by drilling counterbored pilot holes and driving 1" screws through the side panels, into the center unit.

Step K: INSTALL THE STILES & RAILS.

1. Measure and cut the 1 × 3 vertical face frame stiles for the center (G) and end cabinets (F) to length. Attach the stiles to both units, using glue and finish nails driven through pilot holes. The edges of the stiles should be flush with the outside edges of the

side panels.

2. Cut 1 × 3 horizontal face frame rails to fit between the stiles, along the edges of the permanent shelves and bottom panels. Anchor the rails to the stiles by drilling pilot holes diagonally through the rails and into the stiles and driving 2" finish nails into the holes.

Step L: INSTALL THE TOP PANEL.

Lay a sheet of ¼" oak plywood on the entertainment center, and outline the top of the cabinets onto the plywood. Also mark cutouts for the wire organizer notch and ventilation screen. Cut the plywood along the marked lines, using a jig saw. Sand the panel smooth then attach it to the top of the entertainment center with ¾" wire brads.

Step M: APPLY THE FINISHING TOUCHES.

1. Trim the top of the entertainment center with mitered ornamental molding to cover the exposed edges of the plywood. Attach the moldings by drilling pilot holes and driving 1¼" finish nails into the top rails and side panels.

2. Cover gaps along the wall and floor with base shoe molding, attached with 1" finish nails driven through pilot holes.

J. *Shim under the side panels of the end units if necessary to align the top of each end unit with the center unit.*

K. *Measure and cut 1 × 3 vertical face frame stiles and attach them.*

L. *Lay a sheet of ¼" oak plywood on the entertainment center, and outline the top of the entertainment center onto the plywood.*

3. Fill and plug the nail and screw holes, then sand and finish the entertainment center.

4. Insert ventilation screens into the cutouts in the shelf panels, then attach an electrical outlet strip to the back panel on the center cabinet, just above the double-layer middle shelf.

5. If you need to run wires between the units for electronic equipment, drill an access hole through the side panels into the center cabinet using a hole saw or forstner bit. Install grommets in the holes.

Step N: MAKE THE OVERLAY DOORS.
1. Build folding overlay doors for the center unit by framing two pairs of ½" plywood panels with door-edge molding (see Basic Doors, page 40). Finish the doors to match the entertainment center, then join each pair with butt hinges attached to the backs of the panels.
2. Mount the folding doors to the center unit face frame with semiconcealed hinges (see page 40). Build, finish, and install the remaining overlay doors. Install door pulls if desired.

Step O: MAKE THE DRAWERS.
1. Build and finish the overlay drawers for the center unit and end units, following the information on ba-

sic drawers on page 30. The drawer design for this project varies slightly from standard design by using framed plywood panels, not solid hardwood, for the drawer faces.

2. Attach drawer pulls to the faces of the drawers, if desired, and slide the drawers into the cabinets.

TIP:

Installing edge moldings and smaller trim pieces and building drawers is faster and easier with an electric powered brad nailer. Electric brad nailers are much less expensive than pneumatic nailers, and operate just like an electric stapler. Many electric brad nailers shoot a variety of brad lengths for different thicknesses of material.

M. *Install mitered ornamental molding along the top edge and base-shoe molding along the bottom edge of all the cabinets.*

N. *Build folding overlay doors for the center unit. Join each pair with butt hinges attached to backs of panels.*

O. *Build, finish, and install remaining overlay doors and drawers for the center unit and end units.*

Food & Dishware Storage

Well-designed food and dishware storage usually goes unnoticed. A poorly designed kitchen, on the other hand, is likely to cause one aggravation several times every day. Kitchens include more things to store, and we need ready access to those things more often than anywhere else in the home. They serve as storage centers for many different types of supplies, including food, dishware, pots and pans, cooking utensils, cleaning products, silverware, and a variety of appliances. The ultimate goal is to make all of these items easily accessible every time they are needed, without taking up more of the available space than is absolutely necessary.

Good cabinet storage is essential to a well-organized kitchen. Deep cabinets should be equipped with sliding drawers or lazy Susans that allow access to the items forced to the back. Otherwise, as a rule, kitchen cabinets should be shallow (about twelve inches deep). The shelving inside each cabinet should be properly spaced to store specific items, while eliminating wasted vertical space.

If your kitchen cabinet space is limited, it may be time to start storing items in alternate areas. Many types of food can be shown off in a bowl on the counter or in a hanging display, such as the colander fruit rack. Containers placed against the backsplash provide excellent storage for dry goods like pasta and flour. Pots and pans can be put on display near the stove with pot racks. Consider placing extra canned goods and non-perishable items in a closet near the kitchen or in a pantry.

IN THIS SECTION:

Food & Dishware Storage Ideas

Modular wall *mounting systems free up cabinet space and keep your most-used items visible and hanging within easy reach.*

A breakfast table *can be stored in a wall cabinet that opens downward when needed, saving space in small kitchens.*

A floor-to-ceiling *pullout rack reclaims the space at the back of your cabinet so that your pots and pans no longer have to pile on top of one another.*

A simple wooden lattice *adorned with S-hooks is a clever way to store your pots and pans.*

135

A slim pullout bottle rack utilizes that tight corner space under the counter.

A mini-pantry makes efficient use of the full depth of a cabinet with an array of glide-out shelves and drawers.

A deep drawer in a base cabinet supported by steel glides keeps root vegetables in a cool and dark environment, which delays sprouting.

Built-in shelves *and cabinets in this bump-out alcove provide all necessary storage in this small kitchen. Open shelving can be especially pleasing in small spaces.*

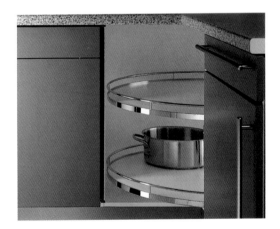

With one simple spin *a lazy Susan lets you reach the items stored deep in the back of an otherwise inaccessible corner space.*

Modular shelving *units form an efficient pantry storage space. Mix and match various units to meet your needs.*

Colander Fruit Rack

The colander fruit rack is a great storage solution for fruits and vegetables that would otherwise take up valuable countertop or refrigerator space. The rack was designed to utilize a previously unused space over a kitchen island or in the corner, displaying fruits and vegetables decoratively. Each colander is adjustable and removable for easy access and cleaning, and the rack is simple to adapt for any decor.

Keep your fruits and vegetables within easy reach with this industrial-style, multi-purpose rack.

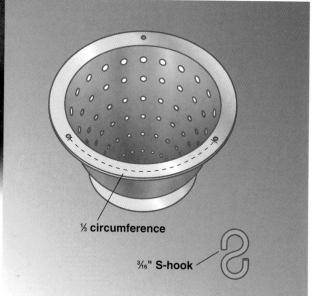

⅓ circumference

³⁄₁₆" S-hook

TOOLS & MATERIALS

- Drill with bits
- (1) 15 ft. decorative chain
- (1) 2-, 4-, & 8-quart colanders
- (1) ³⁄₁₆" threaded J-hook screw
- (1) Heavy-duty key chain ring
- (9) ³⁄₁₆" S-hooks
- Cotton string
- Permanent marker

Step A: DRILL THE HANGING HOLES.
To properly hang the colanders from the chains, drill holes in the top lip of each colander at increments of ⅓ the total circumference.
1. To find ⅓ of the circumference of each colander lip, place the colanders upside down on a flat surface and wrap a piece of string around the underside of the top lip. Cut the string where it meets around the colander. Fold it into thirds.
2. Use a permanent marker to mark both folded ends of the string. Then place the string back around the top edge and use the marks on the string as reference points for marking the spots to be drilled on the colander lip.
3. Drill the holes on the marked spots of the lip, using a ³⁄₁₆" drill bit.

Step B: MOUNT THE HOOK & THE CHAINS.
Most hardware stores and home centers sell chain by the foot in several different styles. Select a type of chain and have the store personnel cut three 5 ft. lengths for you.
1. Use a stud finder to locate a ceiling joist, or install blocking in the area you plan to hang the rack.
2. Drill a ⅛" hole through the ceiling and into the joist or existing blocking. Then screw the J-hook into the hole.
3. Thread the chain through a heavy-duty key ring just as you would thread car keys onto the ring, and hang the key ring from the ceiling hook.

Step C: HANG THE COLANDERS.
Thread the S-hooks through the holes you drilled in the colanders and then through the chains. Make sure the S-hooks hold the colanders level. If you want to add more storage space, place the colanders closer together and add another one to the bottom of the chain.

VARIATION:

Bowls work well for storing socks, nails and screws, plants, or even magazines.

A. *Drill the holes in ⅓ increments of the perimeter of the colanders.*

B. *Thread the chain onto the heavy-duty key ring.*

C. *Hang the colanders at a uniform height on the chains with S-hooks.*

Dish Rack

The holding capacity and clean vertical lines of this plate drying rack could easily make it a beloved fixture in your kitchen. The efficient, open design lets air circulate to dry mugs, bowls, and plates more efficiently than most in-the-sink types of racks.

The rack is handsome enough to double as a display rack to showcase your dinnerware. Even though it has a small (9¼ × 21½") footprint, the rack lets you dry or store up to 20 full-size dinner plates plus cups or glasses. The tall dowels in the back of the rack are removable so you can rearrange them to accommodate large or unusually shaped dishes. The sides have a slight backward slant that gives you easier access to the dishes. This slant requires cutting a diagonal line from the top to the bottom.

This compact plate drying rack is handsome enough to double as a dinnerware display case.

TOOLS & MATERIALS

- Circular saw
- Drill with bits
- Finish sander
- Combination square
- (1) 1 × 2" × 4 ft. oak
- (1) 1 × 6" × 2 ft. oak
- (1) 1 × 10" × 3 ft. oak
- (3) ¾ × ¾" × 2 ft. oak stop molding
- (7) ⅜"-dia. × 3 ft. oak dowels
- Waterproof glue
- Wood screws (#8 × 1⅝")
- 4d finish nails
- ⅜"-dia. flat oak plugs
- (4) Rubber feet
- Finishing materials

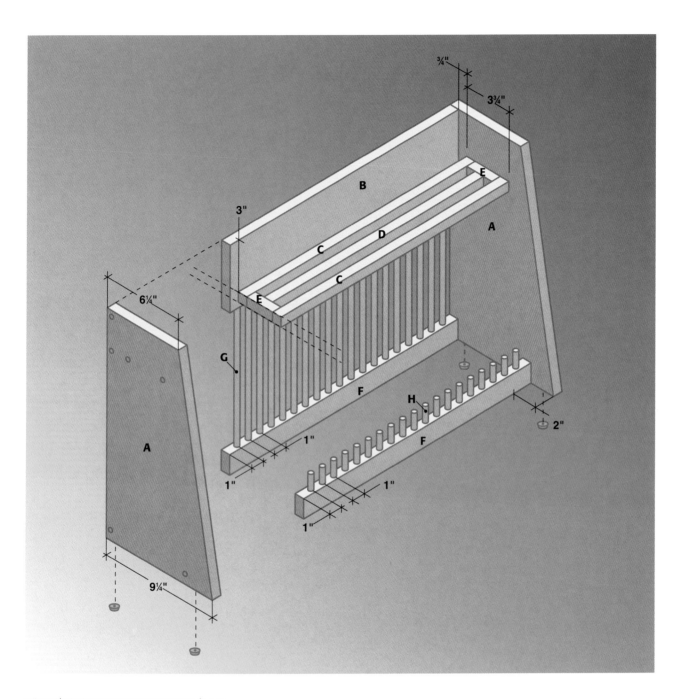

Key	Part	Dimension
A	(2) Side	¾ × 9¼ × 17" oak
B	(1) Back	¾ × 5½ × 20" oak
C	(2) Shelf front/back	¾ × ¾ × 17" molding
D	(1) Shelf divider	¾ × ¾ × 18½" molding
E	(2) Shelf end	¾ × ¾ × 2¼" molding
F	(2) Rail	¾ × 1½ × 20" oak
G	(19) Back dowel	⅜"-dia. × 10½" dowel
H	(19) Front dowel	⅜"-dia. × 1⅝" dowel

Directions: Dish Rack

Step A: SMALL CAPS PREPARE THE SIDES, BACK & RAILS.
The sides have a slight backward slant that gives you easier access to the dishes. This slant requires cutting a diagonal line from the top to the bottom of the side pieces.
1. Cut the sides (A) to length. Measure in 3" from the front top corner and make a reference mark with a pencil. Use a straightedge to draw a reference line from this point to the bottom front corner.

TIP:

If you plan on consistently using dishes of unusual size, you may choose to change the location of the front rail. The location specified will work well for plates as small as 7" and as large as 11".

---

2. Cut along the diagonal line, using a circular saw, and sand the side panels smooth.
3. Cut the back (B) and rails (F) to length and sand the edges smooth.
4. Clamp the back and rails together, as shown in photo A. Use a combination square to measure and mark the dowel holes at 1" intervals. Drill ¼"-deep dowel holes in the two rails. Then reset the depth of your drill to ½" and drill the deeper dowel holes in the back piece.
5. Drill ⅜"-dia. counterbored pilot holes through the sides where the back piece and back rail will be attached. Apply waterproof glue, and assemble the pieces, using wood screws.

Step B: SMALL CAPS BUILD THE SHELF.
1. Cut the shelf front and back pieces (C), divider (D), and ends (E) to length.

A. *Clamp the back and the rails together, then measure and mark the dowel locations.*

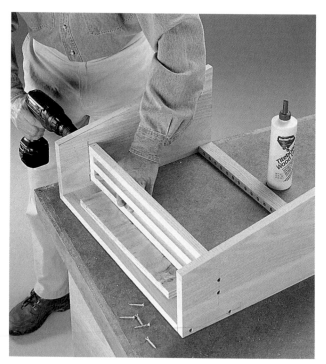

B. *Use a ¾" spacer to position the shelf from the back while you drill counterbored pilot holes.*

2. Position the shelf front, back, and ends together, and drill pilot holes for 4d finish nails. Apply glue, and nail the pieces together.

3. Glue and nail the divider in place. Then carefully drill counterbored pilot holes through the sides where the shelf will be attached.

4. Lay the entire unit on its back and position the shelf 3" down from the top of the rack. Use a ¾"-thick piece of scrap material as a spacer between the shelf and the back, and drill counterbored pilot holes. (Be sure to drill the pilot holes into the long shelf pieces, not through the dividers.) Apply glue to the joints, and secure the shelf with wood screws.

Step C: CUT & INSERT DOWELS.

1. Cut the back dowels (G) to length, and install them by inserting one of the ends into the holes in the back, then dropping them down into the back rail.

2. Cut the front dowels (H) to length, and sand the edges of one end of each dowel. Use waterproof glue to secure the unsanded end of each dowel in a front rail hole.

Step D: ATTACH THE FRONT RAIL & APPLY FINISHING TOUCHES.

1. Position the front rail 2" back from the front edge of the rack, then drill counterbored pilot holes through the sides. Apply waterproof glue, and screw the front rail in place.

2. Fill all screw holes with oak plugs, and sand the entire rack and all dowels with 150-grit sandpaper until smooth.

3. Apply a water-based polyurethane finish, and attach rubber feet to the bottom of the rack.

TIP:

Dowel sizes have a tendency to vary in size due to expansion of the wood. To determine which size hole works best for your dowels, drill three holes in scrap wood using a ⅜" brad-point bit as well as one just slightly larger and one slightly smaller. Then test each dowel length in each hole to ensure a proper fit.

C. *Insert dowels into the holes under the back first, then drop them down into the holes in the rail.*

D. *Clamp the front rail, drill pilot holes, and then glue and screw the rail into place.*

Pot Racks

These inexpensive, easy-to-build pot racks are wonderful organizers and great additions to any kitchen, especially kitchens that suffer from limited cabinet or countertop space. Most busy cooks have one or more overhead racks in their kitchens to keep frequently used cooking utensils within reach. Overhead racks also give proud cooks an opportunity to show off copper pans and other gourmet cooking equipment.

We've included construction options for a ladder rack with wood dowels and a rack made with metal electrical conduit. When sanded, the conduit has a matte finish similar to brushed aluminum or stainless steel.

Add a space-saving cooking center to your kitchen with these versatile pot racks.

TOOLS & MATERIALS

- Circular saw
- Drill with bits
- Finish sander
- Tubing cutter
- Clamps
- Portable drill guide
- Channel-type pliers
- Pot hooks
- 10" adjustable wrench
- 16 ft. decorative chain
- (4) J-hooks
- (4) Screw eyes
- 4d finish nails
- Finishing materials

Wooden rack
- (1) 1 × 3" × 8 ft. oak
- (3) 1"-dia. × 3 ft. oak dowel

Variation rack
- (1) 1 × 3" × 8 ft. poplar
- (1) ¾" × 10 ft. thin-wall electrical conduit
- (10) ¾" compression couplings
- (10) ⅞" chrome furniture caps
- (20) ¼ to 1" reduction washers

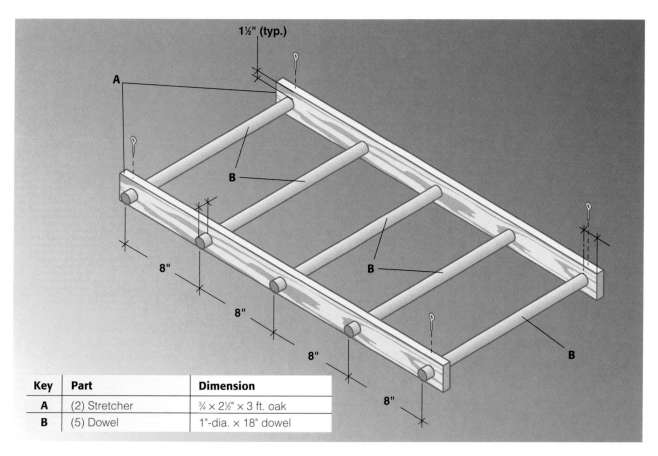

1½" (typ.)

A

B

B

B

8"

8"

8"

8"

Key	Part	Dimension
A	(2) Stretcher	¾ × 2½" × 3 ft. oak
B	(5) Dowel	1"-dia. × 18" dowel

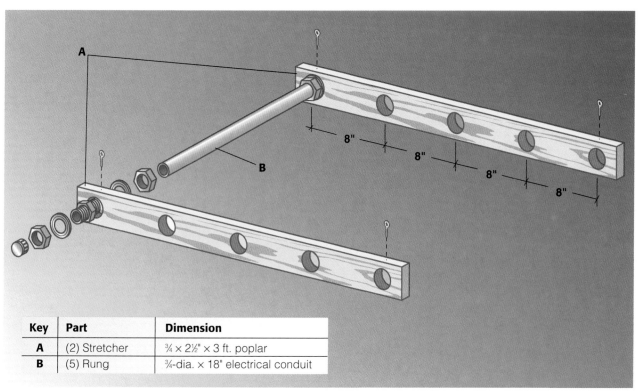

A

B

8"

8"

8"

8"

Key	Part	Dimension
A	(2) Stretcher	¾ × 2½" × 3 ft. poplar
B	(5) Rung	¾-dia. × 18" electrical conduit

145

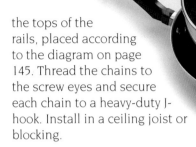

Directions: Wooden Ladder Rack

Step A: PREPARE THE STRETCHERS & DOWELS.
The stretchers hold the dowels in place and create the outside frame of the pot rack, so it is important that each stretcher be free of cracks, checks, and knots. Otherwise, the stretchers may crack or break under a heavy load.

1. Cut the stretchers (A) to length, using a circular saw. Mark the dowel locations on one stretcher. See the diagram on page 145 for proper spacing of the holes. Clamp the stretchers together so all edges are flush. Drill 1" holes, using your drill equipped with a drill guide.

2. Cut the dowels (B) to 18" lengths, and check to make sure they fit through the holes you have drilled. If needed, shape the ends of the dowels with a sander until they fit into their respective holes.

Step B: ASSEMBLE THE RACK & APPLY FINISHING TOUCHES.
1. To secure the dowels to the stretchers, drill 1/16" pilot holes through the top edges of the stretchers and into the 1"-dia. dowel holes. Position the dowels so they extend 1" past the stretchers, then glue and fasten them in place with 4d finishing nails.

2. Sand the entire project smooth and apply a water-based polyurethane finish. Thread four screw eyes into the tops of the rails, placed according to the diagram on page 145. Thread the chains to the screw eyes and secure each chain to a heavy-duty J-hook. Install in a ceiling joist or blocking.

Variation: Metal/Wood Combination

The layout and size of the metal/wood combination pot rack utilizes the same size stretchers as the wooden pot rack. The only difference between the stretchers in the two projects is the size of the holes for the dowels. The metal couplings require

TIP:

Typically, hardwoods shrink substantially when kiln-dried. When this happens, it is common for the ends to develop checks or cracks. Even if the boards look fine, trim 1/2" to 1" off the ends to ensure that your project is free of checks and cracks.

A. *Place a scrap of plywood under the stretchers to prevent tearouts, and drill 1" holes in each stretcher.*

B. *Insert the dowels into the holes, securing each with glue and a 4d finish nail driven through a pilot hole.*

larger holes to fit into the stretchers. For the project shown, 1⅛"-wide holes were necessary. However, hole size will vary with couplings made by different manufacturers.

Step A: PREPARE THE STRETCHERS.
Cut and drill the holes in the stretchers, using the same construction methods as for the wooden rack, except using a 1⅛" spade bit to make the holes. Sand the stretchers smooth, and apply a clear water-based polyurethane finish. Let the stretchers dry before assembling the rack.

Step B: CUT THE RUNGS & ASSEMBLE THE RACK.
1. Using 120-grit sandpaper, by hand or with a finish or random-orbital sander, sand a 10 ft. length of ¾" electrical conduit until you achieve the finish you desire.
NOTE: Sand the conduit only as much as necessary— if you sand through the galvanized finish, the pipe will rust over time.
2. Cut the electrical conduit into five 18" lengths, using a tubing cutter. Unscrew and remove the compression nuts and rings from all compression couplings. Slide a compression nut and ring onto the end of a piece of conduit, followed by a 1" to ¾" reduction washer.

3. Cap the end of the conduit with a coupling, and tighten the coupling nut and ring back on the fitting until it cannot be removed with moderate hand pressure. Repeat this step until the ends of each piece of conduit are capped.
4. Slide the capped ends of the pipes into the holes of each stretcher, and slide a reduction washer over the threads of the coupling extending from the outside edge of the stretcher.
5. Screw a compression ring and nut onto the threads of the coupling, and repeat the assembly process on one stretcher until all fittings are in place. Then install the nuts and washers on the other stretcher.
6. Tighten all the compression nuts, using a large adjustable wrench and a channel-type pliers.

Step C: APPLY THE FINISHING TOUCHES.
Snap a chrome furniture cap into the end of each coupling nut. The chrome cap may need to be adjusted with a pliers to fit snugly into the end of the coupling. Thread four screw eyes into the tops of the rails according to the diagram on page 145. Attach the chains to the rack and secure each chain to the ceiling joists with J-hooks. If you are concerned about rust appearing on the conduit, coat the conduit with a layer of paste wax.

B. *Insert the sanded pipe into the compression coupling, and tighten the fitting, using a channel-type pliers and an adjustable wrench.*

C. *Finish the rack by plugging the holes in the compression fittings with 1" chrome-plated furniture caps.*

Pantry Cabinet

Most pantries are great for storing kitchen supplies or appliances that you don't use every day. However, if your pantry itself is poorly organized and inconvenient to use, it winds up as wasted space in your home. To get the most from your pantry, we devised a shelving unit that provides maximum vertical storage capacity. Standing 84" high, the shelf features three solid shelves for storing heavy goods and two adjustable shelves to fit large or awkward items.

You can use this project as a freestanding unit against a wall or as a divider within a larger pantry. The open construction also means you can identify what you have on hand at a glance.

Included in the instructions is a simple option for converting an adjustable shelf into a rack that is perfect for stable storage of wine, soda, or other bottled liquids.

*This **adjustable** shelving unit provides the versatility needed to organize your pantry.*

TOOLS & MATERIALS

- Circular saw
- Drill with bits
- Finish sander
- Nail set
- Wood mallet
- (14) 1 × 4" × 8 ft. pine
- (2) ¾ × ¾" × 6 ft. pine stop molding
- Wood glue
- Wood screws (#6 × 1¼", 1¾", #8 × 1⅝")
- (8) ¼" shelf pins
- ⅜"-dia. birch plugs
- Finishing materials
- 4d finish nails

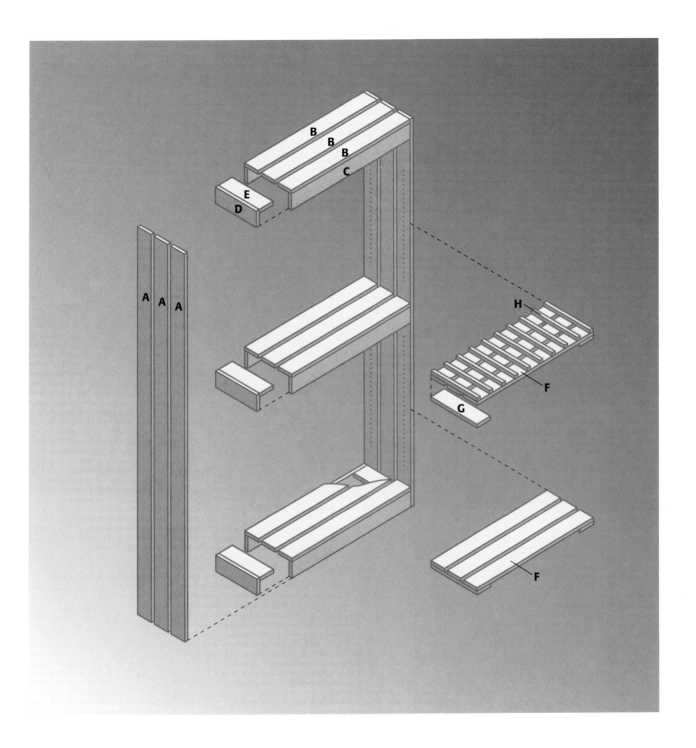

Key	Part	Dimension
A	(6) Side slat	¾ × 3½ × 84" pine
B	(9) Fixed-shelf slat	¾ × 3½ × 30½" pine
C	(6) Fixed-shelf face	¾ × 3½ × 30½" pine
D	(6) Fixed-shelf end	¾ × 3½ × 10½" pine

Key	Part	Dimension
E	(6) Fixed-shelf stretcher	¾ × 3½ × 10½" pine
F	(6) Adjust. shelf slat	¾ × 3½ × 30⅜" pine
G	(4) Adjust. shelf stretcher	¾ × 3½" × 1 ft. pine
H	(10) Wine-shelf cleat	¾ × 3¾" × 1 ft. pine

Directions: *Pantry Cabinet*

Step A: MAKE THE SHELF FRAMES.

1. Cut the fixed-shelf faces (C), shelf ends (D), and shelf stretchers (E) to size. Sand the cuts smooth and position the shelf ends between the shelf faces so the corners are flush.

2. Drill ⅜" counterbored pilot holes through the shelf faces into each shelf end. Try to keep all the counterbores aligned throughout the project to ensure a professional look.

3. Complete the shelf frame by joining the shelf faces and the shelf ends together with wood glue and 1⅝" wood screws driven through the pilot holes. Repeat the shelf frame assembly for the other two fixed-shelf frames.

TIP:

Buy or make wood plugs to fill counterbored screw holes. Building centers usually carry a variety of plug types, sizes, and styles. To cut your own, you can use either a special-purpose plug cutting tool or a small hole saw that mounts to your power drill. The diameter of the plug must match the counterbore.

Step B: INSTALL THE STRETCHERS.

1. Place a stretcher inside the corner of a shelf frame, with the stretcher face flush with the top edges of the frame.

2. Counterbore pilot holes on the shelf faces and ends, and attach the stretcher with glue and 1⅝" screws driven through the pilot holes. Install stretchers on the other side of the shelf frame and on the other two shelves.

Step C: COMPLETE THE FIXED SHELVES.

Three slats are fastened to each shelf frame, completing the fixed-shelf units.

1. Cut the shelf slats (B) to size and sand the edges smooth. Place three slats on your work surface. Turn one shelf frame over so the stretchers are on the bottom of the frame, and place the frame on top of the slats.

2. Move the slats so the corners and edges are flush with the shelf frame. Space the slats ¾" apart, using a piece of scrap 1 × 4 as a spacing guide.

3. Attach the slats with glue and 1¼" screws counter-

A. *Join the shelf faces to the ends by driving 1⅝" screws through counterbored pilot holes.*

B. *Apply glue and drive counterbored screws into the shelf faces and shelf ends to connect the stretchers.*

sunk through the bottom of the stretchers into each of the shelf slats. Repeat this assembly for the remaining two fixed shelves.

Step D: ASSEMBLE THE CABINET.
The fixed shelves are connected directly to the side slats to provide stability. The base of the pantry cabinet is wide enough to allow the cabinet to stand alone, as long as the cabinet is square. Make sure all the joints are square and the edges are flush during this final assembly.

1. Cut the side slats (A) to size, and sand them smooth. Draw a reference line on each side slat, 40" from the bottom end. These lines mark the location of the bottom edge of the middle fixed shelf.

2. To attach the side slats, align all three shelves on end roughly 40" apart, and lay a side slat over them. Adjust the top and bottom shelves so they are flush with the side slat ends and corners. Adjust the lower edge of the middle shelf so it rests on the reference line. Make sure the fixed shelves are correctly aligned and the corners are square.

3. Counterbore pilot holes through the side slats into the fixed-shelf ends, and attach them with glue and 1¼" screws.

4. Position the next side slat flush with the other edge of the fixed shelves, and attach it with glue and

screws driven through counterbored pilot holes.
5. Center the middle slat, using scrap pieces of 1 × 4 as spacers. Attach it with glue and screws.
6. With a helper, carefully turn the assembly over so it rests on the attached side slats. Position a side slat over the fixed-shelf ends. Make sure the corners and edges are flush.
7. Attach the side slat to the fixed shelves using glue and wood screws. Attach the remaining slats to the fixed shelves, making sure they are square as you go.

Step E: DRILL THE PEG HOLES.
The rows of holes on the inner faces of the side slats are used to hold the pegs for adjustable shelving. Make a drilling template to ensure that the holes are perfectly aligned, and the shelves will be level.

C. *Join the fixed-shelf slats to the stretchers with glue and 1¼"
screws driven through the underside of the stretchers.*

D. *When attaching the side slats, position the outer side slats so
the edge is flush with the edges of the fixed shelves.*

Drilling Template Detail

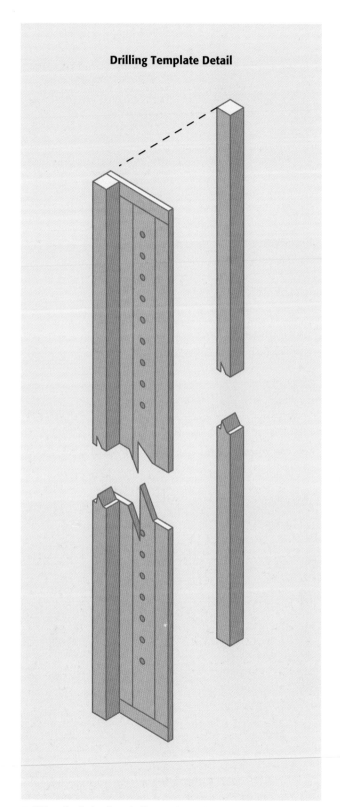

Drilling the holes for shelf pegs is simplified by using a template made from a 4 × 34" strip of ⅛ or ¼" pegboard and two 34"-long strips of ¾ × ¾" scrap wood (you can also use stop molding).

1. Use masking tape to outline a row of holes on the pegboard. Position a ¾" scrap wood strip against the pegboard so the edge is about 1¾" from the outlined holes. Fasten this guide strip with glue.

2. When the glue dries, turn the template over and attach the second ¾" guide strip with screws, aligning it with the first strip.

3. Wrap masking tape around the tip of a ¼" drill bit at a depth of ½". Use it as a reference guide to ensure that you do not drill completely through the side slats. Position the drilling template against the inside face of a side slat with the ¾" guide strip resting flush against the edge of the slat.

4. Drill a row of peg holes along the inner face of the side slat, using the pegboard holes as a guide. Make sure not to drill beyond your masking tape depth guide on the bit.

5. Rotate the template and position it against the other side slat so the other guide strip is resting flush against the edge of the slat and the opposite face of the template is facing out. Drill another row of holes exactly parallel to the first row. Repeat the

E. *Use a pegboard template for uniform placement of peg holes.*

152

process near the back edge of both side slats.
6. When finished drilling, sand the slats to remove any roughness or tearout.

Step F: MAKE THE ADJUSTABLE SHELVES.
Our project includes two adjustable shelves, but you can choose to build more. The adjustable shelves are similar in design to the fixed shelves, but without shelf faces or ends.
1. For each shelf, cut two stretchers (G) and three slats (F), and sand them smooth. Lay three slats on your worksurface and arrange the stretchers over the ends of the slats so the edges and corners are flush. The slats should be spaced ¾" apart.
2. Drill pilot holes through the stretchers into the slats, and fasten them with glue and countersunk 1¾" wood screws.
3. For wine shelving, the design calls for ten wine cleats. Cut the cleats(H) to size from ¾" pine or pine stop molding, using a circular saw and straightedge guide. Sand the cuts smooth.
4. Place the first cleat on the adjustable shelf, ⅛"

from one end. Keep the ends of the wine cleats even with the edges of the shelf slats, and attach them with glue and 4d finish nails. Use a 2½"-wide spacer to guide placement for the rest of the cleats, and nail them in place. Use a nail set to recess all the nail heads on the wine cleats as you go.

Step G: APPLY FINISHING TOUCHES.
1. Using a wood mallet, pound glued ⅜"-dia. birch plugs into all counterbored holes. Carefully sand the plugs flush, and then finish-sand the pantry with fine-grit sandpaper.
2. Wipe the cabinet clean with a rag dipped in mineral spirits. When the wood dries, apply your choice of finish. We brushed a light coat of linseed oil onto our pantry to preserve the natural appearance. If you prefer paint, use primer and enamel.
3. When your finish dries, insert ¼" shelf pins at the desired heights and rest the adjustable shelves on top of the pins.

F. *A 2½"-wide spacer helps ensure uniform placement of the wine shelf cleats.*

G. *Use a wood mallet to pound glued ⅜" birch plugs in place.*

Pine Pantry

Turn a remote corner or closet into a kitchen pantry with this charming pine cabinet.

TOOLS & MATERIALS

- #6 × 1¼", 1½" and 2" wood screws
- 2d, 4d and 6d finish nails
- 16-ga. × 1" wire nails
- turntable hardware
- cabinet handles
- 3 × 3" brass hinges (2)
- cabinet door hinges (4)
- ¾" cove molding
- ⅜ × 1¼" stop molding
- glue
- finishing materials

This compact pantry cabinet is ideal for keeping your kitchen organized and efficient. It features a convenient turntable shelf, or "Lazy Susan," on the inside of the cabinet for easy access to canned foods. A swing-out shelf assembly lets you get the most from the pantry's space. The roominess allows you to store most of your non-refrigerated food items.

But the best feature of the pantry is its appearance. The rugged beauty of the cabinet hides its simplicity. For such an impressive-looking project, it is remarkably easy to build. Even if you don't have a traditional pantry in your home, you can have a convenient, attractive storage center.

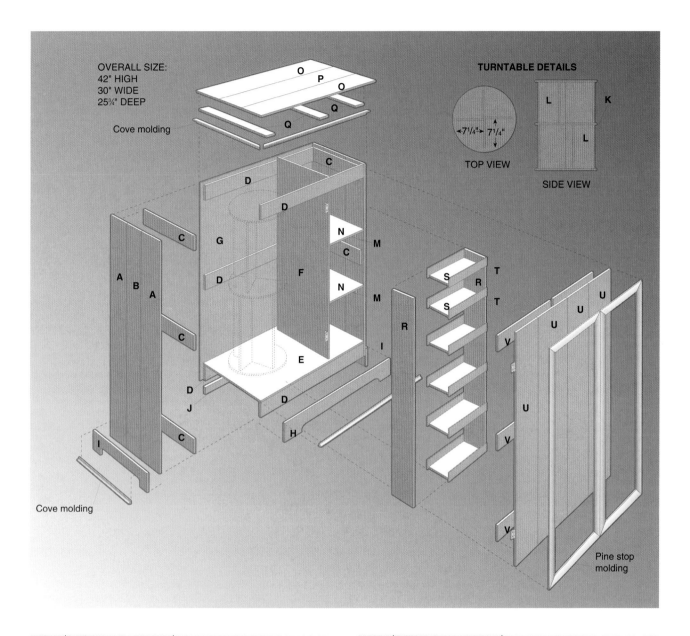

Pine Pantry

OVERALL SIZE:
42" HIGH
30" WIDE
25¾" DEEP

Cove molding

Cove molding

TURNTABLE DETAILS

TOP VIEW

SIDE VIEW

Pine stop molding

Key	Part	Dimension
A	(4) Side board	¾ × 9¼ × 39¼" pine
B	(2) Middle board	¾ × 5½ × 39¼" pine
C	(6) Panel cleat	¾ × 2½ × 22½" pine
D	(5) Stretcher	¾ × 2½ × 26½" pine
E	(1) Floor	¾ × 24 × 26½" plywood
F	(1) Divider	¾ × 22½ × 36" plywood
G	(1) Back	¼ × 28 × 39¼" plywood
H	(1) Base front	¾ × 3½ × 29½" pine
I	(2) Base side	¾ × 3½ × 24¼" pine
J	(1) Base back	¾ × 1½ × 28" pine
K	(3) Turntable shelf	¾ × 16"-dia. plywood

Key	Part	Dimension
L	(8) Supports	¾ × 7¼ × 12" pine
M	(4) Shelf cleat	¾ × 1½ × 22" pine
N	(2) Fixed shelf	¾ × 9 × 23" plywood
O	(2) Top board	¾ × 9¼ × 30" pine
P	(1) Middle board	¾ × 7¼ × 30" pine
Q	(3) Top cleat	¾ × 2½ × 22¼" pine
R	(2) Swing-out end	¾ × 6 × 32" pine
S	(6) Swing-out shelf	¾ × 6 × 10" pine
T	(12) Swing-out side	¼ × 2 × 11½" plywood
U	(4) Door board	¾ × 6⅝ × 35" pine
V	(6) Door cleat	¾ × 2½ × 11" pine

155

A. *Fasten cleats to the side and middle boards, forming the cabinet sides.*

B. *Attach front and back stretchers at the top and bottom, and a middle stretcher at the back.*

Directions: Pine Pantry

For all screws used in this project, drill ⁵⁄₆₄" pilot holes. Counterbore the holes ⅛" deep, using a ⅜" counterbore bit.

Step A: MAKE THE CABINET SIDES.
1. Cut the side boards (A), middle boards (B), and panel cleats (C) to length. Sand all of the parts smooth.
2. Position a middle board between two side boards, with the ends flush. Butt the boards against a framing square to keep them in line. Position a panel cleat flat across the boards so the bottom edge of the cleat is flush with the bottom edges of the boards. The ends of the cleat should be ¾" from the outside edges of the side boards. Fasten the cleat to the boards with glue, and drive 1¼" wood screws through the cleat and into the side and middle boards.
3. Attach the next panel cleat to the boards so its top edge is 21½" up from the bottom edge of the first cleat (photo A). Maintain a ¾" distance from the cleat ends to the board edges.
4. Install the top panel cleat with its top edge 1" down from the board tops.
5. Repeat these steps to make the other cabinet side.

Step B: ATTACH THE SIDES.
1. Cut the side stretchers (D) to length.
2. Connect the cabinet sides by attaching the

stretchers to the ends of the panel cleats. Position bottom stretchers at the front and back of the cabinet, keeping their top and bottom edges flush with the top and bottom edges of the panel cleats. The top two stretchers are each positioned a little differently—the back stretcher is flush with the tops and bottoms of the panel cleats, and the front stretcher is flush with the top edges of the cabinet sides. Apply glue and drive 1½" wood screws through the stretcher faces and into the ends of the cleats.
3. Attach the remaining stretcher at the back of the cabinet, flush with the panel cleats on the middle of the cabinet sides (photo B).

Step C: ATTACH THE FLOOR.
1. Cut the floor (E) to size. Sand the top face smooth, and fill any voids in the front edge of the floor with wood putty.
2. Position the floor on top of the bottom stretchers and panel cleats, with the floor's front edge flush with the face of the front stretcher. Glue the parts. Drive 1½" wood screws through the floor and into the stretchers and panel cleats.

Step D: ATTACH THE DIVIDER.
1. Cut the divider (F) and shelf cleats (M) to size.
2. Draw a reference line across the floor from front to back, 9" from the right cabinet side. This line marks the position of the divider's shelf-side face. Measure and mark shelf cleat position lines on the right cabinet side, 10" and 20¾" up from the cabinet floor. Draw

C. *Install the divider 9" in from the right side of the cabinet.*

D. *Check for square by measuring diagonally between the corners to make sure the distances are equal.*

corresponding lines on the divider. These lines mark the top edges of the shelf cleats.

3. Use glue and 1¼" wood screws to fasten the shelf cleats to the divider and side, aligning their top edges at the lines. Keeping all back edges flush, drive the screws through the cleats and into the divider and side panel.

4. Apply glue to the bottom edge of the divider. Insert the divider into the cabinet with its cleated face toward the cleated cabinet side. Drive 1½" wood screws up through the cabinet floor and into the divider edge. Drill ⁄₁₆" pilot holes through the top stretchers and drive 6d finish nails through the top stretchers and into the divider edges (photo C).

Step E: ATTACH THE BACK.
1. Cut the back (G) to size, and position it on the cabinet.
2. Drive evenly spaced 1" wire nails through the back and into the edge of one side panel.
3. Measure diagonally across the opposite corners to check if the cabinet is square (photo D). Square the cabinet, if needed, by applying pressure to opposite corners. When the diagonal measurements are equal, complete the nailing of the back to the stretchers and the remaining side panel.

Step F: ATTACH THE FIXED SHELVES.
1. Cut the fixed shelves (N) to size. Sand them smooth.
2. Position the shelves on the shelf cleats, with their

ends butted against the cabinet back. Attach the shelves with glue, and drive 1½" wood screws through the shelves and into the cleats.

Step G: MAKE THE BASE.
Three of the four base boards have cutouts that create a foot at each corner.
1. Cut the base front (H), base sides (I) and base back (J) to length. Sand the parts smooth.
2. Use a compass to draw 1¾"- radius semicircles, centered 7¼" from each end of the base front. Hold the point of the compass as close as possible to the bottom edge. Using a straightedge, draw a straight line connecting the tops of the semicircles. Repeat

E. *Cut the round turntable shelves with a jig saw. Each turntable shelf has an 8" radius.*

F. *Assemble the turntable supports in three pairs, joined at right angles.*

G. *Using glue and 4d finish nails, attach the swing-out shelf sides.*

these steps on the base sides, but center the semicircles 4¾" from the front end and 5½" from the back end. Cut along the lines with a jig saw.

3. Mark lines on the rear edges of the base sides, ½" from the bottom edge. These lines mark the position of the bottom edge of the base back.

4. Attach the base sides to the base front with glue, and drive 4d finish nails through the base front and into the ends of the base sides.

5. Attach the base back, between the base sides at the reference lines, using glue and 4d finish nails.

Step H: ATTACH THE CABINET & BASE.

1. Turn the cabinet on its back. Slide the base over its bottom end until the base back meets the bottom cleats. The base should extend 2" beyond the cabinet's bottom edges. Drive 2" wood screws through the bottom cleats and side boards and into the base sides.

2. Drive 1¼" wood screws through the front stretcher and into the base front.

Step I: BUILD THE TURNTABLE SHELVES.

1. Cut the turntable shelves (K) to size. To cut the circular shape, mark the center of the turntable shelves, and use a compass to draw a 16"-dia. circle. Cut the shelves to shape with a jig saw, and sand the cuts smooth (photo E).

2. Cut the turntable supports (L) to length.

3. Attach pairs of turntable supports at right angles by applying glue and driving 1½" wood screws through one support's face and into the other sup-

port's edge, forming simple butt joints (photo F).

4. Use a straightedge to draw a line across the turntable shelves, directly through their centerpoints. Place one pair of turntable supports along the line with the joint at the centerpoint (see Diagram). Make sure the support pair forms a right angle. Then, draw the outline of the supports on the shelf. Position another support pair on the other side of the line and draw the outline. Drill pilot holes through the shelves, centered within the outlines, and fasten the turntable shelves to the turntable supports with glue and 1½" wood screws. The supports should have their spines meeting at the center-point of the turntable. Offset the upper and lower sets of supports on the opposite sides of the middle shelf to allow room for driving the screws.

5. Attach the turntable hardware to the bottom face of the bottom turntable shelf, following manufacturer's directions. The turntable must be centered on the shelf, or the assembly will not rotate smoothly. Install the turntable assembly after you apply the finish to the pantry.

Step J: BUILD THE SWING-OUT RACK.

1. Cut the swing-out shelves (S), swing-out ends (R), and swing-out sides (T) to size. Sand the parts smooth.

2. Draw lines 6" apart starting from the bottom of the swing-out ends. These lines mark the positions of the bottom faces of the swing-out shelves. Apply glue to the shelf edges. Then, attach them to the swing-out ends by driving 1½" wood screws through the ends and into the shelf edges. The bottom shelf should be

H. *Use a circular saw with a straightedge as a guide to rip-cut the door boards to size.*

I. *Attach pine stop molding to create a frame around the edges of the door boards.*

flush with the bottom of the end edges.

3. Attach the swing-out shelf sides (T) on the edges of the shelves with glue and 4d finish nails (photo G).

Step K: MAKE THE TOP.

1. Cut the top boards (O), middle board (P), and top cleats (Q) to length. Sand them smooth.

2. Attach a top cleat across the inside faces of the boards, 1¾" from each end. Make sure that the ends of the boards are flush and that the cleats are centered from front to back. Apply glue and drive 1¼" wood screws through the cleats and into the top and middle boards. Fasten the middle cleat so its right edge is 11½" from the right end of the top.

3. Position the top on the cabinet so it overhangs the front and sides of the cabinet by 1". Fasten the top by driving 4d finish nails into the cabinet sides and toenailing through the middle cleat and into the divider.

Step L: BUILD THE DOORS.

1. Cut the door boards (U) and door cleats (V) to size (photo H). Sand them smooth.

2. Lay the boards in pairs, with their ends flush. Center the top and bottom cleats, keeping them 2" in from the top and bottom ends. Apply glue and drive 1¼" wood screws through the cleats and into the door boards. Attach the middle cleat, centering it between the top and bottom cleats.

3. Miter-cut ⅜" stop molding to frame the front faces of the doors. Fasten the molding with glue and 2d finish nails (photo I).

Step M: APPLY FINISHING TOUCHES.

1. Miter-cut ¾" cove molding to fit around the base and top (see diagram). Attach the molding with glue and 2d finish nails.

2. Set all nails with a nail set, and fill the nail and screw holes with wood putty. Finish-sand the pantry, and apply the finish of your choice.

3. Attach two evenly spaced 3 × 3" butt hinges to the edge of the swing-out rack. Mount the rack to the divider, using ¼"-thick spacers between the rack and divider (photo J).

4. Install the turntable assembly on the floor of the pantry.

5. Attach hinges and handles to the doors. Mount the doors to the cabinet sides.

J. *With spacers in place to help align the parts, attach the swing-out rack to the divider with 3 × 3" butt hinges.*

Wine & Stemware Cart

With our versatile oak wine and stemware cart, you can display and serve wine and other cordials from one convenient station. This cart can store up to 15 bottles of wine, liquor, soda or mix, and it holds the bottles in the correct downward position to prevent wine corks from drying out.

The upper stemware rack holds more than a dozen long-stemmed wine or champagne glasses. The cart carries a removable serving tray with easy-to-grip handles that works well for cutting cheese and for serving drinks and snacks. Beneath the tray is a handy storage area for napkins, corkscrews, and other items. Sturdy swivel casters make this wine rack fully mobile over tile, vinyl, or carpeting.

This beautiful oak cart with a lift-off tray allows you to transport and serve your wine safely, and provides an elegant place to display your vintage selections.

TOOLS & MATERIALS

- Circular saw
- Compass
- Drill with bits & drum sander attachment
- Jig saw
- Finish sander
- Belt sander
- Quick clamps
- Bar or pipe clamps
- (2) 1 × 12" × 6 ft. oak
- (1) 1 × 4" × 8 ft. oak

- (1) 1 × 4" × 6 ft. oak
- (1) 1 × 3" × 2 ft. oak
- (1) 1 × 2" × 4 ft. oak
- (1) ½ × 2¼" × 2 ft. oak
- (1) ½ × 3¾" × 4 ft. oak
- Wood screws (#6 × 1", 1¼" and 1½")
- ⅜"-dia. oak plugs
- (4) Casters
- Wood glue
- Finishing materials

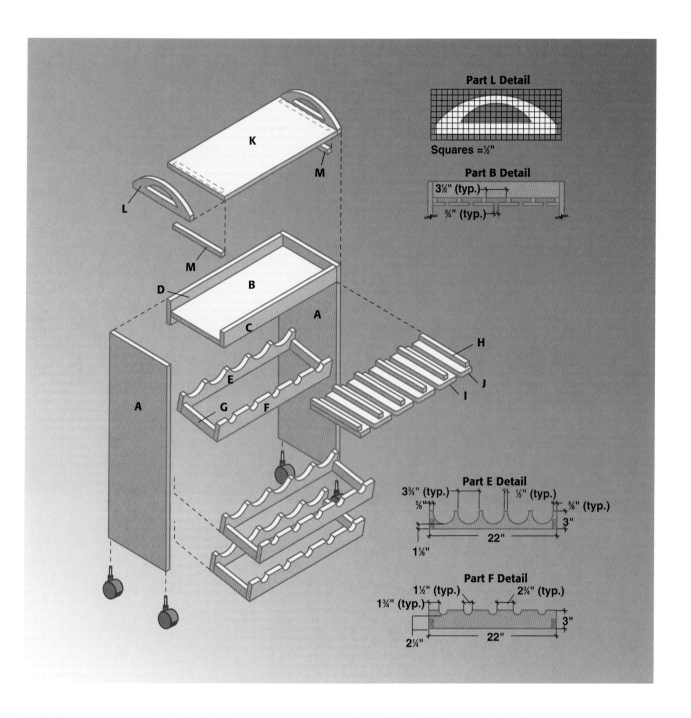

Part L Detail

Squares = ½"

Part B Detail

3½" (typ.)

¾" (typ.)

Part E Detail

3¾" (typ.) ½" (typ.)

⅝" ⅝" (typ.)

3"

22"

1⅛"

Part F Detail

1½" (typ.) 2¾" (typ.)

1¾" (typ.)

3"

2¼" 22"

Key	Part	Dimension	Key	Part	Dimension
A	(2) Side	¾ × 11¼ × 34" oak	**H**	(6) Stemware slat	¾ × ¾ × 9¼" oak
B	(1) Top	¾ × 9¾ × 22" oak	**I**	(4) Stemware plate	½ × 3½ × 9¾" oak
C	(1) Front stretcher	¾ × 2½ × 22" oak	**J**	(2) End plate	½ × 2⅛ × 9¾" oak
D	(1) Back stretcher	¾ × 4 × 22" oak	**K**	(1) Tray	¾ × 11¼ × 22" oak
E	(3) Wine rack back	¾ × 3 × 22" oak	**L**	(2) Tray handle	¾ × 3½ × 11¼" oak
F	(3) Wine rack front	¾ × 3 × 22" oak	**M**	(2) Tray feet	¾ × ¾ × 9½" oak
G	(6) Wine rack cleat	¾ × 1½ × 6½" oak			

Directions: Wine & Stemware Cart

Step A: CONSTRUCT THE SIDES & RACK ASSEMBLY.
Before fastening the frame parts together, make sure the assembly is square (see Tip on page 163).
1. Cut the cart sides (A), top (B), and back stretcher (D) to size from 1 × 12 oak. Cut the front stretcher (C) from 1 × 3 oak. Cut the stemware slats (H) from 1 × 4 oak. Cut the plates (I) and end plates (J) from ½"-thick oak.
2. Clamp a belt sander to your worksurface, and use it as a grinder, as shown on page 17, to round over the front corners of the stemware plates, and one front corner of each end plate.
3. Sand all of the pieces smooth.
4. Place the top (B) flat on your worksurface. Arrange the stemware slats on its bottom face, flush with the back edge. Space the slats 3½" apart, using a piece of scrap wood as a spacer. See Part B Detail on page 161 for more layout information. Keep the outer slats flush with the ends of the top. Drill ³⁄₃₂" pilot holes through the slats, and counterbore the holes ⅛" deep, using a ⅜" counterbore bit. Attach the slats with glue and 1¼" wood screws.

Step B: BUILD THE WINE RACKS.
Assemble each wine rack individually and attach them to the sides of the cart.
1. Cut the wine rack backs (E) and fronts (F) from 1 × 4 oak, and cut the cleats (G) from 1 × 2 oak.
2. To lay out the cutouts on the front and back pieces of the wine rack (see Part E and F Detail on page 161), mark points along one long edge of each board, and use a compass to draw the semicircles. Measuring from one end, mark points at 2½", 6¾", 11", 15¼", and 19½".
3. The rack back has 1⅞"-radius semicircles, and the rack front has ¾"-radius semicircles. Set the point of the compass on each reference mark, as close as possible to the edge, and draw the semicircles. Carefully make the cutouts with a jig saw.
4. Position the cleats between the rack fronts and backs, and drill two pilot holes through the faces of

A. *Use a spacer to keep the slats aligned properly, and attach them with glue and screws.*

B. *Use a drum sander attached to your portable drill to smooth the jig saw cuts on the wine racks.*

the fronts and backs and into the ends of the cleats. Counterbore the holes ¼" deep. Join the pieces with glue and 1½" wood screws.

5. Fill the counterbores with glued oak plugs. Sand the plugs flush with the surface, and sand any rough edges smooth. Clamp each completed rack to your worksurface, and sand the cutouts smooth with a drum sander attached to a drill.

Step C: Set the rack pitch.
On the inside face of each side panel, measure up ½" from the bottom, and make a mark at the front edge. Then measure up 2½" from the bottom, and make a mark at the back edge. Draw an angled reference line between the marks.

Step D: Attach the wine racks.
1. With one of the side pieces laying flat on your worksurface, position a wine rack so the bottom edge is on the reference line and the front edge is set back ¾" from the front edge of the side panel. Drill pilot holes through the rack cleats, and counterbore the holes ⅛" deep. Attach the rack to the side with glue and 1¼" wood screws.

2. Attach the middle and top racks in the same way, using a 4 × 10" spacer to position them correctly.
3. Use clamps to hold the remaining side panel in position. Make sure the bottom rack is on the reference line, and use the spacer to set the positions of the middle and top racks. Fasten the racks to the other side panel.
4. Arrange the stretchers between the sides so their top and outside edges are flush with the tops and outside edges of the sides. Drill pilot holes through the sides and into the ends of the stretchers. Counterbore the holes ¼" deep. Attach the stretchers with glue and 1½" wood screws.

TIP:

To check for square, measure your project from one corner diagonally to its opposite corner. Repeat the procedure for the other two corners. If the two diagonal lines are equal, your assembly is square.

C. *Measure ½" along the front and 2½" along the back of each side, and connect the marks for the bottom rack alignment.*

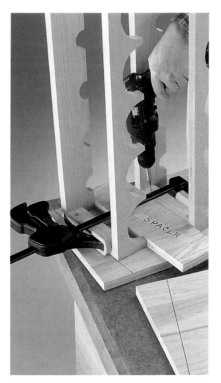

D. *Clamp a 4 × 10" spacer between the top and middle racks for proper positioning.*

E. *Drive screws through the slats to secure the top to the sides.*

Step E: ATTACH THE TOP ASSEMBLY.

1. Lay the cart on its side, and clamp the top panel between the side pieces. The bottom face of the top should be flush with the bottom edge of the front stretcher.

2. Measure the distance between the top panel and the top ends of the sides to make sure the top panel is level. Drill pilot holes through the outer slats and into the sides, and counterbore the holes ⅛" deep. Apply glue to the edges of the top and to the outside edges of the outer slats. Position the top, and drive 1¼" wood screws through the outer slats and into the sides.

3. Drill three evenly spaced pilot holes, counterbored ¼" deep, through both stretchers and into the edges of the top. Secure the pieces with 1½" wood screws.

Step F: COMPLETE THE RACK.

Attach the stemware plates to the slats to complete the stemware rack.

TIP:

Applying a thin coat of sanding sealer before staining helps the wood absorb stain evenly, which can eliminate blotchy finishes. Sanding sealer is a clear liquid, usually applied with a brush. Read the labels of the products you plan to use to make sure the finishes are compatible.

1. Set the cart upside down on your worksurface. Position an end plate on an outside slat, with its square side flush against the side panel and its square end flush against the back stretcher. Drill two pilot holes down through the end plate, taking care to avoid the screws in the slat beneath. Counterbore the holes ⅛" deep, and fasten the plate with glue and 1" wood screws.

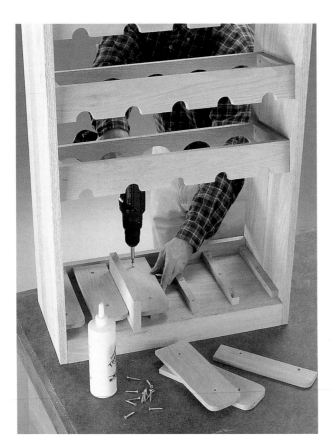

F. *Use a ¾" spacer to guide the placement of the stemware plates.*

G. *Drill holes for the casters in the bottom edges of the sides. Consider using a right-angle drill guide to ensure the holes are perpendicular to the sides.*

2. Repeat these steps to position and attach the remaining plates. Use a ¾"-thick spacer between the plates to ensure uniform spacing.

Step G: FIT THE CASTERS.
Using the proper size drill bit, drill holes into the bottom edges of the cart sides, and test-fit the casters. Position the holes so they are centered on the edge from side to side and are no less than 1" from the front and back side edges. For the casters to work properly, the holes must be perpendicular to the bottom edges of the sides.

Step H: MAKE THE TRAY & APPLY FINISHING TOUCHES.
1. Cut the tray (K) from 1 × 12 oak, and cut the tray handle (L) blanks from 1 × 4 oak. Cut the ¾ × ¾" feet (M) from leftover 1 × 12.
2. Transfer the pattern for the handles onto one of the blanks (see Part L Detail on page 161).
3. Using a backer board to prevent splintering, drill a starter hole on the inside portion of the handle. Then use a jig saw to cut along the pattern lines.
4. Trace the outline of the shaped handle onto the remaining handle blank. Cut the pattern on the second handle. Clamp the two handles together, and gang-sand them so their shapes are identical. See page 17 for more information on gang-sanding.
5. Position the tray between the handles, and drill five evenly spaced pilot holes through the side of each handle. Counterbore the holes ¼" deep. Attach the handles to the ends of the tray with glue and 1½" wood screws.
6. Position the tray feet on the bottom edge of the tray, ⅛" from the side edges and ⅞" from the front and back edges. Drill pilot holes through the feet, and counterbore the holes ⅛" deep. Attach the feet with glue and 1" wood screws.
7. Glue oak plugs into all visible ¼"-deep counterbored holes, and sand the plugs flush with the surface.
8. Finish-sand the entire cart and apply the finish of your choice. Add a polyurethane topcoat to seal and protect the surface.
NOTE: If you will be using the tray as a cutting board, be sure to use a nontoxic finish.
9. When the finish is dry, install the casters.

H. *Drill a pilot hole, then cut the inside handle profile with a jig saw. Use scrap wood as a backer board to prevent splintering.*

TIP:

Jig saw blades cut on the upward stroke, so the top side of the workpiece may splinter. To protect the finished or exposed side of a piece, make the cut with the exposed side face down. This way, if the edge splinters, it will remain hidden on the unexposed side. Remember to maintain a fast blade speed if you are cutting with a coarse-tooth blade. When cutting curves, use a narrow blade, and move the saw slowly to avoid bending the blade. Some jig saws have a scrolling knob that allows you to turn the blade without turning the saw.

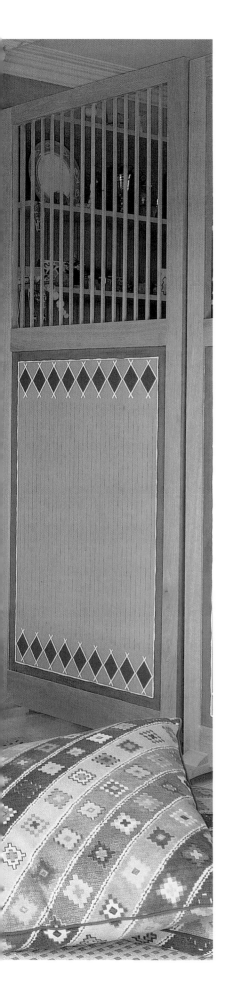

Recreation Storage

Recreation storage isn't just about an orderly home; it's about our well-being. A child that can't find a toy cries aloud, but he or she is no more miserable than the busy adult who has a few free hours in which to relax, but can't find the fishing tackle, golf club, hobby bin, or favorite CD that he or she wants. It's as true for adults as it is for kids: toys tend to get lost unless they are always returned to the same place.

Pre-made storage units for specific recreational equipment can be expensive, and they don't always suit your storage needs. Building your own recreational storage units allows you to customize projects for oddly shaped items, or to accommodate the right combination of growing collections of CDs, DVDs/Game ROMs, or videotapes.

Recreational storage can be as simple as a large box to house a variety of items. However, the more specific your activities are, the more complex and specialized your projects will tend to be. Location, size, and adaptability are all important aspects to consider for recreational storage projects.

Positioning a storage unit is a matter of common sense. If the kids tend to drop their athletic equipment, toys, or games in one particular area, try to build the new recreation storage near that location; you won't have to fight against existing habits to get them to use it. Whenever possible, build each project slightly oversized to make it easy to put things away and to retrieve them.

Remember that as time goes on, recreational activities change; and in the case of music, video, and gaming media, so do technologies. Take into considerations that your project may ultimately hold items you don't currently own. Build your projects so they can be adapted as new interests or new media formats come along.

IN THIS SECTION:

Recreation Storage Ideas

Slotted shelving *for compact discs is trim and compact, and it doesn't take up floor space.*

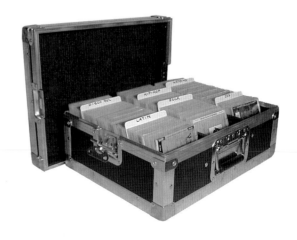

Discarding CD *jewel cases and storing the discs and all artwork in full-size sleeves allows four-times as much music to fit in the same amount of space.*

Slotted shelving brackets at the back of this closet create a versatile media storage unit that can be hidden away when not in use.

Slide-out drawers with slotted racks are ideal for storing CDs and DVDs out of sight but within easy reach.

The increasing need for media storage has produced a staggering array of towers, boxes, books, bags, bins, cabinets, crates, and novelty items; if you can dream of it, you can probably find it for sale.

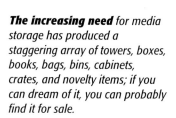

An inexpensive system of wire drawers, bins, shelves, and hooks can convert any small area in your hall, entryway, or basement into a well-organized storage space for toys and sports equipment.

Knee-wall high shelving with colorful, open crates is an easy way for kids to store their toys, clothing, books, and drawing supplies.

170

Metal shelving standards anchored to studs make an ideal storage system for sports equipment. Make sure to buy a system that accepts many different styles of hangers.

An expandable bike rack telescopes to lock into position between the floor and ceiling. It works well in either a basement or garage.

A moveable loft with a powered cable system supports up to 1000 lbs., and smoothly lowers to the floor along the metal wall tracks with the turn of a key.

Sports Locker

If you or your children are active in sports, you know how valuable a good sports locker can be. Six feet tall and broad in the shoulders, this locker can handle just about anything thrown at it. But don't be afraid that this storage project will make your house smell like a locker room—the pegboard doors provide plenty of ventilation.

If, like most people, your interest in sports is confined to a few activities, you can easily customize this sports locker to meet your needs. Add extra shelves to store smaller-scale equipment or clothing; if you play a lot of softball, put an extra row of bat hangers in the open side; if you are an outdoors person, replace the bat hangers with a piece of closet rod so you can store your hunting or fishing apparel in one location where it won't pass its outdoorsy fragrance along to your other outerwear; if your family enjoys golf, eliminate the bottom two shelves to create space for two more sets of clubs.

By using a little imagination, you can turn this versatile project into a real team player.

Whatever your game—basketball, skiing, golf, hockey, baseball, cricket— this roomy sports locker will become a most valuable project.

TOOLS & MATERIALS

- Circular saw
- Drill with bits & hole saw
- Jig saw
- Finish sander
- Compass
- Power miter saw or miter box and backsaw
- (2) ¾" × 4 × 8 ft. plywood
- (1) ¼" × 4 × 8 ft. plywood
- (1) 2 × 4" × 6 ft. pine
- (6) 1 × 2" × 6 ft. pine
- (1) ⅛" × 4 × 8 ft. pegboard
- (4) ½ × 1⅛" × 8 ft. wainscot cap
- Wood glue
- Wood screws (#6 × 2", #8 × ¾")
- 1" brads
- (4) 1½" × 2" butt hinges
- (2) Door pulls or handles
- (4) Magnetic door catches
- (4) Shaker-style pegs
- Finishing materials

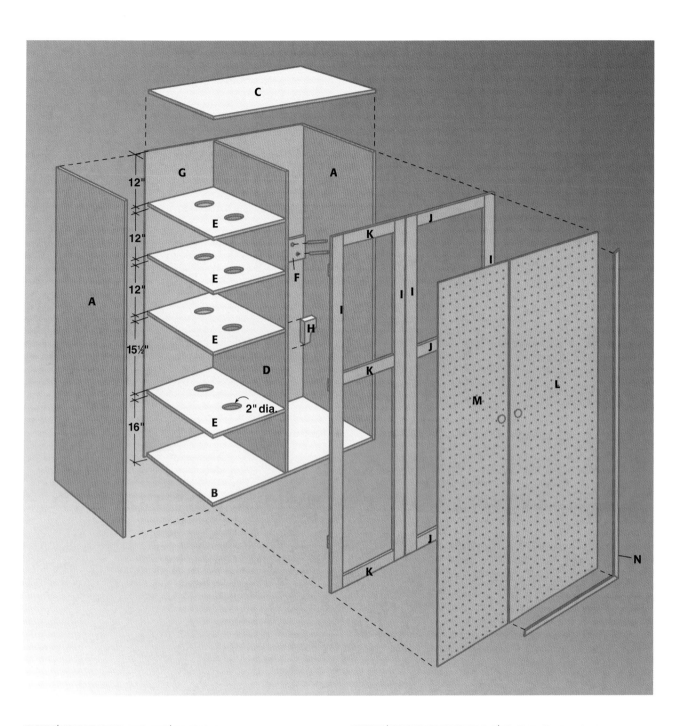

Key	Part	Dimension
A	(2) Side	¾ × 20 × 71¼" plywood
B	(1) Bottom	¾ × 20 × 38½" plywood
C	(1) Top	¾ × 20 × 40" plywood
D	(1) Divider	¾ × 20 × 70½" plywood
E	(4) Shelf	¾ × 16 × 20" plywood
F	(1) Stretcher	¾ × 6 × 21¾" plywood
G	(1) Back	¼ × 40" × 6 ft. plywood

Key	Part	Dimension
H	(8) Hanger	1½ × 3½ × 4" pine
I	(4) Door stile	¾ × 1½ × 71¼" pine
J	(3) Long rail	¾ × 1½ × 19¹³⁄₁₆" pine
K	(3) Short rail	¾ × 1½ × 14¹⁄₁₆" pine
L	(1) Wide door	⅛ × 22¾ × 71¼" pegboard
M	(1) Narrow door	⅛ × 17 × 71¼" pegboard
N	(3) Door trim	½ × 1⅛ × 11"* cap molding

*Cut to fit

Directions: Sports Locker

Step A: BUILD THE FRAME.
1. Cut the components of the locker to size: the sides (A), bottom (B), and top (C) from ¾"-thick plywood. Sand the surfaces with medium (100- or 120-grit) sandpaper to smooth out the rough spots. Then clamp the bottom between the side panels and drill counterbored pilot holes through the side panels and into the bottom. Fasten the pieces, using glue and 2" wood screws.
2. Attach the top to the sides with glue and screws driven down through the top and into the top edges of the side panels.
3. Cut the divider (D) to size. Lay the locker on its back, and fasten the divider between the top and bottom panels of the box, 16" from the right side. Make sure the back and front edges of the divider are flush with the edges of the top and bottom panels.

Step B: BUILD THE SHELVES.
Cut the shelves (E) to size. Each shelf has two optional 2"-dia. holes to keep balls from rolling around in the locker. Cut two holes in each shelf using a 2"-dia. hole saw mounted on a drill. The centerpoint of each hole is located 5" from the front or back edge of the shelf, and centered from side to side. Place a

piece of scrap wood under the project when using a hole saw, to prevent damage to your worksurface and tearout on your workpiece. Smooth out the edges on the shelves, and sand any rough surfaces smooth.

Step C: ATTACH THE SHELVES, BACK & STRETCHER.
1. Mark the shelf locations on the side and divider (see diagram on page 173). Cut four scraps of wood the same length as the shelf height to support each shelf while you install it. Install the shelves by driving #6 × 2" screws through the divider, into the edges of the shelves.
2. Cut the back (G) to size. Mark a horizontal reference line for positioning the top of the stretcher, 39" up from the bottom. Fasten the back to the sides, top, and bottom with evenly spaced 1" brads. Nail along one side first, making sure the frame is square before nailing the remaining edges.
3. Cut the stretcher (F) to size from ¾" plywood. Drill holes for Shaker-style pegs in the stretcher. Align the stretcher with the reference marks on the back and attach it with #6 × 2" screws driven through the side and divider panels, and into the ends of the stretcher.

A. *Install the divider panel between the top and bottom panels, separating the locker into an open area and a shelf area.*

B. *Using a hole saw, cut 2"-dia. holes in the shelves to keep balls from rolling inside the locker.*

C. *Use wood spacers to support each shelf while you fasten it with screws.*

Step D: ATTACH THE HANGERS.

1. Cut eight hangers (H) to size from 2 × 4 pine. Set the legs of a compass to a 2" radius, and position the point of the compass at one corner of each hanger. Draw a ¼-round cutting line at the corner, then cut along the line with a jig saw and sand the cut smooth.

2. Draw reference lines for two rows of hangers 30" and 52" up from the bottom panel. Space the hangers so they are 1¼" apart—a good distance for hanging bats or paddles. Fasten the pieces by driving two screws through the divider and into each hanger.

Step E: BUILD THE DOORS & APPLY FINISHING TOUCHES.

1. Cut the door stiles (I), long rails (J), and short rails (K) from 1 × 2 pine. Apply glue to the ends of the rails, and fasten them between the stiles by driving wood screws through the stiles and into the rails, completing the door frames.

2. Cut the wide door (L) and narrow door (M) to size from ⅛"-thick pegboard. Position the pegboard panels over the door frames, making sure they fit squarely on the frames. Screw the panels to the frames with ¾"-long wood screws, keeping the frames flat on the worksurface as you go.

3. Miter-cut 2" wainscot cap molding to fit around the edges of each door. Tape the cap pieces to the

door so they hold their position, and drill pilot holes through the molding and the pegboard. Attach the cap frame to the doors with glue and 1" brads.

4. Fill all screw holes and exposed plywood edges with wood putty, and sand all rough edges and surfaces smooth. Apply glue to the tips of the Shaker-style pegs and insert them into the stretcher. Prime and paint the locker—we used enamel paint for a hard finish.

5. Hang the doors with two 1½ × 2" butt hinges per door, then attach a pull or handle to each door.

6. Install magnetic door catches for each door at the top and bottom of the divider.

TIP:

Pegboard can be tricky to paint with a brush or roller—no matter how hard you try, the peg holes always seem to clog with paint, creating a ragged appearance. For best results, paint pegboard with spray paint or a paint sprayer.

D. *Attach the hangers by driving screws through the divider and into the ends of the hangers.*

E. *Assemble the rails and stiles to make the two differently sized door frames.*

Sewing Chest

With this clever sewing chest, you can move from room to room in pursuit of your hobbies, without leaving a trail of tools and materials in your wake. The padded lid flips up for access to a removable tray and the generous storage compartment below. The upholstered top can be used as a footrest, a seat, or even a temporary pincushion—just be careful not to mix the uses. This sewing chest is designed to be the perfect size for most sewing, knitting, and fabric-art projects. It's big enough to hold all your tools and supplies, but still lightweight and portable.

Soft lines, a spacious interior, and a removable tray make this chest a perfect companion for sewing, knitting, or needlepoint hobbyists.

TOOLS & MATERIALS

- Circular saw
- Drill with bits, drum sander, & 1½"-dia. hole saw
- Jig saw
- Miter box and backsaw
- Bar or pipe clamps
- Nail set
- Finish sander
- Scissors
- (1) ¾" × 4 × 8 ft. plywood
- (1) ½ × 2¼" × 8 ft. beaded molding
- Wood glue
- Wood screws (#6 × 1¼", 2")
- 4d finish nails
- 1" wire brads
- 1"-thick foam
- Upholstery fabric
- Upholstery tacks or staples
- 1½ × 1¼" butt hinges
- Finishing materials
- Velcro® strips

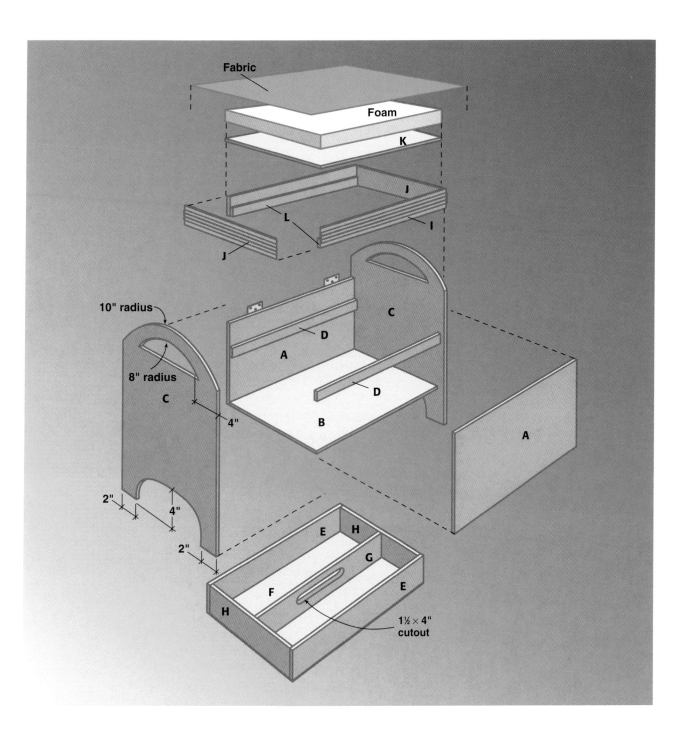

Fabric

Foam

K

J

L

I

J

10" radius

8" radius

C

4"

C

A

D

D

B

A

2"

4"

2"

E   H

G

F

E

H

1½ × 4"
cutout

Key	Part	Dimension
A	(2) Front/back	¾ × 9¾ × 18½" plywood
B	(1) Bottom	¾ × 14 × 18½" plywood
C	(2) Chest end	¾ × 16 × 20" plywood
D	(2) Tray cleat	¾ × 1½ × 18½" plywood
E	(2) Tray side	¾ × 3 × 18" plywood
F	(1) Tray bottom	¾ × 9¾ × 18½" plywood

Key	Part	Dimension
G	(1) Tray divider	¾ × 3 × 16½" plywood
H	(2) Tray end	¾ × 3 × 12¼" plywood
I	(2) Side molding	½ × 2¼ × 18¼" molding
J	(2) End molding	½ × 2¼ × 15½" molding
K	(1) Seat board	¾ × 14⅜ × 17⅛" plywood
L	(2) Seat cleat	¾ × 1 × 17¼" plywood

Directions: *Sewing Chest*

Step A: ASSEMBLE THE CHEST.

1. Cut the end panels (C) to size from ¾"-thick plywood. Use a straightedge to draw a centerline from top to bottom on each panel (to be used as a reference for drawing the curved cutting lines).

2. To make the curved top on the end panels, tack a finish nail 10" down from the top, on the centerline. Tie a string to the nail, measure out 10" on the string, and tie a pencil at this point. With the string pulled taut, draw a curve from one side of the panel to the other.

3. To draw cutting lines for the handle cutouts, adjust the pencil so it is 8" from the nail, and draw a semicircle below each top curve. To create the straight bottom of the handle cutouts, use a straightedge to draw a line intersecting the points where the 10" curves meet the edges of the panel.

4. To make the bottom cutting lines for the feet of the chest, mark points 2" in from the side edges of each end panel, at the bottom edges. Mark another point 4" up from the bottom edge along the centerline of both panels. Then draw a line 8" long at the 4" mark parallel to the bottom edge of each panel. Connect the endpoints of these lines with a smooth arc to the 2" reference marks.

5. Cut along the marked lines for the curves, using a jig saw. To make the handle cutouts, drill starter holes, then slip the jig saw blade into position and complete the cutout. Sand the curves smooth, using a drill and a drum sander attachment or a sanding block.

6. Cut the front and back panels (A), bottom panel (B), and tray cleats (D) to size. Attach the cleats to the inside faces of the front and back panels using glue and 1¼" wood screws. The top of each cleat should be 6½" above the bottom of the front and back panels.

7. Attach the bottom to the front and back panels with glue and 2" screws, making sure the ends of the front and back are flush with the face of the bottom panel. Add the end panels to the assembly. The underside of the bottom should be flush with the tops of the cutouts on the bottoms of the end panels. The front and back panels should each be recessed ¼" from the edges of the end panels. Use glue and 2" counterbored screws driven through the outside faces of the end panels and into the front, back, and bottom panels.

Step B: PREPARE THE DIVIDER.

1. Cut the tray sides (E), tray bottom (F), tray divider (G), and tray ends (H) to size.

A. *Make the handle cutouts and the curves at the top and bottom of the end panels with a jig saw.*

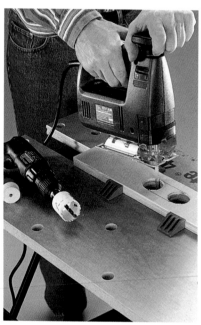

B. *Make the ends of the handle cutout in the divider with a hole saw, then connect with a jig saw.*

C. *After making the handle cutout in the divider, attach it between the tray ends with glue and finish nails.*

2. Mark a centerpoint on one face of the divider. Draw a 4"-long line through the centerpoint, parallel to the top and bottom edges. Then mark points on the line 1¼" on each side of the centerpoint. Install a 1½"-dia. hole saw on your portable drill and drill holes at these points. Complete the cutout with a jig saw, then sand it smooth, using a drill and drum sander attachment.

Step C: ASSEMBLE THE DIVIDER.
Fasten the tray sides to the tray ends with glue and 4d finish nails. Attach the tray bottom in the same way. Attach the divider between the ends. Use a nail set to set all exposed nail heads.

Step D: BUILD THE SEAT & MAKE THE CUSHION.
1. Cut the beaded molding to make the sides and ends (I, J) of the seat frame. Use a hand miter box and backsaw to cut 45° miters so the pieces fit together to form a square frame. Assemble the frame and drill pilot holes. Join the pieces, using glue and 1" brads at each joint. Clamp the frame from both directions with bar or pipe clamps, making sure the corners are square.
2. Cut the seat cleats (L) and seat board (K) to size. Make sure the cleats are flush with the bottom edges

of the seat frame, and attach them to the sides of the frame, using glue and 4d finish nails.
3. Fill the plywood edges with putty. Finish-sand and paint the chest before proceeding.
4. Cut a piece of 1"-thick foam rubber to cover the seat board. Cut a piece of upholstery material large enough to cover the foam and the seat board and overhang by at least 4" on each side. Fold the upholstery over the foam and seat board, and tack or staple it along the edges. NOTE: Trim off excess material. Set the seat onto the seat cleats in the frame, and attach it by driving 4d finish nails through the frame and into the seat board.

Step E: ADD VELCRO® STRIPS.
For a handy touch, cut self-adhesive Velcro® strips and stick them to the underside of the seat. Stick a piece of upholstery fabric to the matching part of each Velcro® strip. Use the strips to secure knitting needles or other light crafting items.

Step F: ATTACH THE SEAT.
Attach the seat to the chest with 1½ × 1¼" butt hinges.

D. *After stapling or tacking the upholstery material over the foam-rubber padding, trim off the excess material with scissors.*

E. *Store knitting needles or other light items between strips of Velcro® attached to the underside of the seat. Cover the backs of the strips with upholstery.*

F. *Attach the seat to the back of the chest with two evenly spaced 1½ × 1¼" butt hinges.*

Stackable Storage Blocks

I f you are looking for a multi-purpose storage project that is easy to build and usable in any room, stackable storage blocks are the answer. Made from finish-grade ¾" birch plywood, the size, color, and style of these blocks are easy to adapt to any space. If you plan to stack the blocks, install the optional 1 × 3 slats to hold each block safely in place. Be creative. The possibilities are endless.

Stackable blocks provide unique storage space limited only by your imagination.

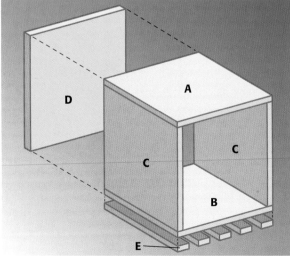

TOOLS & MATERIALS

- Circular saw with plywood blade
- Drill with bits
- Utility knife
- Straightedge guide

- Combination square
- (1) ¾" × 4 × 8 ft. birch plywood
- (3) 1 × 3" × 8 ft. pine

- Wood screws (#6 × 1½, #6 × 1¼)
- Finishing materials

Key	Part	Dimension
A	(1) Top	¾ × 21¾ × 21" birch plywood
B	(1) Bottom	¾ × 21¾ × 21" birch plywood
C	(1) Sides	¾ × 21¾ × 22½" birch plywood
D	(1) Back	¾ × 22½ × 22½" birch plywood
E	(9) Slats*	¾ × 2½ × 22½" pine

* Optional

180

Directions: Stackable Storage Blocks

Step A: MEASURE & CUT THE PIECES.
1. Lay out the cutting lines for each piece of the block separately, using a straightedge to make accurate, straight lines. Before making any cuts across the grain of the plywood, score the top layer of veneer several times with a sharp utility knife to avoid splintering.
2. Cut the top (A), bottom (B), sides (C), and back (D) from ¾" plywood using a plywood cutting blade on a circular saw. Sand the edges smooth.

Step B: ASSEMBLE THE BOX FRAME.
Screw the top and bottom of the box to the side pieces with 1½" wood screws driven through counterbored pilot holes. Space the screws approximately every 5", making sure all connecting edges are flush and that the side pieces cap the top and bottom.

Step C: ATTACH BACK & APPLY THE FINISHING TOUCHES.
1. To attach the back of the block, drill counterbored pilot holes near each corner, through the back panel only. Then turn the frame assembly on its front edge and position the back panel on top, making sure the sides of the frame are flush with the edges of the back.
2. Drive a screw into one of the pilot holes of the back panel, rotate the block 90°, and check the block

for square, using a combination square. Make any necessary adjustments and drive the next screw. After each corner screw, check the block for square.
3. Drill counterbored pilot holes spaced approximately every 5" around the perimeter of the back panel, and then drive screws into the holes.
4. Cut the slats (E) to size and install them so they interlock when the blocks are stacked. Use a scrap piece of 1 × 3 as a spacer, and install the slats using 1¼" screws driven through the interior of the block and into each slat. Finish the slats prior to installing them if you plan to paint them.
5. Finish the blocks as you prefer. You may want to cover the screw heads with wood plugs or putty for a cleaner look.

VARIATIONS:

Install casters with locking wheels to make portable blocks. Or, consider multiple blocks that decrease in size for stacking variations. Use a template to cut out decorative shapes for a child's room, or apply veneer tape to the front edges of the blocks, stain them, and use them as end tables.

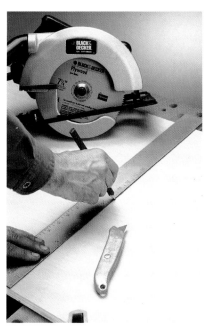

A. *Lay out the block pieces. Score all crosscuts with a utility knife, then cut out the pieces.*

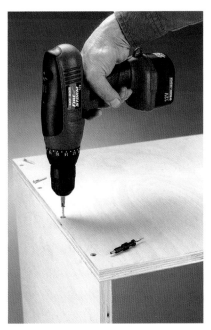

B. *Screw the top and bottom to the sides, spacing the screws approximately every 5".*

C. *Drive in a corner screw, making sure the block is square before driving each additional corner screw.*

Treasure Chest

Treasures are in the eyes of the beholder. One child's old bottle caps are another child's gold dubloons. Whatever perceived valuables your kids may have, they'll enjoy keeping them safe and secure in this trusty treasure chest.

Built entirely of pine and beaded pine paneling, this chest incorporates simple construction designs that give the appearance of more complicated counterparts. The lid is held open by a lid support and, when closed, is kept structurally sound by the side and end lips. The treasure chest is suitable for either a natural or painted finish and can be accented with decorative trunk hardware.

Keep cherished toys and prized belongings in a safe place with this beaded pine treasure chest.

TOOLS & MATERIALS

- Circular saw
- Drill with bits
- Finish sander
- Bar clamps
- (6) 1 × 3" × 8 ft. pine
- (1) ½ × 1¼" × 8 ft. pine stop molding
- (1) ¾" × 2 × 4 ft. plywood
- (6) 5/16 × 4" × 8 ft. beaded pine paneling
- Wood glue
- Wood screws (#6 × ¾", 1¼", & 1½")
- Button plugs
- Hinges
- Lid support
- Latch
- Finishing materials

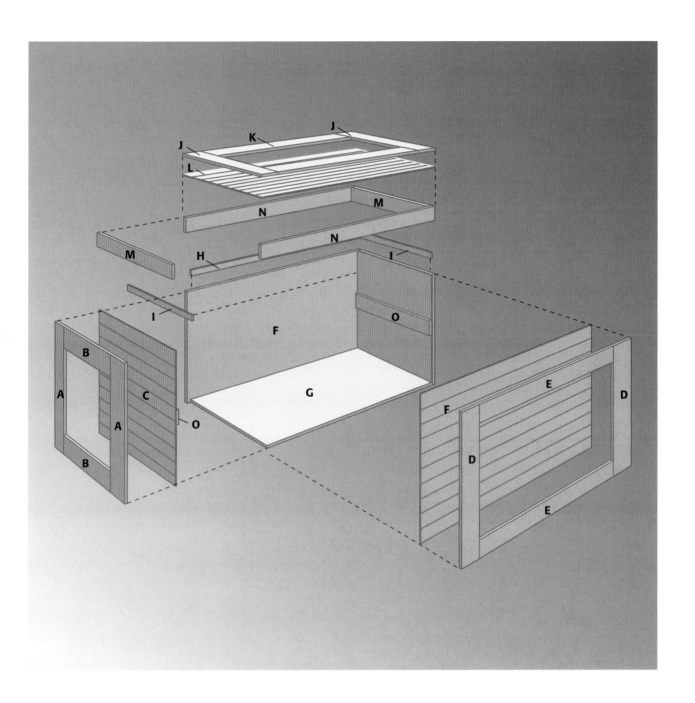

Key	Part	Dimension
A	(4) End stile	¾ × 2½ × 16" pine
B	(4) End rail	¾ × 2½ × 10½" pine
C	(2) End panel	⁵⁄₁₆ × 14½ × 15½" beaded pine
D	(4) Side stile	¾ × 2½ × 16" pine
E	(4) Side rail	¾ × 2½ × 25" pine
F	(2) Side panel	⁵⁄₁₆ × 14½ × 28" beaded pine
G	(1) Bottom panel	¾ × 15½ × 28" plywood
H	(2) Side lip	½ × 1¼ × 28½" pine molding

Key	Part	Dimension
I	(2) End lip	½ × 1¼ × 15" pine molding
J	(2) Cover stile	¾ × 2½ × 15½" pine
K	(2) Cover rail	¾ × 2½ × 23½" pine
L	(1) Cover panel	⁵⁄₁₆ × 15½ × 28½" beaded pine
M	(2) End frame	¾ × 2½ × 15½" pine
N	(2) Side frame	¾ × 2½ × 30" pine
O	(2) Handle cleat*	¾ × 2½ × 15" pine

*Optional

Directions: Treasure Chest

Step A: BUILD THE END FRAMES.
1. Cut the end stiles (A) and end rails (B) to length from 1 × 3 pine, and sand the edges and surfaces with medium-grit sandpaper.
2. Lay the rails and stiles face down on a flat surface, positioning the rails so their outside edges are flush with the ends of the stiles. Apply wood glue to the ends of the rails and clamp the components. Set the clamped assemblies aside to dry.

Step B: CUT & INSTALL THE END PANELS & SIDE PANELS.
1. Cut the end panel pieces (C) to length from beaded pine paneling and sand the edges with medium-grit sandpaper. Unclamp the end rail and stile assemblies after they have sufficiently dried, and place the end panel pieces on the rail and stile assemblies, flush with the stile edges and ¾" in from the rail edges. Fasten the end panels to the rail and stile assemblies with glue and ¾" wood screws.
2. Cut the side stiles (D) and side rails (E) to length from 1 × 3 pine and sand with medium-grit sandpaper. Glue and clamp the rails and stiles as done previously for the end assemblies and set them aside to dry.
3. Cut the side panel pieces (F) to size from beaded pine paneling and sand with medium-grit sandpaper. Unclamp the side rail and stile assemblies after they have dried and place the side panels on the rail and stile assemblies, 1" in from the stile edges and ¾" in from the rail edges. Fasten the side panels to the rails and stile assemblies, using glue and ¾" wood screws.

Step C: ASSEMBLE THE CHEST FRAME.
1. Stand the end panel assemblies and a side panel assembly on their bottom edges on a flat worksurface. Position the end panel assemblies flush with the ends of the side panel assemblies and clamp the panels in place. Drill counterbored pilot holes through the side stiles into the end stiles. Unclamp the panels and join them with glue and 1½" wood screws.
2. Cut the bottom panel (G) to size from ¾"-thick plywood and sand it smooth with medium-grit sandpaper. Position the bottom panel and secure it with glue and counterbored wood screws.
3. Cut the side lips (H) and end lips (I) to length from ½ × 1¼" pine stop molding. Leave one lip slightly shorter to allow room for the lid support. Sand the

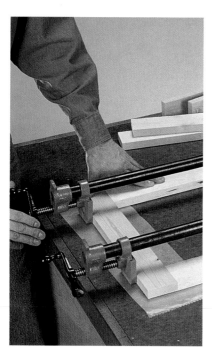

A. *Apply glue to the end rails and position them between the end stiles, then clamp in place until dry.*

B. *Fasten the end panels to the end rails and stiles.*

C. *Secure the end panel assemblies between the side panel assemblies.*

edges and surfaces smooth with medium-grit sand-paper. Fasten the lips to the end and side rails with their bottom edges ¾" below the top edge of the rails, using glue and 1¼" wood screws.

Step D: BUILD THE COVER.
1. Cut the cover stiles (J) and cover rails (K) to length from 1 × 3 pine. Sand the edges and surfaces smooth with medium-grit sandpaper. Position, glue, and clamp the rails and stiles as done for the end and side assemblies. Then cut the cover panel piece (L) to size from beaded pine paneling.
2. Unclamp the cover rail and stile assemblies after they have dried and lay them face down on a flat sur-face. Place the cover panel piece on the rail and stile assemblies, flush with the stile and rail edges. Fasten the cover panel piece to the rail and stile as-semblies, using glue and ¾" wood screws.
3. Cut the end frames (M) and side frames (N) to length from 1 × 3 pine to fit the perimeter of the cover panel assembly. Attach the end and side frames to the cover panel assembly with glue and counterbored wood screws.

Step E: INSTALL THE HANDLE CLEATS.
If you choose to have handles on the chest, you'll need handle cleats to mount the handles. Cut the handle cleats (O) to size from 1 × 3 pine and fasten them 7" down from the top of the end lips, using glue and 1½" screws driven into the end stiles.

Step F: APPLY FINISHING TOUCHES.
Finish-sand the entire chest and fill all open pilot holes with wood plugs. Sand the plugs flush, and ap-ply several coats of quality primer and enamel paint, or varnish and polyurethane, letting each coat dry thoroughly between applications. Place the cover on the chest. Mark the hinge locations with a pencil on the back side of the chest and cover, 3" in from each end. Attach the hinges to the side frame and side rail with the hinge screws included with the hardware. In-stall the handles, latch, and lid support.

TIP:

Beaded pine paneling is available in both panels and in packages of tongue-and-groove planking. We used planks, which tend to be more durable, but you could easily use panels, if you prefer.

D. *Attach the end and side frames to the cover panel assembly with glue and counterbored screws.*

E. *Fasten the handle cleats to the insides of the end panels with glue and screws.*

F. *Mount the hinges to the back side of the chest and cover.*

Rod & Tackle Center

Anyone who loves to fish knows that fishing rod storage can be a big problem. Lines become tangled together; rods tip over and spill out in all directions; fragile (and expensive) reels stick out into traffic areas, where they are vulnerable to being kicked or bumped; and worst of all, hooks and lures can creep out dangerously into your living spaces. With this simple storage unit, you can keep your fishing rods and tackle well organized, tangle free, and out of harm's way.

Designed with a sleek profile so it fits against a wall, this rod and tackle center makes efficient use of your space. The slide-out tackle tray and the open tackle box storage area can be accessed from either side. The rod racks feature cutouts in both the upper and lower racks so rods will not slip out or rub together.

The rod and tackle center can be positioned flat against the wall to use the minimum amount of floor space, or you can set it with a side panel against the wall for maximum accessibility. Either way, at least one side panel will be exposed, so you can attach hooks for hanging landing nets or even your favorite fishing hat.

This two-sided equipment storage unit can hold up to eight fishing rods, plus spare tackle and a pair of tackle boxes.

TOOLS & MATERIALS

- Circular saw
- Drill with a 1½"-dia. hole saw
- Jig saw
- Finish sander
- Compass
- Pipe or bar clamps

- (1) ¾" × 4 × 8 ft. plywood
- (1) ¼" × 2 × 2 ft. lauan plywood
- Wood glue
- Deck screws (#6 × 1⅝")
- ¾" wire brads
- Finishing materials

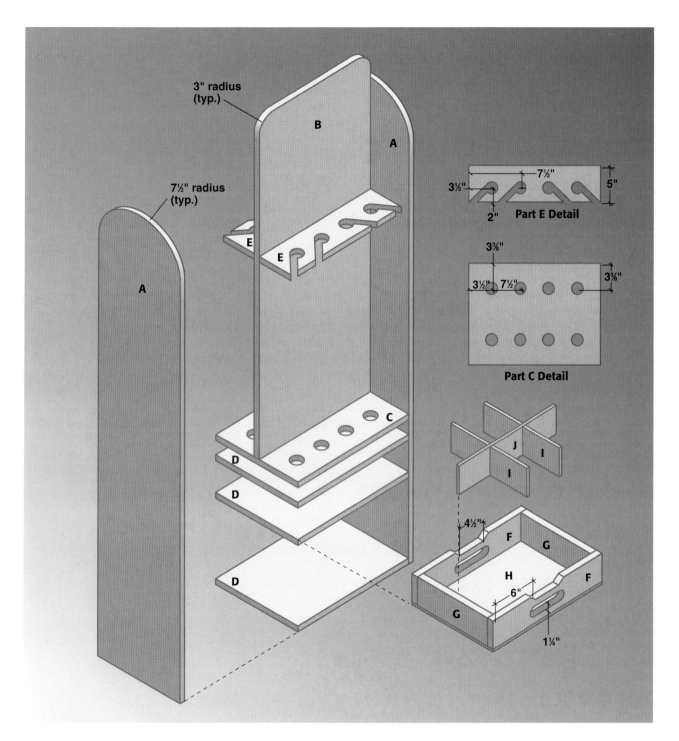

3" radius (typ.)

7½" radius (typ.)

B

A

A

E

E

7½"

3½"

2"

5"

Part E Detail

3⅜"

3½" 7½"

3⅜"

Part C Detail

C

D

D

D

J

I

I

4½"

F

G

H

F

G

6"

1¼"

Key	Part	Dimension
A	(2) Side	¾ × 13½ × 65¼" plywood
B	(1) Divider	¾ × 18½ × 48" plywood
C	(1) Lower rack	¾ × 13½ × 18½" plywood
D	(3) Shelf	¾ × 13½ × 18½" plywood
E	(2) Upper rack	¾ × 5 × 18½" plywood

Key	Part	Dimension
F	(2) Tray front/back	¾ × 4⅛ × 18¼" plywood
G	(2) Tray side	¾ × 4⅛ × 11½" plywood
H	(1) Tray bottom	¼ × 13 × 18¼" lauan plywood
I	(2) Short tray divider	¼ × 4 × 11½" lauan plywood
J	(1) Long tray divider	¼ × 4 × 16¾" lauan plywood

187

Directions: Rod & Tackle Center

Step A: MAKE THE SIDES.
Cut the sides (A) to size from ¾"-thick plywood. Draw a 7½"-radius roundover at the top of each side panel, using a compass. Cut along the marked lines on both panels with a jig saw, and then sand any rough spots smooth.

Step B: ATTACH THE SHELVES.
1. Cut the lower rack (C) and shelves (D) to size. Mark centerpoints for two rows of four 1½"-dia. holes on the lower rack, according to the positioning shown on the Part C Detail on page 187. Cut the holes with a 1½"-dia. hole saw and a drill.
2. Set the side panels on edge, about 20" apart. Apply glue to the edges of one shelf, and position it between the sides so the bottom face is flush with the bottom edges of the sides. Drill counterbored pilot holes, and drive 1⅝" screws through the sides and into the shelf.
3. Glue and clamp the lower rack between the sides, 20" up from the bottom edges of the side panels. Drill counterbored pilot holes, then drive 1⅝" screws through the sides and into the shelves. Install the remaining two shelves, positioning the lower edge of one at 12" and one at 17½" above the bottom edges of the side panels.

Step C: INSTALL THE DIVIDER.
1. Cut the divider (B) to size. Mark reference lines across both faces of the board, 28" from the bottom. Then use a compass to draw 3" radius roundovers on both top corners of the divider. Cut along the roundover lines with a jig saw and sand the edges smooth.
2. Apply beads of glue to the bottom and outer edges of the divider. Position it so it is centered between the side panels, front to back, resting squarely on the top of the lower rack. Clamp the divider between the sides with pipe clamps or bar clamps. Then drive screws at 8" intervals through countersunk pilot holes in the side panels, into the edges of the divider.

Step D: INSTALL THE UPPER RACKS.
The upper racks support the tips of fishing rods with a row of four 1½"-dia. holes. Each hole has an angled slot cut from the front edge of the board to the hole so you can slip the fishing rod into the hole.
1. Cut the upper racks (E) to size, and mark centerpoints for four evenly spaced 1½" holes in each shelf,

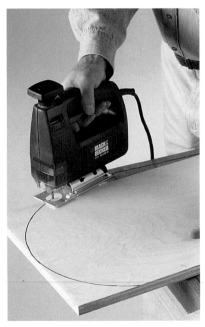

A. *Use a jig saw to cut the 7½"-radius curves on the tops of the side panels.*

B. *Glue and clamp the lower rack between the sides, then reinforce the joint with wood screws.*

C. *Install the shelves and lower rack, then clamp the side panels around the divider.*

as shown in Part E Detail on page 187. Drill these holes, using a drill and a 1½" hole saw.

2. Draw cutting lines to mark the angled, ½"-wide slots from the front edge of each rack to each hole. Cut the slots, using a jig saw and sand any rough edges smooth.

3. To attach the upper racks, position them between the side panels so the tops are flush with the reference lines. Make sure the upper racks butt flush against the divider. Drill counterbored pilot holes through the sides, and attach the upper racks with glue and 1⅝" screws driven through the side panels, into the ends of the racks.

Step E: MAKE THE TRAY BOX.

1. Cut the tray front/back pieces (F), tray sides (G), and tray bottom (H) to size.

2. The finger-grip slots on the front and back pieces of the tray are 1¼"-high × 6¼" long. To lay out the cutting lines for the finger-grips, refer to the diagram of the tray on page 187. The top edge of the cutout should be 2¼" down from the top edges of the front and back pieces. Use a drill with a 1¼" spade bit to create the rounded ends of the cut, then connect the holes with a jig saw to form the slot on each panel. Sand the edges of the cutouts smooth with medium-grit sandpaper.

3. To make the layout for the ¾"-deep access notches in the top edges of the front and back pieces, refer to the diagram of the tray on page 187. The access notches start 6" in from each end of the pieces. The sides of the notch should angle in at about 45°. Cut the notch out with a jig saw and sand the cutline smooth.

4. Drill pilot holes, and attach the tray sides between the tray front and back with glue and 1⅝" screws, forming a rectangular frame. Attach the tray bottom to the frame with glue and ¾" wire brads.

Step F: MAKE TRAY DIVIDERS & APPLY FINISHING TOUCHES.

1. The tray dividers are made from lauan plywood strips that fit together with half-lap joints. Cut the tray dividers (I, J) to size from ¼"-thick lauan plywood. Use a jig saw to cut a ¼"-wide × 2"-long notch in the center of each of the two shorter dividers (I). Cut a pair of ¼"-wide × 2"-long notches in the longer divider (J), 5¼" in from each end. Fit a short divider notch over each long divider notch to make sure the parts fit together, then glue them in place in the bottom of the tray.

2. Fill all screw holes with putty. Sand the entire project, and apply primer and paint. Paint the tray section separately, then insert it in the shelf area when the finish has completely dried.

D. *Lay out the angled slots connecting the holes to the front edges of the upper racks rods.*

E. *Cut access notches and finger-grip cutouts into the front and back of the tray.*

F. *Cut out the tray dividers, then notch them to form half-lap joints. Test-fit them, then glue the dividers in place.*

Garden Center

This garden center eliminates the clutter of gardening supplies, and does double duty as a functional gardening workstation. Positioned at a comfortable working height, the plywood worksurface lets you repot plants or blend soils without straining your back. The main cabinet is large enough to hold most of your fertilizers, seeds, and other supplies. A soil cart housed in the cabinet rolls out to make transporting heavy materials a snap. The tubes at the sides of the cabinet organize your long-handled gardening tools. And the high shelves at the top of the cabinet are perfect for storing pesticides and other products that should be kept out of the reach of children.

This combination worksurface and cabinet lets you centralize your gardening tools & supplies in one convenient location.

TOOLS & MATERIALS

- Circular saw
- Drill with bits
- Jig saw
- Finish sander
- Combination square
- Clamps
- (1) ¼" × 4 × 4 ft. hardboard
- (1) 1 × 2" × 8 ft. pine
- (2) ¾" × 4 × 8 ft. AC plywood
- (1) 4"-dia. × 4 ft. PVC drainpipe

- Wood glue
- Wood screws (#6 × 1¼")
- ¼"-dia. × 1½" carriage bolts with nuts and washers
- 2d finish nails
- (4) Glide feet
- (4) 2½"-dia. casters
- (4) Self-closing cabinet hinges
- (2) Door pulls
- Wood putty
- Finishing materials

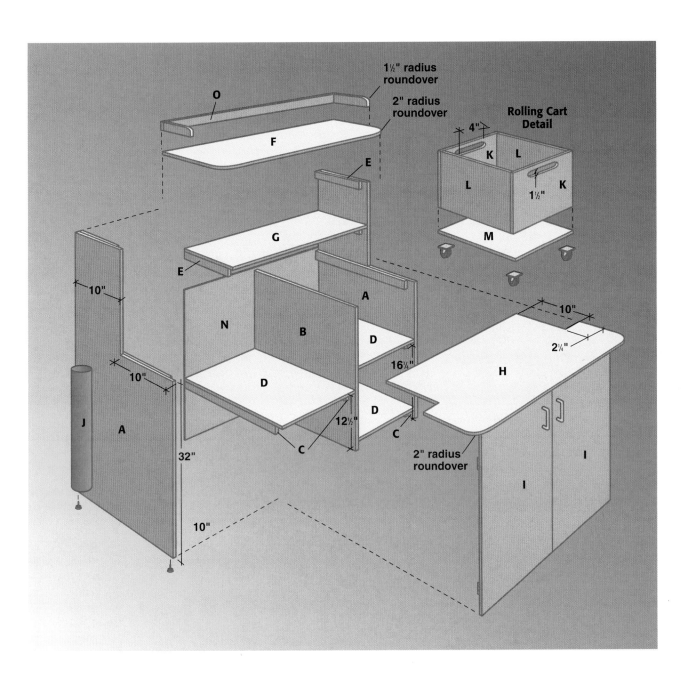

Key	Part	Dimension
A	(2) Side panel	¾ × 20" × 4 ft. plywood
B	(1) Center partition	¾ × 20 × 32" plywood
C	(8) Shelf cleat	¾ × 1½ × 18" plywood
D	(3) Cabinet shelf	¾ × 13⅞ × 20" plywood
E	(4) Upper shelf cleat	¾ × 1½ × 8" pine
F	(1) Top shelf	¾ × 13 × 33" plywood
G	(1) Upper shelf	¾ × 10 × 28½" plywood
H	(1) Work surface	¾ × 23 × 33" plywood

Key	Part	Dimension
I	(2) Door	¾ × 14¾ × 31⅞" plywood
J	(2) Tool holder	4"-dia. × 2 ft. PVC pipe
K	(2) Box end	¾ × 12 × 10" plywood
L	(2) Box side	¾ × 16 × 10" plywood
M	(1) Box bottom	¾ × 12 × 17½" plywood
N	(1) Back panel	¼ × 30 × 32¾" hardboard
O	(3) Shelf skirt	¾ × 1½ × * pine

*Cut to fit

Recreation Storage

Directions: Garden Center

Step A: MAKE THE SIDE PANELS.

The L-shaped side panels of the gardening center support shelf cleats and the worksurface.

1. Cut the side panels (A) to size. Mark a reference point on the front edge of one of the panels, 32" from the bottom. Using a combination square as a guide, draw a 10" line perpendicular to the side edge at this point. Then place the combination square on the top edge of the panel and draw a reference line from the end of the 10" reference line to the top edge of the panel. These two lines indicate the cutout area on the panel.

2. Use a jig saw or circular saw to make the cutout. Sand the edges smooth, then use the cut panel as a template to draw a matching cutout on the other side panel. Cut out the second side panel and sand the edges smooth.

Step B: INSTALL THE SHELF CLEATS.

The cabinet shelves are supported by 1 × 2 cleats mounted on the inside faces of the cabinet sides and on the center divider panel. There are two shelves on the right side of the unit and one shelf on the left side.

1. Cut the divider (B) to size from ¾"-thick plywood.

Then cut the shelf cleats (C) and upper shelf cleats (E) to size from 1 × 2 pine. Sand the plywood surfaces and edges with medium-grit sandpaper on a power sander.

2. Begin installing the cleats (C) on the interior face of the left side panel and the left face of the divider. Measure up 12" from the bottom edge of the side panel and divider and draw reference lines parallel to the bottom edge, using a combination square. Install the cleats for the shelf on the left side using wood glue and 1¼" wood screws.

3. To install the cleats for the bottom shelf on the right side, position the cleats flush with the bottom and back edges of the right side panel and the divider.

4. Measure up 16¼" from the bottom edge of the side panel and divider and draw reference lines for the bottom edges of the cleats for the middle shelf. Install these cleats flush with the back edges of the side panel and the divider and flush with the reference lines, using glue and 1¼" wood screws.

5. The cleats for the worksurface of the cabinet are

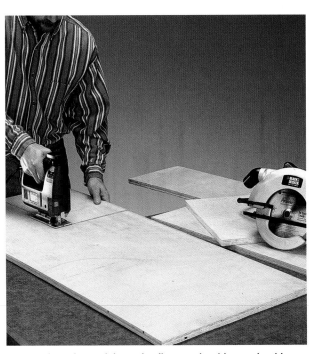

A. *Cut along the straight cutting lines on the side panels with a circular saw, then use a jig saw or hand saw to finish the cuts at the corners.*

B. *Measure up from the bottom cabinet cleats to mark positions for the other cabinet shelf cleats.*

192

installed flush with the back edges of the divider and right side panel and flush with the cutout line made in Step A.

6. The upper shelf cleats (E) are supports for the upper (G) and top (F) shelves that run the width of the cabinet. Mark lines for the upper shelf cleats in the area above the worksurface, 9" above the tops of the cleats at the worksurface cutout. Attach the shelf cleats just below the lines, flush with the back edges of the sides using glue and 1¼" wood screws. Attach additional cleats flush with the tops of the side panels to help support the top shelf.

Step C: INSTALL THE SHELVES.
1. Cut the cabinet shelves (D) and upper shelf (G) to size. Prop the side panels in an upright position, about 33" apart, with their cleated surfaces facing in.
2. Attach the upper shelf in the area above the worksurface, using glue and 1¼" wood screws—counterbore pilot holes for the screws so the heads can be covered with wood putty.
3. Prop the divider up between the sides, making sure the cleats are lined up correctly with the matching cleats on the side panels. Attach the cabinet shelves, making sure the front and back edges are flush with the edges of the side panels.

Step D: MAKE THE TOP SHELF.
1. Cut the top shelf (F) to size from plywood. Draw cutting lines for roundovers on the front corners of the shelf, using a compass set for a 2" radius. Cut the roundovers with a jig saw and use a sander to smooth out the cuts.
2. For decorative appeal and to prevent items from slipping off the top shelf, we added skirt boards (O) to the back and ends of the shelf. First measure the shelf and cut a 1 × 2 to the same length.
3. Cut two pieces of 1 × 2 to 4" in length. Draw a 1½"-radius roundover at one end of each piece (see diagram on page 191).
4. Cut the roundovers and sand them smooth. Attach the back skirt board to the back of the shelf, on edge and flush at each end, using glue and 1¼" wood screws driven up through the shelf and into the skirt board.
5. Fasten the side skirts to the ends of the shelf, with the square end of each piece butted up against the back skirt board. Fasten the top shelf to the top cleats on the side panels.

Step E: BUILD & ATTACH THE WORKSURFACE.
The worksurface is notched to fit around the top shelf sections of the side panels. Rounded over at the

C. *Attach the cabinet shelves and upper shelves to the sides and the divider to stabilize and strengthen the garden center.*

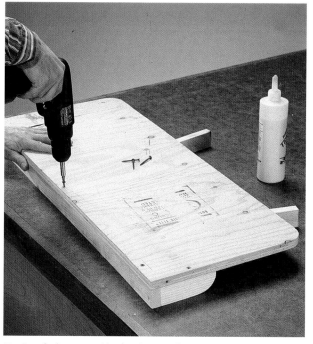

D. *Attach the 1 × 2 skirt that frames the top of the top shelf, screwing the pieces together from below.*

front corners, it overhangs the lower sections of the side panels on the front and sides.

1. Cut the worksurface (H) to size from ¾"-thick plywood. Mark 10"-deep × 2¼"-wide notches at the back corners to fit around the sides (see the diagram on page 191).

2. Use a compass set for a 2" radius to mark roundover cutting lines at the front corners of the worksurface. Make the cutouts with a jig saw, then smooth them out with a sander.

3. Test-fit the worksurface and check to make sure the cabinet assembly is square. Set the worksurface onto the horizontal arms of the side-panel cutouts, with the notches fitting around the sides, and the overhang equal from side to side. Attach the worksurface to the cleats, using glue and screws.

Step F: MAKE THE TOOL HOLDERS & BACK PANEL.
We mounted 2 ft.-long sections of PVC drainpipe to the outside faces of the side panels to create holders for long-handled garden tools.

1. Cut a section of 4"-dia. PVC drainpipe into two 24" lengths to make the tool holders (J). A hacksaw is a good tool choice for cutting PVC. Smooth out the cuts with emery paper or very fine sandpaper. If you plan to paint the PVC tool holders, buff the pipes

with medium-grit sandpaper to create a better bonding surface for the paint, an activity known as scarifying.

2. Draw reference lines for hanging the tool holders on the outer faces of the side panels. The lines should be parallel to the back edges, 7" in from the back edge. On the reference lines, mark drilling points 4" and 24" up from the bottom edges of the side panels.

3. Drill ¼"-dia. guide holes for carriage bolts at these points. Then mark matching guide holes on the tool holders by positioning the pipes on the centerlines so the holes in the side panels fall 2" in from each end of the pipe. Insert a pen through the guide holes in the side panels and mark the hole locations onto the surface of the pipes. Drill a ¼"-dia. hole at each of these points.

4. Place the pipes in position, with the guide holes aligned, and insert carriage bolts from inside each pipe, through the side panels. Attach washers and nuts to the ends of the carriage bolts and tighten them securely, but do not overtighten them.

5. Cut the back panel (N) to size from ¼" hardboard, using a circular saw. Position the back panel at the back of the cabinet assembly but do not attach it until you have squared the cabinet—one of the main jobs of the back panel is to keep the cabinet from

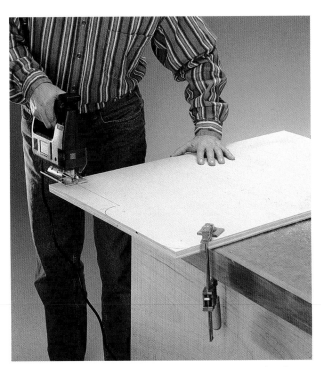

E. Use a jig saw to cut notches into the sides of the worksurface so it fits around the side panels.

F. Insert a pen or pencil into the guide holes in each side panel and mark drilling points on the pipes.

slipping out of square. The cabinet is square if the diagonal measurements are equal. Once you have squared the cabinet, attach the back panel with 2d finish nails. Keep the edges of the back panel flush with the outside surfaces of the side panels and the top of the worksurface.

Step G: ATTACH THE DOORS.
1. Cut the doors (I) to size from ¾"-thick plywood.
2. Attach self-closing cabinet door hinges sized for ¾"-thick wood to the outside back faces of the doors. One hinge should be positioned 2" down from the top edge of each door, and another 4" up from the bottom.
3. Position the doors over the front of the cabinet, maintaining a ⅛" gap between them. Mark the hinge screw locations onto the inside faces of the side panels, then remove the doors and drill pilot holes at the screw locations. Hang the doors.

Step H: MAKE SOIL CART & APPLY FINISHING TOUCHES.
The rolling soil cart lets you transport blended potting soils from the work area to the garden without straining your back.
1. Cut the box sides (L), box ends (K) and box bottom (M) to size from ¾" plywood.
2. Mark hand-grip cutouts on the box ends. The bottom of each cutout should be 3½" down from the top edge of the box end; the top should be 2" down; the ends of the cutouts should be 4" in from the side edges.
3. Draw roundovers at the ends of the cutouts, then drill a starter hole inside the cutout line and make the cutouts with a jig saw. Sand the edges smooth.
4. Attach the box ends to the box sides with glue and screws driven to form butt joints (see the diagram on page 191). Attach the box bottom to the sides and ends.
5. Attach casters to the underside of the box bottom. The casters (we used 2½"-dia. casters) should be positioned an inch or two inside each corner. If the screws that come with the casters are more than ¾" in length, substitute shorter screws with the same shank size.
6. Attach nail-on glide feet to the bottom edges of the garden center's side panels. Fill counterbored screw holes with wood putty, sand all wood surfaces smooth, and apply varnish or paint. You may wish to remove the doors before applying the finish. Once the finish is dry, attach door pulls about 3" down from the top of each door.

G. *Hang the cabinet doors with self-closing cabinet hinges to keep the doors from swinging open.*

H. *Fasten the casters to the bottom corners of the soil cart, using screws that are no more than ¾" long.*

Clothing Storage

For many of us, just finding space to store the various costumes we wear for the different roles and occasions in our lives is a challenge. Organizing the clothing so that you can actually find what you're looking for is even more difficult. It's hard to know what you have to wear in the morning when you can't see beyond the mess in your closet, dresser, or wardrobe. On the bright side, there is actually a lot of unused space in a bedroom, adjacent hallway, and even the clothes closet, which can be utilized by tailoring it to cater to your specific needs. Consumers are catching on: we spend more money on commercial closet organizers and elaborate chests and dressers than almost any other storage category.

Many commercial clothing storage systems work well, but are surprisingly expensive. And when a professional organizing service is involved, the costs skyrocket. The projects in this section offer attractive, practical and cost-effective alternatives. To decide which projects would benefit you the most, we recommend you simply look around your closets and into your drawers on the day after the laundry has been done. At this moment, it will become clear if you need more space for hanging shirts, blouses, and trousers (try the Armoire), a place to hang outerwear (the Copper Coat Rack), or spaces for storing everyday clothes (the Chest of Drawers or the Under-Bed Storage Box). Or perhaps your storage needs are more specialized: try the hanging Tie & Belt Rack to make some order of the tangled mass of leather and silk ribbons in your dresser drawer; or the Entryway Chest to store linens, blankets, and quilts.

Clothing storage affects our daily lives as we prepare for the workday, change for after-work activities, or slip into something more comfortable at night. The right clothing storage should make everything you have visible at a glance so that finding a matching outfit becomes more of a pleasure and less of a scavenger hunt.

Clothing Storage Ideas

A modular closet system, with high and low rails and tailored to your needs, can hold 50-75% more than a traditional one-rail closet, and make everything in your wardrobe readily accessible and easy to find.

The right freestanding modular wardrobe can feel like a built-in if it's well chosen for the space and style of a room.

A stylish open closet, like this one, used as an elegant room divider and held in place by adjustable poles that exert pressure against the floor and ceiling, proves that a closet doesn't always have to be kept behind closed doors.

An open portable closet—whether it's a "leaning closet" or a freestanding closet on wheels—provides extra garment storage instantly anywhere.

Closed portable closets are perfect for rooms without adequate closet space, or for storage of your out-of-season clothing. And because they are lightweight and oftentimes on wheels, they make moving a snap. You'll hardly need to unpack.

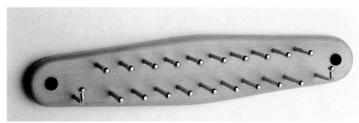

A tie and belt rack can be purchased or built yourself. Mount it to the inside of a closet wall or door.

"Vacuum-pack" plastic storage bags, perfect for long-term storage, compress clothing to a fraction of their size, and protect them from mildew, insects, and dust.

An over-the-door, *hanging-clothes rack provides quick and easy additional storage space at a budget price.*

Over-the-door *shoe racks keep shoes visible and easy to find—without taking up closet or floor space.*

A rolling pants *hanger fits underneath your regular clothes rack, freeing up space to use for shirts.*

201

Tie & Belt Rack

Keep your ties and belts in order and available in one handy location with this inexpensive hanging rack. Made of aromatic cedar, the rack also adds a pleasant fragrance to your closet.

By eliminating the tie and belt hooks, you can make heavy-duty cedar hangers that will protect your winter coats and other favorite clothing from moth damage. Perfect for your closet or as a gift to a friend, these simple pieces will only take a few hours to make.

Directions: Tie & Belt Rack

Step A: MAKE THE HANGER BODY.
1. Trace the outline of the body of a standard plastic or metal hanger onto a piece of 1" aromatic cedar. Use a jig saw to cut along the outline.
2. Sand the entire hanger body, using 120-grit sandpaper, rounding the edges and smoothing the faces.

Made of aromatic red cedar, the tie and belt rack organizes your accessories.

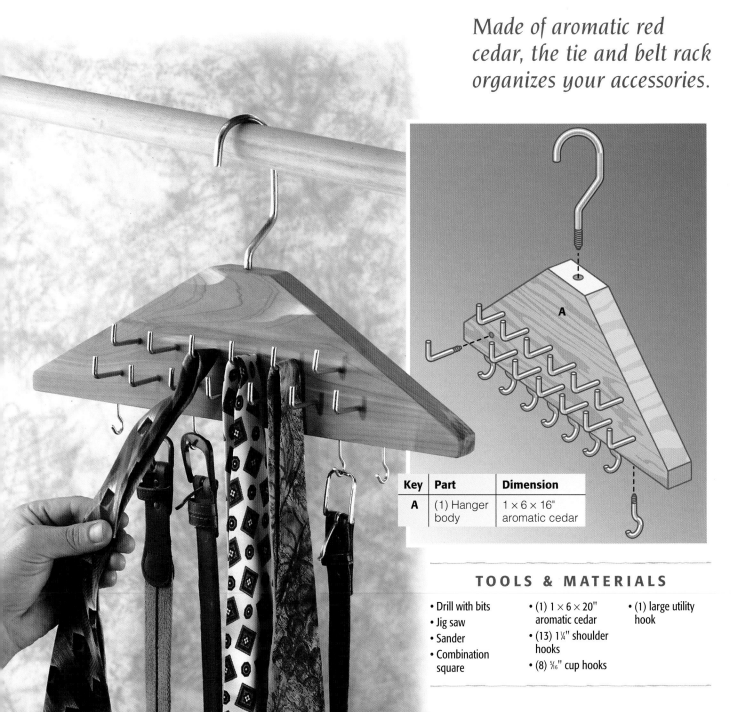

Key	Part	Dimension
A	(1) Hanger body	1 × 6 × 16" aromatic cedar

TOOLS & MATERIALS

- Drill with bits
- Jig saw
- Sander
- Combination square
- (1) 1 × 6 × 20" aromatic cedar
- (13) 1¼" shoulder hooks
- (8) ⁵⁄₁₆" cup hooks
- (1) large utility hook

Step B: LAY OUT THE BELT HOOK LOCATIONS.
1. Mark a center line across the face of the workpiece, using a combination square. Extend the line across the bottom and top edges.
2. To make the layout for the belt hooks, measure 2" on ether side of the centerline mark and draw reference marks across the bottom edge of the workpiece. Then, measuring toward the outside edges from your reference marks, draw additional marks in 1½" increments for each belt hook.
3. Set a combination square to half the thickness of the hanger, and use the end of the ruler as a guide to draw reference marks through the previous marks for each belt hook location. This process will create an "X" in each hook location.

Step C: LAYOUT THE TIE & HANGING HOOK LOCATIONS.
1. Position one edge of a combination square ruler flush with the lower edge of the workpiece so the end of the ruler is flush with the center line. Draw a horizontal line 1" from the bottom edge, then without moving the ruler, make a vertical reference mark 1" from the center line. Make additional reference marks in 1½" increments toward the outer edge for as many hooks as desired.
2. Make an additional horizontal reference line 1"

above the first horizontal line and repeat the previous step, of making reference marks. To stagger the layout of the tie hooks, the first mark should be ¾" from the center mark and in 1½" increments to the outer edge.
3. Repeat the steps taken to lay out the hook locations on the other side of the center line, and the back of the workpiece if desired.
4. To find the location of the hole for the large utility hook on the top of the workpiece, set the combination square ruler to half the thickness of the workpiece. Then position the square flush with the front side of the workpiece and make a reference line through the center line across the top edge.
5. Drill ¼"-deep pilot holes at every reference mark for a tie or belt hook. Drill a ½"-deep pilot hole for the utility hook at the intersection of the two reference lines on the top edge of the hanger.
6. Erase all the reference marks and screw the shoulder hooks in the tie holes and the cup hooks in the belt holes. Then screw the utility hook in place. Do not apply a finish to the hanger body or the cedar will lose its scent. Sand the hanger body on occasion with fine sandpaper to replenish the scent.

A. *Cut the aromatic cedar with even pressure applied to the saw, or your cuts will be rough and more difficult to sand.*

B. *Use a combination square to make straight, accurate reference marks.*

C. *Offset the reference marks in the second tier of tie hooks by measuring out ¾" from the center mark.*

Copper Coat Rack

For many people, finding a place to hang coats is a problem. Entryway closets can quickly fill with other storage items, or there may be no closet in the entryway at all. Whether you need it for the capacity to store coats, or you simply like its style, the copper coat rack will help you organize your entryway.

Built with sturdy, ½" rigid copper pipe and ⅜" soft copper, the rack is both functional and decorative. A large upper shelf is a great place for your hat and gloves. And the cross support at the base is inset for tidy storage of shoes and boots.

Decorate the copper coat rack any way you like. We have provided detailed descriptions for the decorations shown here, but feel free to experiment. For more information on working with copper pipe, see page 14.

Organize your entryway with the distinctive appearance of the copper coat rack.

TOOLS & MATERIALS

- Pipe cutter
- Propane torch
- 3-in-1 pipe tool
- Tape measure
- Locking pliers
- Pliers
- Flux brush
- Hammer
- (26) ½" copper tee
- (4) ½" 90° elbow
- (4) ½" copper cap
- Flux
- Solder
- (2) ¾" to ½" reduction coupling
- (50 ft.) ⅜" water-rated thin-wall soft copper
- Nylon scouring pad
- (6) ½ × 10 ft. rigid copper, type L
- (1) ¾ × 10 ft. rigid copper, type L
- Light-gauge wire
- Masking tape

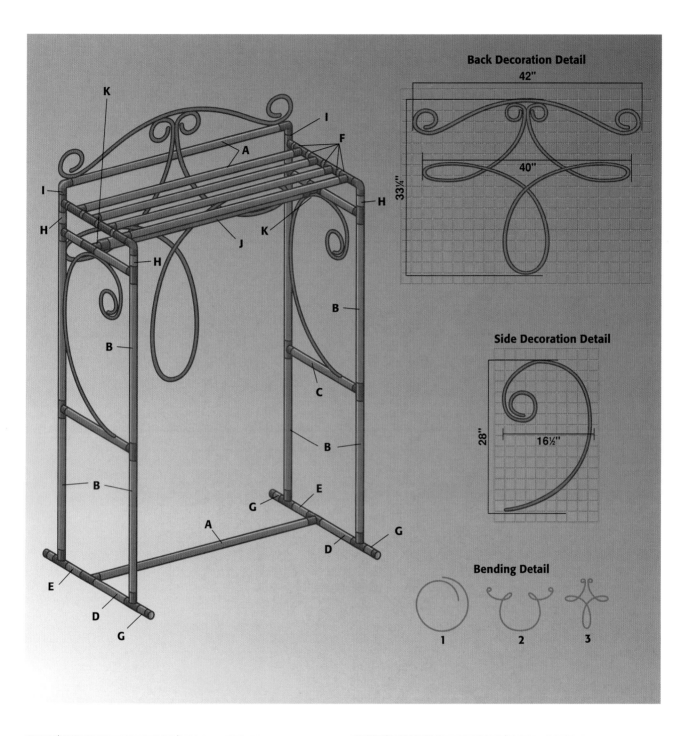

Back Decoration Detail

42"

33¼"

40"

Side Decoration Detail

28"

16½"

Bending Detail

1   2   3

Key	Part	Dimension
A	(6) Cross extension	½"-dia. × 40" copper pipe
B	(8) Leg extension	½"-dia. × 28" copper pipe
C	(2) Leg brace	½"-dia. × 16" copper pipe
D	(4) Leg brace	½"-dia. × 9" copper pipe
E	(4) Leg brace	½"-dia. × 5¾" copper pipe
F	(10) Extension pipe	½"-dia. × 2¼" copper pipe

Key	Part	Dimension
G	(4) Foot extension	½"-dia. × 2¾" copper pipe
H	(4) Bar extensions	½"-dia. × 2¾" copper pipe
I	(2) Risers	½"-dia. × 1½" copper pipe
J	(1) Hanging bar	¾"-dia. × 35¼" copper pipe
K	(2) Hanging bar extension	½"-dia. × 2¼" copper pipe

Directions: *Copper Coat Rack*

Step A: PREPARE THE FRAME.
1. Following the cutting list, cut all pieces of pipe for the frame of the rack to length. Minimize the waste of copper by cutting the longest pieces possible from each length of pipe first, and moving down the cutting list until all the lengths are cut. Sort the lengths as you go, placing pieces of equal length together.
2. Test-fit the rack together to ensure the pieces are cut to the proper length. Make sure each connection of the frame fits correctly before continuing. Hold each connection together with masking tape as you assemble the rack. It's easier to complete the assembly if you start at the base of the rack and work your way up.
3. After test-fitting the pieces of the hanging bar, assemble the entire shelf area separately. Once the shelf assembly is pieced together, place the entire assembly on top of the lower assembly. Keep in mind that at this point, the rack is held together with masking tape and will fall apart if you place any weight on it.

Step B: SOLDER THE FRAME.
See page 14 for more information on preparing and soldering pipe.

1. Solder the frame together starting with the base of the leg assemblies and working your way up. Solder each cross extension for the shelf to the adjoining tees separately. Then solder the tees together with the extension pipes to form the shelf.
2. When the shelf assembly has been soldered together, place it on top of the lower assembly and complete the frame by soldering the connection between the shelf and legs (this connection is shown in photo A).

Step C: CREATE THE SOFT COPPER DECORATIONS.
The dimensions of each decoration are given in the diagram on page 205. Feel free to create your own decorations, using the techniques described. Remember that the copper tube is flexible, so you will be able to make small adjustments in the size of each decoration after completing the overall shape.
1. To make the decorations on the sides of the rack, clamp a piece of 2¼"-dia. PVC pipe to your worksurface. Use a locking pliers to hold the end of the soft copper tubing in place, and wrap approximately 5 feet of tubing around the pipe. Crimp the end of the tubing with a pliers, and break it off.
2. Unwrap the copper from the pipe, molding it into the approximate dimensional shape provided in the

A. *Test-fit each length together, making sure the pieces are cut to the proper length. Use masking tape to hold the joints in place.*

B. *Solder the joints of the frame from the base up. Solder the upper shelf assembly separately to make the assembly process easier.*

Side Decoration Detail. The copper will be easier to shape if you unwrap it to form each shape. To make other style shapes and sizes, experiment by wrapping the soft copper tubing around various-sized cylindrical shaped pipes, buckets, or cans.

3. The back decoration is made up of two pieces of soft copper tubing. To make the lower part of the decoration, start with approximately 16 feet of soft copper tube. Unwrap the factory-made coil and form it into a circle with a 40" circumference. The soft copper should complete 1¼ rotations of the circle.

4. Follow the Bending Detail, steps 1 through 3, in the diagram on page 205 to create the decorative shape. Make the rounded curls on each end by wrapping the tube around a length of PVC pipe.

5. To make the upper part of the back decoration, start with a 5-ft. length of ⅜" soft copper. Repeat the process of wrapping one end of the tube around a piece of PVC pipe so the wrapped section completes 1½ rotations of the pipe. Unlock the pliers, and mold the copper tubing into the shape provided in the Back Decoration Detail on page 205.

6. To complete the last ring on the upper part of the back decoration, wrap the other end of the soft copper tubing around the PVC pipe, and use a pliers to crimp and break off the excess.

Step D: SOLDER THE DECORATIONS TO THE FRAME.

1. Before soldering each decorative piece to the frame of the rack, line up the joints where you plan to solder them, and tap the soft copper joint area lightly with a hammer to produce a flat space with more surface area for adhering the solder.

2. Wrap a light-gauge copper wire around each joint of the decorative pieces and the rigid frame to hold them in place while soldering.

3. Solder the decorative pieces of copper to the rigid frame, following the basic technique of soldering covered on page 14. The copper wire will provide a pocket for the warm solder to flow into, holding the soft copper decorations in place.

VARIATION:

Make additional decorations with pieces of sheet copper, by stenciling a decorative shape on paper and punching the design into the sheet with a hammer and a small nail. Sheet copper is available at most roofing supply stores, and is easily bent to attach to the frame of the unit with machine screws or rivets.

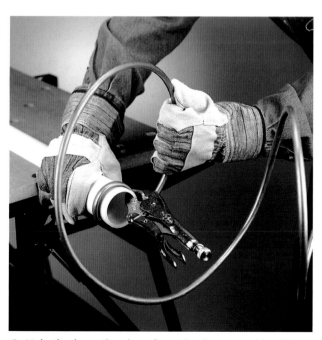

C. *Make the decorative pieces from ⅜" soft copper tubing. Wrap the tubing around a scrap piece of PVC, and unwrap it to create each specific shape. Refer to page 205 for specific dimensions of each piece.*

D. *Solder the decorations to the rigid frame at the designated locations, centering them on the rack. Tap each soldering area with a hammer prior to soldering the joint to create a flatter area for adhering the solder.*

Chest of Drawers

Children's furniture is notoriously expensive, but you can build this simple chest of drawers for a fraction of the cost of a dresser from most specialty shops. To make it, you'll use only the most basic carpentry techniques to achieve a result with a clean, attractive appearance.

This chest of drawers features all wood parts—there is no need to purchase metal drawer slides or other hardware. Not quite full-size, this chest of drawers will fit nicely into your child's bedroom, while still offering plenty of clothing storage space. It also makes a great nightstand.

This petite chest of drawers brings clothing perfectly into reach for young children, yet provides generous storage space for an older child's wardrobe.

TOOLS & MATERIALS

- Circular saw
- Drill with bits
- Finish sander
- Hammer
- Router
- Miter box with backsaw
- (1) ¾" × 4 × 8 ft. plywood
- (1) ¾" × 2 × 4 ft. plywood
- (1) ½" × 4 × 4 ft. plywood
- (1) ½" × 2 × 4 ft. plywood
- (1) ¾ × ¾" × 8 ft. cove molding
- (1) ½ × ½" × 8 ft. quarter-round
- Wood glue
- Wood screws (#6 × 1¼", 2")
- 4d finish nails
- 1" brad nails
- (24) Plastic drawer glides
- (6) 2"-dia. cabinet drawer knobs
- Finishing materials

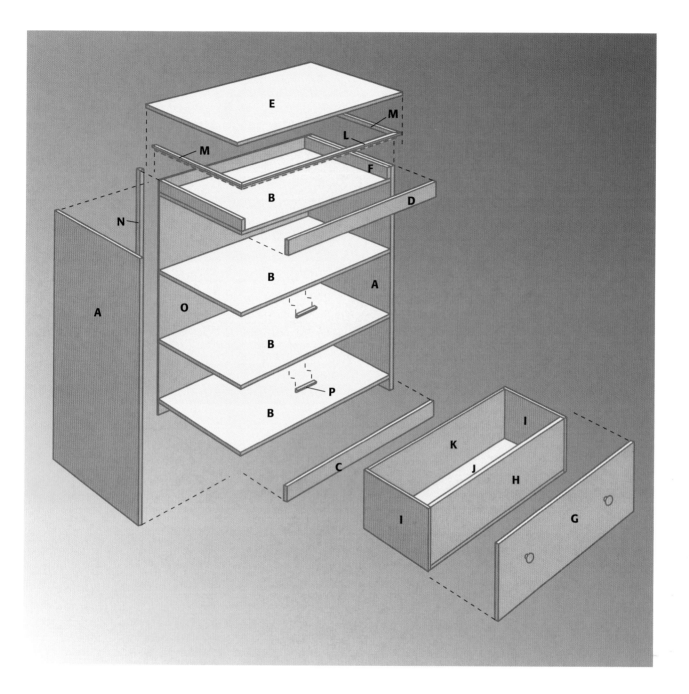

Key	Part	Dimension
A	(2) Side	¾ × 15¼ × 31" plywood
B	(4) Duster	¾ × 14½ × 20½" plywood
C	(1) Bottom rail	¾ × 2 × 22" plywood
D	(1) Top rail	¾ × 1½ × 22" plywood
E	(1) Top	¾ × 17" × 2 ft. plywood
F	(2) Top cleat	¾ × 1½ × 14½" pine
G	(3) Drawer face	¾ × 9 × 22" plywood
H	(3) Drawer front	¾ × 7¼ × 19¼" plywood

Key	Part	Dimension
I	(6) Drawer side	½ × 8 × 14¼" plywood
J	(3) Drawer bottom	¾ × 13¾ × 19¼" plywood
K	(3) Drawer back	½ × 8 × 19¼" plywood
L	(1) Front cove	¾ × ¾ × 23½" molding
M	(2) Side cove	¾ × ¾ × 16¾" molding
N	(2) Back cleat	½ × ½ × 29⅜" molding
O	(1) Back	¼ × 20½ × 29⅜" plywood
P	(3) Stop block	½ × ½ × 4" molding

Directions: *Chest of Drawers*

Step A: BUILD THE CHEST.
1. Cut the sides (A) and duster panels (B) to size from ¾"-thick plywood. Cut the back panel (O) from ¼"-thick sheet goods (¼"-thick plywood or hardboard). Sand all parts smooth. Mark guidelines for the duster positions on the inside faces of the sides, 1⅜", 10¾", 19⅞", and 29" from the bottoms.
2. Stand the side pieces on their back edges and set ¾"-thick spacers between them. Position the duster panels so their lower edges are flush with the marked guidelines and their front edges are flush with the front edges of the side panels.
3. Drill pilot holes, counterboring them just enough so that the screwheads can be covered with wood putty during the finishing process. Fasten the duster panels into place, using glue and 2" wood screws.

Step B: INSTALL THE BACK.
Lay the back in place so its top edge is flush with the top edges of the sides. Fasten it with 1" brads driven through the back and into the duster panels. Cut the back cleats (N) to size from ½" quarter-round molding, then attach these cleats to the back edges of the sides, using 1" brads.

Step C: ATTACH THE RAILS & TOP.
1. Cut the bottom rail (C) and top rail (D) to size. Position each rail so its ends are flush with the outer faces of the sides. The top edge of the top rail should be flush with the tops of the sides, and the lower edge of the bottom rail should be flush with the bottoms of the sides. Fasten the rails to the front edges of the sides and duster panels, using glue and counterbored wood screws driven through the rails, into the sides.
2. Cut the top (E) and the top cleats (F) to size. Attach the cleats to the inside faces of the side panels, flush with the top of the chest, by driving 1¼" screws through the cleats, into the sides. Position the top on the chest so it is flush with the back, and the overhang is equal on both sides. Drill and counterbore pilot holes through the top and into the cleats. Attach the top, using glue and 2" wood screws.
3. Use a router with a ¼" roundover bit, or use a detail sander to smooth the edges of the top.
4. Tack four ⅛"-thick plastic drawer glides to the ends of each drawer opening to eliminate friction between the drawers and the chest.

A. The duster panels support the drawers. Attach them with glue and screws driven through the sides.

B. Attach cleats made from ½" quarter-round molding at the outside edges of the back panel to give it extra strength.

C. Tack plastic drawer glides to the inside faces of the drawer openings to eliminate friction.

Step D: BUILD THE DRAWER BOXES.
1. Cut the drawer fronts (H), drawer bottoms (J), drawer sides (I) and drawer backs (K) to size. Fasten each drawer bottom to a drawer front with glue and counterbored 1¼" wood screws, driven through the bottom and into the bottom edge of the drawer front.
2. Fasten the sides to the front and bottom with glue and 1" brads, driven through the sides. Fasten the drawer backs to the back edges of the drawer sides and bottom, using glue and 1" brads.

Step E: ATTACH THE DRAWER FACES & KNOBS.
1. Cut the drawer faces (G), and round over all the edges with a router or sander. Mark drilling centers on each face to use as guides for the holes for the drawer knobs or pulls. Center a mark 4" from each end of the drawer faces and drill holes at these points. Size the guide holes to match the bolts on the knobs.
2. Tape a ¼"-thick spacer to the back of each drawer, and slide the drawers into the openings in the chest. The glides should keep each drawer centered on a duster panel and the spacers will keep the front edges of the drawer fronts aligned with the front edges of the sides.
3. Starting with the bottom drawer, attach the drawer

faces. Tape or clamp the drawer face in place on the drawer front. Drive 1¼"-long screws through the guide holes and into the drawer front to hold the drawer face temporarily in place. Remove the drawer and drive 1¼" wood screws through the back side of the drawer front and into the drawer face. Remove the screws in the knob holes, and position the bottom drawer in the frame. Attach the drawer faces to the two remaining drawers, maintaining ⅛"-wide gaps between each drawer face.
4. Attach knobs to the drawer faces. Most drawer knobs have a bolt in the center that is inserted through the drawer front to secure the knob.

Step F: APPLY THE FINISHING TOUCHES.
1. Miter-cut the front cove (L) and side cove (M) with matching 45° angles, and install them into the frame where the top is joined to the chest, using 4d finish nails.
2. Cut the stop blocks (P) to size. Remove the drawers, and fasten the blocks on the duster panel bottoms, ¾" from their front edges, using 1" brads.
3. Fill all nail and screw holes and exposed plywood edges with wood putty, then sand all the surfaces smooth. Prime and paint the dresser as desired.

D. *Fasten the sides to the front with wire nails driven through pilot holes in the sides.*

E. *Drive screws through the knob holes in the drawer face to temporarily attach it to the drawer front.*

F. *Turn the frame upside down, and use 1" brads to attach the stop blocks.*

Armoire

Long before massive walk-in closets became the norm in residential building design, homeowners and apartment-dwellers compensated for cramped bedroom closets by making or buying armoires. The trim armoire design shown here reflects the basic styling developed during the heyday of the armoire, but at a scale that makes it usable in just about any living situation.

At 60" high and only 36" wide, this compact armoire still boasts plenty of interior space. Five shelves on the left side are sized to store folded sweaters and shirts. You can hang several suit jackets or dresses in the closet section to the right.

With a simple, rustic appearance, this movable closet blends into almost any bedroom.

TOOLS & MATERIALS

- Circular saw
- Drill with bits
- Jig saw
- Finish sander
- Framing square
- Bar or pipe clamps
- Hammer
- Utility knife
- Household iron
- (3) ¾" × 4 × 8 ft. birch plywood
- (1) ¼" × 4 × 8 ft. birch plywood
- (1) 1 × 2" × 8 ft. pine
- (6) 1 × 3" × 8 ft. pine
- (1) 1 × 6" × 8 ft. pine
- (1) 1½"-dia. × 2 ft. fir dowel
- Wood screws (#6 × 1¼")
- 3d, 6d finish nails
- Compass
- Wood glue
- Nail set
- Closet rod hangers
- (6) Hinges
- (3) Door pulls
- Finishing materials

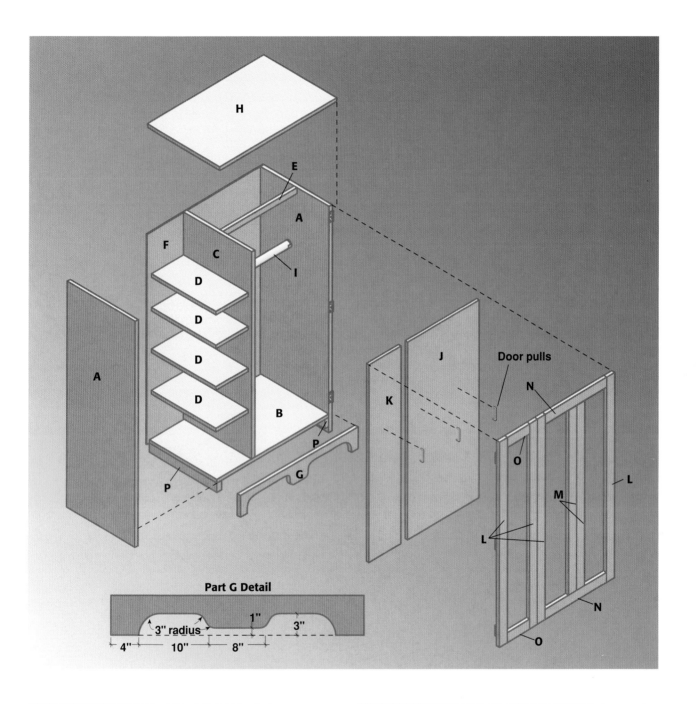

Part G Detail

3" radius · 1" · 3"
4" · 10" · 8"

Key	Part	Dimension
A	(2) Side panel	¾ × 21 × 59¼" plywood
B	(1) Bottom panel	¾ × 21 × 34½" plywood
C	(1) Center panel	¾ × 21 × 53¾" plywood
D	(4) Shelf	¾ × 10⅞ × 20¼" plywood
E	(1) Stringer	¾" × 1½ × 22⅞" pine
F	(1) Back	¼" × 36 × 54½" plywood
G	(1) Front skirt	¾" × 5½" × 3 ft. pine
H	(1) Top panel	¾ × 22" × 3 ft. plywood

Key	Part	Dimension
I	(1) Closet rod	1½"-dia. × 22⅞" fir dowel
J	(1) Closet door panel	¾ × 22⁷⁄₁₆ × 52⅛" plywood
K	(1) Shelf door panel	¾ × 10⁷⁄₁₆ × 52⅛" plywood
L	(4) Door stile	¾ × 2½ × 53⅝" pine
M	(2) False stile	¾ × 2½ × 48⅝" pine
N	(2) Closet door rail	¾ × 2½ × 18¹⁵⁄₁₆" pine
O	(2) Shelf door rail	¾ × 2½ × 6¹⁵⁄₁₆" pine
P	(2) Cleat	¾ × 1½ × 21" pine

Directions: Armoire

Step A: PREPARE THE PLYWOOD PANELS.
Careful preparation of the plywood panels that become the sides, bottom, top, and shelves is key to creating an armoire with a clean, professional look. Take the time to make sure all the parts are perfectly square. Then apply self-adhesive veneer edge tape to all plywood edges that will be visible. If you plan to paint the armoire, you can simply fill the edges with wood putty and sand them smooth before you apply the paint.

1. Cut the side panels (A), bottom panel (B), center panel (C), and shelves (D) to size, using a circular saw and a straightedge as a cutting guide. We used birch plywood because it is easy to work with and takes wood stain well. Smooth the surfaces of the panels with medium-grit sandpaper.

2. Apply self-adhesive veneer edge tape to the front edges of the center panel, side panels, and shelves. Cut the strips of edge tape to length and position them over the plywood edges. Then press the strips with a household iron set on a low to medium heat setting, letting the heat from the iron activate the adhesive.

3. Trim the excess tape with a sharp utility knife or veneer edge trimmer. Sand the trimmed edges and surfaces of the edge tape with medium-grit sandpaper.

Step B: ASSEMBLE THE CARCASS.
The main box for the armoire (or any type of cabinet) is called the "carcass." For this project, the carcass includes the side, bottom, and center panels. Fasten the panels together with wood glue and finish nails. Make sure all of the joints are square and the edges are flush.

1. Lay out the cleat positions on the lower sections of the side panels. Measure up 4¾" from the bottom edges of the side panels, and draw a reference line across the inside face of each side panel.

2. Cut the cleats (P) to length and position them just below the reference lines. Secure them with glue, and drive 3d finish nails through the cleats and into the side panels.

3. Stand the side panels upright on their bottom edges and apply a bead of wood glue to the top of each cleat. Place the bottom panel between the side panels on top of the cleats, and clamp it in place. Make sure the taped front edges of the side panels

A. *Apply veneer edge tape to the exposed plywood edges. Trim off excess tape with a sharp utility knife.*

B. *Clamp the bottom panel between the sides and fasten it to the cleats, using glue and finish nails.*

C. *Fasten the shelves between the side panel and center panel with glue and 6d finish nails.*

and bottom panel are flush. Drive 6d finish nails through the bottom panel and into each cleat. Then drive nails through the side panels and into the edges of the bottom panel.

4. Lay the assembly on its back edges. Use a pair of shelves as spacers to set the correct distance between the center panel and the left side panel (as seen from the front of the carcass). Make sure the taped panel edges are at the front of the carcass. Fasten the center panel to the bottom panel with glue, and drive 6d finish nails through the bottom panel and into the edge of the center panel.

Step C: INSTALL THE SHELVES.

1. Draw reference lines for the shelves on the inside face of the left side panel and on the left face of the center panel. Measure up from the top of the bottom panel, and draw lines at 13", 23⅜", 33¾", and 44⅛". Use a framing square to make sure the lines are perpendicular to the front and back edges of the panels.

2. Arrange the shelves so the tops are just below the reference lines, flush with the back edges of the carcass (creating a ¾" recess in front of each shelf). Attach the shelves with glue, and drive 6d finish nails

through the side panel and center panel, and into the edges of the shelves. Brace each panel from behind as you drive the nails.

Step D: ATTACH THE STRINGER AND BACK PANEL.

1. Cut the stringer (E) to length. Center the stringer between the fronts and backs of the center and side panels, flush with the tops. Fasten the stringer, using glue and 6d finish nails.

2. Cut the back panel (F) to size from ¼"-thick plywood. Measure the distances between diagonal corners of the carcass to make sure it is square (the distances should be equal). Adjust the carcass as necessary. Then position the back panel over the back edges of the carcass so the edges of the back panel are flush with the outside faces and top edges of the side panels. Fasten the back panel by driving 3d finish nails through the back and into the edges of the side, center, and bottom panels.

Step E: MAKE & ATTACH THE FRONT SKIRT.

1. Cut the front skirt (G) to length.

2. To lay out the curves that form the ends of the decorative cutouts on the skirt board (see Part G De-

D. *Nail the ¼"-thick back panel to the back edges of the carcass to help keep it square.*

E. *Use a compass to mark the decorative cutout at the bottom of the front skirt board. Then cut the curves, using a jig saw.*

tail on page 213), start by making a mark 7" in from each end. Use a compass to draw a 3"-radius curve to make the outside end of each cutout, holding the point of the compass on the 7" mark, as close as possible to the bottom edge of the board. Then make a mark 11¾" in from each end of the skirt board. Holding the compass point at the bottom edge, draw a 3"-radius curve to mark the top inside end of each cutout. Measure 16⅜" in from each end of the skirt board, and mark points that are 1¾" down from the top edge of the board. Set the point of your compass at each of these marks and draw 3"-radius curves that mark the bottom inside ends of the cutouts. Then at the middle of the bottom edge of the board, measure up 1" and draw a line parallel to the bottom edge, intersecting the inside ends of the cutout lines. Draw lines parallel to the bottom edge of the board, 3" up, to create the top of each cutout. Make the cutout on the skirt board with a jig saw. Sand the cut edges, using medium-grit sandpaper.

3. Position the skirt board against the front of the armoire carcass to make sure the ends of the skirt are flush with the outside faces of the side panels, and the top of the skirt is flush with the top of the bottom panel. Fasten the front skirt to the front edges of the side panels and bottom panel with glue and 6d finish nails.

Step F: MAKE & ATTACH THE TOP PANEL.
1. Stand the armoire upright, and measure the distance between the outside faces of the side panels—it should be 36".
2. Cut the top panel (H) to size.
3. Test-fit the top panel to make sure the edges are flush with the outside faces of the side panels. The back edge should be flush with the outside face of the back panel, and the front edge of the top should overhang the front of the carcass panels by ¾". Apply veneer edge tape to all four edges of the top panel.
4. Fasten the top panel to the center panel, side panels, and stringer with glue and 6d finish nails, making sure it is in the same position as when you test-fit the piece.

Step G: BUILD THE DOORS.
1. Cut the closet door panel (J) and shelf door panel (K) to size. Sand the edges and surfaces of the door panels to smooth out the saw blade marks and any rough spots. Apply edge tape to the edges of each door panel. Trim off the excess tape, and sand the edges smooth.

F. Fasten the top panel with glue and 6d finish nails.

G. Attach the rails and stiles to the door panels with glue. Drive 3d finish nails through the frames into the panels.

2. Cut the door stiles (L), false stiles (M), closet door rails (N), and shelf door rails (O) to length. Rails are the horizontal frame pieces; stiles are the vertical frame pieces.

3. Position the rails and stiles on the front faces of the door panels so they overhang all edges of the panels by ¾". Make sure the rails and stiles meet at right angles to make perfectly square frames. Attach the rails and stiles to both door panels with glue, and drive 3d finish nails through the frame pieces and into the panels.

4. Turn the door panels over on your worksurface. To reinforce the joints between the stiles and rails and the door panels, drill ⁵⁄₆₄" pilot holes through the panels and into the stiles and rails. Counterbore the holes ⅛" deep, using a ⅜" counterbore bit. Fasten the pieces together with 1¼" wood screws.

Step H: HANG DOORS & APPLY THE FINISHING TOUCHES.
1. To hang the doors, mark points along the outside edge of each outer door stile, 8" down from the top and 8" up from the bottom. Mount door hinges to the edges of the stiles at these points. Then install the third hinge, centering it between the top and bottom hinges. Position the doors and fasten the hinges to the side panels. Be sure to adjust the hinges to allow for a ⅛"-wide gap between the doors. Also leave a slight gap between the top end of the doors and the top panel, and between the bottom of the doors and the front skirt.

2. It is easiest to finish the parts of the armoire before you attach the rest of the hardware. Set all the nails with a nail set. Fill all the nail and screw holes with wood putty, and sand the dried putty flush with the surface. Sand all of the wood surfaces with medium (150-grit) sandpaper. Finish-sand the surfaces with fine sandpaper (180-or 220-grit).

3. Wipe the wood clean, and then brush on a coat of sanding sealer; let it dry. Read the manufacturer's directions before applying any finishing products. Apply a wood stain and let it dry completely. Then apply several coats of topcoat—we used two thin

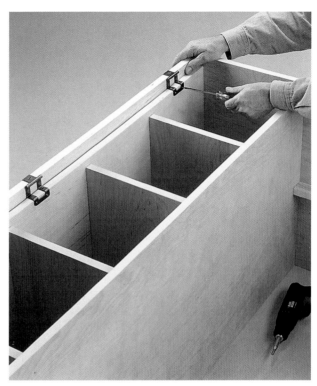

H. *Position the doors and fasten the hinges to the side panels.*

coats of water-based, satin polyurethane. If you prefer, you can leave the wood unstained and simply apply a protective topcoat.

4. Install door pulls on the door panels, 25" up from each bottom rail and centered between the stiles.

5. Mount closet rod hangers to the sides of the closet compartment, 11" down from the top panel. Cut the closet rod (I) to length, and set it into the closet rod hangers.

6. To keep the doors closed when the armoire is not in use, install magnetic door catches and catch plates on the upper inside corners of the doors and at the corresponding locations on the bottom of the top panel. For extra holding power, install catches at the bottoms of the doors as well.

Entryway Chest

This roomy chest makes the most of valuable floor space in your entryway. It's large enough to hold all your family's mittens, hats, and scarves. Move it to your den or family room and it also makes a fine coffee table. This is a very simple project, made from six plywood panels and some decorative trim molding.

For a contemporary appearance, paint the chest in soft pastel tones. Be sure to use glossy enamel paint—the finish is easy to clean.

Another finishing option for the chest is to line the interior with aromatic cedar liners to ward off moths and give your hand and head gear a fresh scent. Aromatic cedar kits are available in various lengths.

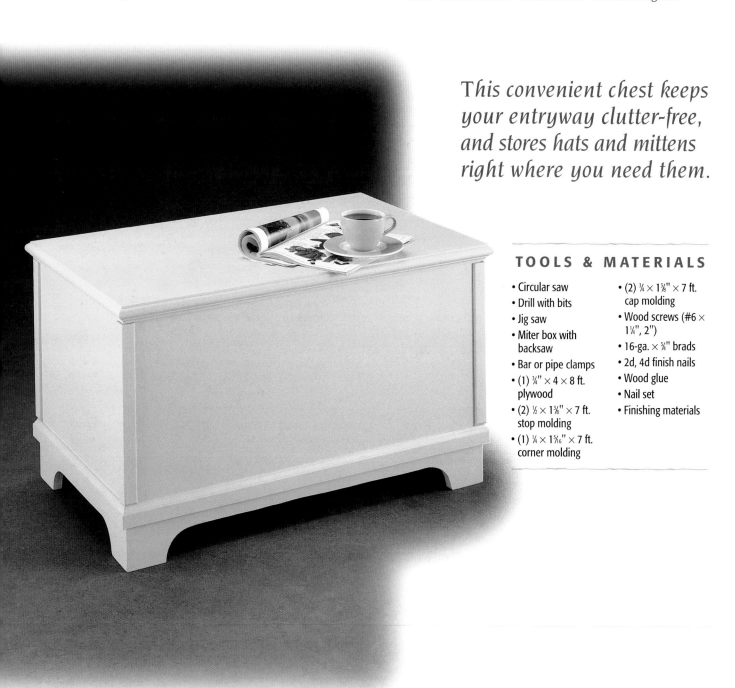

This convenient chest keeps your entryway clutter-free, and stores hats and mittens right where you need them.

TOOLS & MATERIALS

- Circular saw
- Drill with bits
- Jig saw
- Miter box with backsaw
- Bar or pipe clamps
- (1) ¾" × 4 × 8 ft. plywood
- (2) ½ × 1⅜" × 7 ft. stop molding
- (1) ¼ × 1⁵⁄₁₆" × 7 ft. corner molding
- (2) ¾ × 1⅜" × 7 ft. cap molding
- Wood screws (#6 × 1¼", 2")
- 16-ga. × ¾" brads
- 2d, 4d finish nails
- Wood glue
- Nail set
- Finishing materials

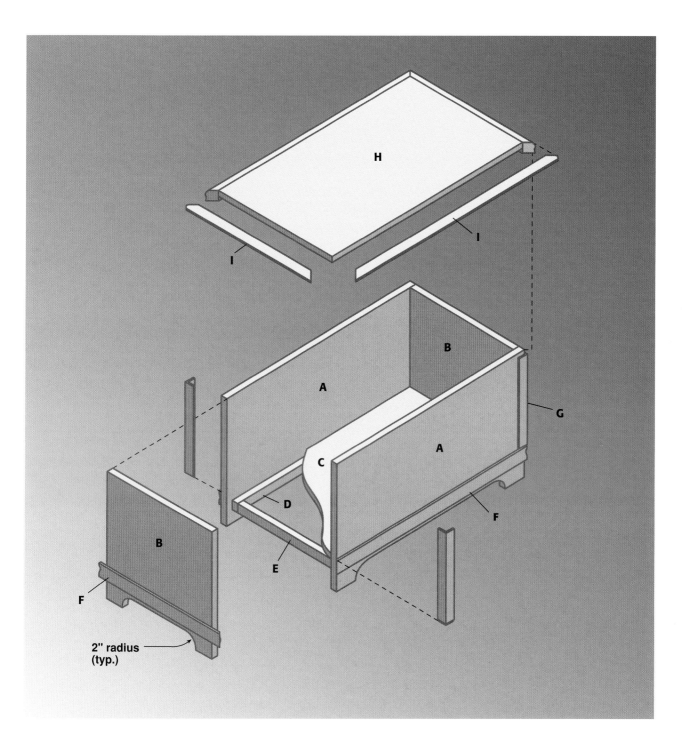

2" radius (typ.)

Key	Part	Dimension
A	(2) Side panel	¾ × 17¼ × 30" plywood
B	(2) End panel	¾ × 17¼ × 16½" plywood
C	(1) Bottom panel	¾ × 16½ × 28½" plywood
D	(2) Side cleat	¾ × 1½ × 15" plywood
E	(2) End cleat	¾ × 1½ × 15" plywood

Key	Part	Dimension
F	(4) Bottom molding	½ × 1⅜ × * stop molding
G	(4) Corner molding	¼ × 1⁵⁄₁₆ × 12" corner molding
H	(1) Lid	¾ × 18⅛ × 30⅛" plywood
I	(4) Top cap	¾ × 1⅜ × * shelf cap

*Cut to fit

219

Clothing Storage

Directions: Entryway Chest

Step A: MAKE THE SIDE & END PANELS.

1. Cut the side panels (A) and end panels (B) to size.

2. To make the cutouts, or kick spaces, on the bottom edges of the sides, draw cutting lines 2" in from one long edge. Use a compass to draw the curved cutting lines at the ends of each kick space. Set the compass to draw a 2"-radius semicircle, and position the point of the compass as close as possible to the bottom edge, 5" in from the ends of the side panels. Draw the semicircles and clamp the sides to your worksurface. Then make the cutouts with a jig saw, using a straightedge to guide the long, straight portion of the cut. Sand the edges to smooth any rough spots.

3. To draw the cutting lines for the kick spaces on the end panels, first draw cutting lines 2" up from one short edge. Set the compass to draw a 2"-radius semicircle, and position the point of the compass as close as possible to the bottom edge, 4¼" in from the side edges of the end panels. Draw the curved semicircles, and make the cutouts with a jig saw. Sand the edges to smooth any rough spots.

Step B: INSTALL THE CLEATS.

Cleats are installed on the interior of the chest to support the bottom panel, so it is important to attach them with their top edges aligned.

1. Cut the side cleats (D) and end cleats (E) to size.

2. To help you position the cleats, draw reference lines on the side and end panels, 3½" up from the bottom edges and ¾" in from the side edges. Position the cleats so their top edges are flush with the reference lines. Drill ⁵⁄₆₄" pilot holes through the cleats and into the panels. Counterbore the holes ⅛" deep, using a ⅜" counterbore bit. Fasten the cleats, using glue and 1¼" wood screws.

Step C: ASSEMBLE THE CHEST.

1. With the cleats facing in, position the end panels between the side panels. Drill counterbored pilot holes through the side panels and into the end panels, and fasten them in place, using glue and evenly spaced 2" wood screws. Make sure the top and bottom edges are flush, and the outside faces of the

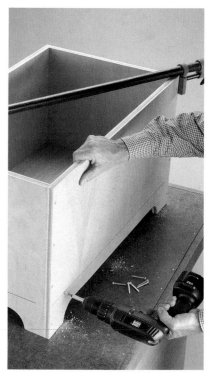

A. *Use a jig saw and a straightedge as a guide to make the kick space cuts in the end and side panels.*

B. *Center the end cleats over the kick spaces, leaving ¾" at each end where the side cleats will fit.*

C. *Hold opposite chest corners together with a bar or pipe clamp to keep the chest square.*

ends are flush with the side edges.

2. Cut the bottom panel (C) to size, and sand it smooth. Test-fit the bottom panel by setting it on top of the cleats. Remove the panel and apply glue to the top edges of the cleats and along the underside edges of the panel. Then reposition the panel inside the chest.

3. Clamp diagonal chest corners with a bar or pipe clamp to hold the piece square while you fasten the bottom panel. To make sure you drive the screws directly into the bottom, mark the screw center points 3⅞" up from the bottoms of the sides and ends. Drill counterbored pilot holes through the sides and ends and into the edges of the bottom panel. Attach the bottom panel to the frame, using 2" wood screws.

Step D: ATTACH THE MOLDING.

1. Cut the bottom molding (F) to fit around the chest, miter-cutting the ends at 45° angles so they will fit together at the corners.

2. Position the moldings so the top edges are 4⅜" up from the bottom edges of the sides and ends. Fasten them with glue and 4d finish nails, driven through 1/16" pilot holes. Apply glue, and drive 2d nails through

the joints where the molding pieces meet, lock-nailing the pieces together.

3. Cut the corner molding (G) to length. Use glue and ¾" brads to fasten the corner molding over the joints between the end and side panels. Make sure the bottom edges of the corner molding butt against the top edges of the bottom molding. Sand the bottom edges of the corner molding to meet the bottom molding. Sand the top edges of the ends and sides to smooth the edges and corners.

Step E: MAKE THE LID & APPLY FINISHING TOUCHES.

1. Cut the lid (H) to size, and sand it smooth.

2. Miter cut four pieces of top cap (I) to fit around the perimeter of the lid.

3. Drill 1/16" pilot holes. Use glue and 4d finish nails to attach the top cap pieces, keeping the top edges flush with the top face of the lid. Glue and lock-nail the mitered corner joints. Set the lid onto the top opening—no hinges are used.

4. Use a nail set to set all nails and brads on the chest. Fill all visible holes with wood putty. Sand any rough spots smooth. Finish the chest as desired.

D. *Fasten the corner molding over the corners to conceal the joints and screw heads.*

E. *Attach the top cap around the perimeter of the lid. Drive nails in partially before positioning the strips.*

Home Office Storage

If you're one of the millions of people who work out of a home office—either by running your own business or by telecommuting to a corporate office—you know that keeping this kind of modern work space organized is a major challenge. Even the traditional family home office, used primarily to pay bills and organize paperwork, has become a much more complicated place than it once was. Even family home offices have begun to rely upon an array of computers, monitors, keyboards, scanners, and printers that overwhelm traditional furniture pieces.

This section focuses on space-saving office furniture and specially built cabinets and supply holders for the home office. Depending upon your storage needs, you may want to consider building the Threaded-rod Table (page 105), as well.

Before you start building office storage, measure the items you plan to store, and adapt the projects to suit your needs. Not all computer equipment is the same size.

Keep in mind that office supply stores, furniture stores, and home centers nationwide sell a wide variety of office furniture. If you plan to build your own, these stores can be a valuable source of ideas.

Home Office Storage Ideas

Ready-to-assemble (RTA) or semi-custom "kitchen" cabinets and countertops can be combined to create a coordinated and attractive office space with drawers, cupboards, and shelving storage catered exactly to your needs.

If you don't require a computer station, a narrow desk in a kitchen or hallway with a compartmentalized desk hutch and upper cabinet may be all you need to sort through your mail, write letters, pay bills, jot notes, or set appointments—keeping stray projects from cluttering up the rest of your home.

A variety of hooks, *clips, and enclosures is available to keep computer cords tidy, out of the way, and un-entangled.*

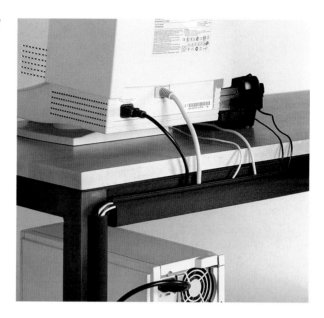

A home office *needn't be elaborate. If it's thoughtfully designed, a shallow reach-in closet or standalone cabinet is all the space needed for a modest home office. And when the room is being used for another purpose, it can be hidden from view with a bi-fold door or pivot door slide.*

An office with little floor space but high ceilings might benefit from a floor to ceiling bookshelf with access by a library ladder.

Plenty of drawer space keeps papers and supplies from cluttering your desk.

A U-shaped desk arrangement allows a computer station, writing desk, and sewing center to all be accommodated within arm's reach of one another. A mix of open and closed storage, and narrow to oversized shelving keeps the accoutrements for all of your activities neatly in place.

A simple magnet strip can keep important projects prioritized and within plain view so they don't get overlooked.

The same thermoplastic ribbed wallboard that can help you keep your tool room or kitchen organized may also help create a versatile and functional office space. A variety of hooks, shelves, bracketed baskets, bins, file sorters, and hanging folder racks can be quickly arranged and re-arranged to suit your needs.

Project Organizer

Organize and store important papers and supplies with the project organizer. No one likes a messy desk, especially when the desk is in your home. With the project organizer, you'll be able to shape up your home office in no time. With nine storage compartments and a depth of only 9¼" you won't have to give up much desk space to organize and add precious storage.

A compact storage unit with multiple bins frees you from the clutter without sacrificing workspace.

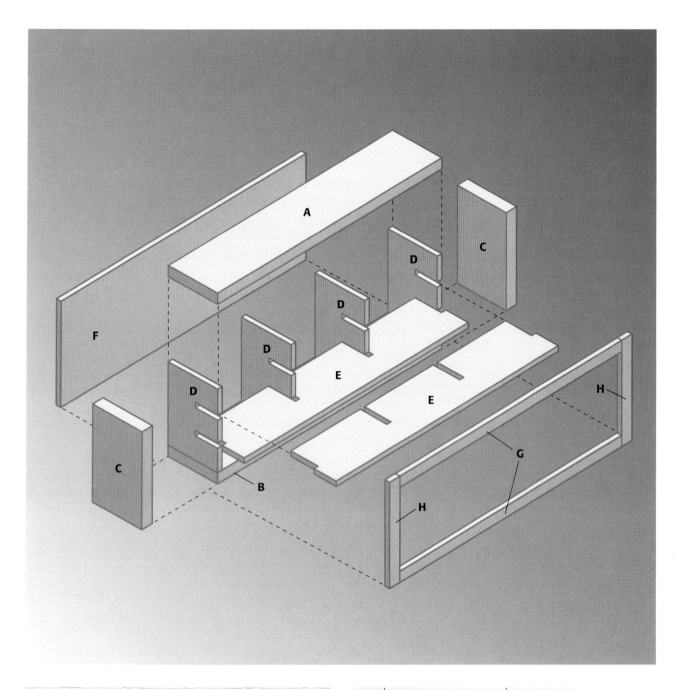

TOOLS & MATERIALS

- Circular saw
- Jig saw
- Household iron
- Drill with bits
- Combination square
- Finishing materials
- Rubber mallet
- Hammer

- Utility knife
- Clamp
- Wood glue
- Straightedge guide
- (1) ¾" × 4 × 4 ft. birch plywood
- (1) ¼" × 4 × 8 ft. lauan plywood

- (1) ½ × 4" × 6 ft. birch
- 20 ft. birch veneer tape (¾")
- Wood screws (#6 × 1½")
- Walnut wood plugs
- Wire brads (1, ½")

Key	Part	Dimension
A	(1) Top	¾ × 9 × 35½" birch plywood
B	(1) Bottom	¾ × 9 × 35½" birch plywood
C	(2) Side	¾ × 9 × 16¼" birch plywood
D	(4) Vertical dividers	¼ × 9 × 14¾" lauan plywood
E	(2) Horizontal divider	¼ × 9 × 35½" lauan plywood
F	(1) Back	¼ × 16¼ × 37" lauan plywood
G	(2) Rail	½ × ¾ × 35½" birch
H	(2) Stile	½ × 1 × 16¼" birch

Directions: Project Organizer

Before making any crosscuts on plywood in this project, score the top layer of veneer with a utility knife, to avoid splintering the surface.

Step A: PREPARE THE BOX PANELS.
1. Cut the top (A), bottom (B), sides (C), and back (F) to size, using a straightedge guide and a circular saw with a plywood blade. Sand the edges smooth with medium-grit sandpaper.
2. Clean the edges of each panel with a wet rag and let them dry. Then apply self-adhesive birch veneer tape to the edges of the top, bottom, and side panels. Press the tape into place with a household iron set to medium heat. After the adhesive is set, use a utility knife or a veneer edge trimmer to trim the veneer; sand the edges smooth.

Step B: ASSEMBLE THE BOX.
1. Stand the top, bottom, and side panels on their back edges. Position the sides so that they cap the top and bottom panels, making sure the corners are flush and the front edges are flush. You may want to clamp the panels in position before driving the first few screws, to make the assembly easier.
2. Assemble the box by drilling counterbored pilot holes through the corners of each side panel and into the top and bottom panels. Then fasten the panels together with glue and 1½" wood screws.
3. Tack the back panel in place, using 1" wire brads spaced about every 6". Make sure the edges of the back panel are flush with the edges of the top, bottom, and side panels.

Step C: CUT THE INTERIOR GRID & TRIM PIECES.
1. Cut the vertical dividers (D) and horizontal dividers (E) to size, using a straightedge guide and a circular saw with a plywood blade.
2. The vertical and horizontal dividers are held together with lap joints. To make the lap joints in the horizontal dividers, measure in 12¼" and 12½" from each end of the panels and make reference marks indicating the location of the notches. Use a combination square to extend those marks 4½" across the dividers. Cut out ¼" notches, using a jig saw with a fine-tooth blade.

A. *Apply veneer tape to the edges of the panels, using a household iron.*

B. *Assemble the panels of the box with 1½" wood screws driven through counterbored pilot holes.*

C. *Mark and cut out the ¼" notches in the dividers.*

3. To make the lap joints in the vertical dividers, measure in 4¾" and 5" from both short ends and make reference marks. Extend these marks 4½" across the vertical dividers, using a combination square as a guide. Cut out the ¼" notches, using a jig saw.

4. Cut the rails (G) and the stiles (H) to size from birch dimensional lumber. Use a circular saw and a straightedge guide to cut the rails and stiles to the proper width. Sand the pieces smooth with medium-grit sandpaper.

Step D: APPLY THE FINISHING TOUCHES.
1. Place a drop of wood glue on each wood plug and insert the plugs into each counterbored screw hole, tapping the plugs into place with a rubber mallet.
2. Sand the plugs flush with the face of the box, using medium-grit sandpaper and a sanding block. Then sand the faces and edges of the box.
3. Stain or paint the project as you desire. We used a few coats of polyurethane on the exterior and a dark stain and polyurethane on the trim pieces and dividers to create a two-tone look, complementing the walnut plugs.

Step E: INSTALL THE DIVIDERS & TRIM.
1. After the finish has sufficiently dried, assemble the divider panels and slide them into the box. You may need to tack the end vertical panels into place with a few ½" wire brads.
2. Install the stiles and rails flush with the front edges of the box frame, using glue and 1" wire brads. Wipe away the excess glue with a damp rag immediately. Let the glue dry before using the project.

> **TIP:**
>
> We used ½" × 4" birch dimensional lumber cut down to size for the trim pieces on this project. The trim needed to be cut to fit flush with the top and bottom panels and ¼" wider than the side panels to hold the dividers in place. You can purchase decorative trim pieces rather than birch dimensional lumber for this project, but keep in mind that the width of the rails and stiles are different.

D. *Insert glued walnut plugs into the counterbored pilot holes. Then sand until the the plugs are flush with the face of the box.*

E. *Slide the completed dividers into the box and install the stile and rail trim around the front edge.*

231

Locker/Filing Cabinet

With a sturdy, legal-sized filing cabinet and a locker cabinet above, this unit is designed with just the right mix of work and play in mind. Solid brass hardware and honey-glazed oak plywood give this cabinet a sophisticated appearance, while the basic construction provides a skill-builder for the first-time router user. Add shelves to the upper cabinet to store extra office supplies, such as printer paper and ink cartridges, and you'll wonder how you stayed organized without this cabinet in your home office.

Whether you're going out for a jog or paying the bills, the locker/filing cabinet will prove its usefulness again and again.

TOOLS & MATERIALS

- Circular saw with plywood blade
- Router with bits
- Quick clamps
- Tape measure
- Drill with bits
- Hammer
- (2) ¾" × 4 × 8 ft. oak plywood
- (1) ½" × 4 × 4 ft. oak plywood
- (1) ¼" × 2 × 4 ft. oak plywood
- (30 ft.) Veneer tape
- (2) Legal hanging file frames
- (1) Coat hanging hook
- (2 sets) Side-mounted drawer glides
- (3) Decorative door pull
- (2) Fully concealed hinges
- (2) Decorative card holders
- Wood glue
- Finishing materials
- ¾" brads
- 6d finish nails
- Wood screws (#6 × 1")
- Nail set

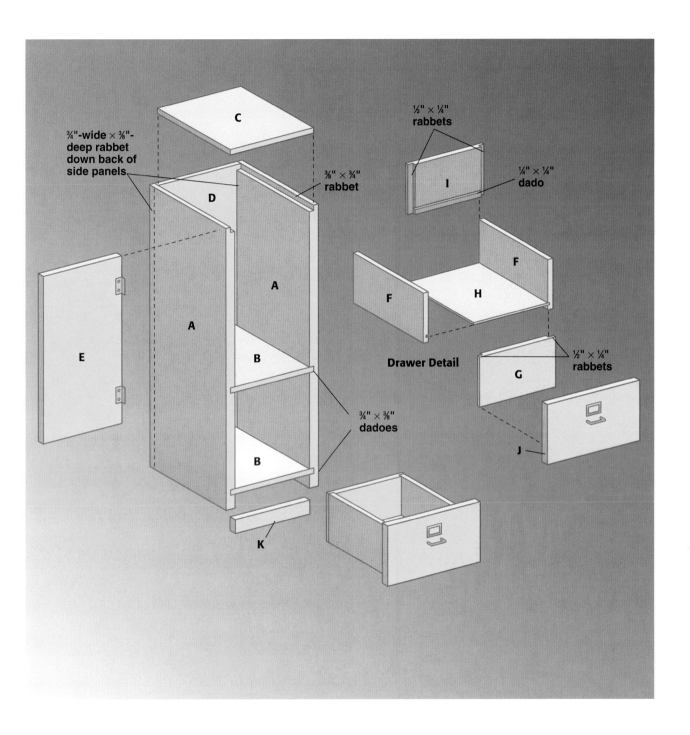

¾"-wide × ⅜"-deep rabbet down back of side panels

⅜" × ¾" rabbet

½" × ¼" rabbets

¼" × ¼" dado

Drawer Detail

¾" × ⅜" dadoes

½" × ¼" rabbets

Key	Part	Dimension
A	(2) Side panel	¾ × 19 × 66" oak plywood
B	(2) Shelf	¾ × 18¼ × 18¾" oak plywood
C	(1) Top	¾ × 18¼ × 18¾" oak plywood
D	(1) Back	¾ × 18¾ × 66" oak plywood
E	(1) Cabinet door	¾ × 38 × 19½" oak plywood
F	(4) Drawer side	½ × 9½ × 17½" oak plywood

Key	Part	Dimension
G	(2) Drawer front	½ × 9½ × 17" oak plywood
H	(2) Drawer bottom	¼ × 16½ × 17½" oak plywood
I	(2) Drawer back	½ × 9½ × 17" oak plywood
J	(2) Drawer face	¾ × 12 × 19½" oak plywood
K	(1) Kickplate	¾ × 18 × 3¾" oak plywood

Directions: Locker/Filing Cabinet

Step A: PREPARE THE FRAME & DRAWER PIECES.
1. Cut the sides (A), shelves (B), top piece (C), and back panel (D) to size, using a circular saw with a plywood cutting blade and a straightedge cutting guide (page 18). Score the plywood with a utility knife before making the cuts to avoid splintering the veneer.
2. Sand all the edges smooth with medium-grit sandpaper and use a household iron to apply oak veneer tape to the front edges of the shelves and top panel, and the top, front, and back edges of the side panels.
3. Using a router and a straightedge guide, cut the dado and rabbet grooves in the side panels, as shown in the diagram on page 233.
4. Cut four strips of ½" plywood 9½" wide and 4 ft. long. Then use a router with a straightedge guide (page 18) to rout a ¼"-wide, ¼"-deep dado groove ¼" from the bottom edge of each piece.
5. Cut the dadoed pieces to size to make the back (I), sides (F), and front drawer pieces (G). The front and back pieces of each drawer require ½"-wide, ¼"-deep rabbet grooves on both short edges as well. See the Drawer Detail on page 233 for more information. Cut the bottom of the drawer to size from ¼" plywood and sand all pieces smooth.

Step B: INSTALL THE SHELVES.
1. Position the sides panels so the dado and rabbet grooves face each other, and the front edge of each panel rests on the worksurface.
2. Apply glue to the side edges of the shelf panels, and slide each panel into the dado grooves so the front edges of the shelves and sides are flush against the worksurface. Temporarily clamp the cabinet frame near both dado joints to hold them in place while installing the top panel.

Step C: INSTALL THE TOP, BACK PANELS & KICKPLATE.
1. Apply glue to the side and back edges of the top panel and set the panel into the rabbet grooves on the side panels so the front edge is flush with the worksurface. Then drill pilot holes through the top panel into the sides, and tack the top into place with 6d finish nails.
2. Remove the temporary clamps near the dadoes and apply glue to the edges of the back panel, positioning it in the rabbet grooves on the back of the cabinet. Make sure the bottom edges of the back and sides are flush.
3. Clamp the cabinet assembly together and drive 6d finish nails through pilot holes in the back panel, into the sides. Make sure the edges of the back panel are flush with the sides of the cabinet.

A. *Use a router with a straightedge guide to cut the dado and rabbet grooves shown in the diagram on page 233.*

B. *Assemble the cabinet frame with glue in each joint and clamp the joints tight. Make sure the front edges of the panels are flush.*

C. *Attach the back panel with glue and 6d finish nails. Countersink the nail heads with a nail set.*

4. Cut the kickplate (K) to size and sand any rough edges smooth. Apply glue to the top and side edges of the kickplate and tack it in place with 6d finish nails driven through pilot holes in the side panels. Let the glue dry.

Step D: MAKE THE DRAWERS & PREPARE THE FACES.
1. While the glue dries on the cabinet, assemble the drawers. Apply glue to the rabbet grooves on a front drawer panel and attach it to the side panels by driving ¾" brads through the front into the side panels. Make sure the edges are flush and the dado grooves near the bottom edges line up.
2. Slide the bottom panel of the drawer into place and attach the back panels to the side panels with glue and ¾" brads. Repeat this process to build the second drawer.
3. Before cutting the faces for the drawers and the cabinet door, make sure the wood grain runs in the same direction for each panel. Cut the drawer face panels and door to size and apply veneer tape to all edges. Trim any excess veneer with a utility knife.

Step E: FINISH THE CABINET & INSTALL HARDWARE.
1. After the glue has dried, apply the finish of your choice to the frame, face panels, and drawer assemblies. Let the finish dry, and install the drawer face hardware. Center the drawer pulls on the face panels.
2. Install the face panels by driving 1" wood screws

through the front panel of the drawer assemblies into the face panels. The bottom drawer face should overlay the drawer assembly by 1¼" on the top and bottom edges, and approximately 1⅛" on the side edges. The top drawer should overlay the drawer assembly by 2" on the top edge, and ½" on the bottom edge. These overlay measurements will line up the edges of the drawer faces with the side panels of the cabinet and the upper shelf.
3. Using a pencil and a combination square, draw reference lines on the inside faces of both side panels 1½" and 12¾" up from the bottom shelf. Install the side-mounted drawer glides to the cabinet with ½" mounting screws, so the top edge of each glide is flush with a reference line. Then attach the remaining drawer glide pieces flush with the bottom edges of the drawers.
4. Install the hanging hook in the cabinet where desired. Predrill pilot holes for the mounting screws, taking care not to puncture the cabinet's exterior.

Step F: HANG THE CABINET DOOR & INSERT FILE FRAMES.
1. Hang the cabinet door following the instructions provided by the hinge manufacturer. Adjust the hinges so the door sits precisely over the cabinet frame.
2. Install the hanging file frames, adjusting the frames until they are snug in the drawer.

D. *Assemble the drawers using glue and brads on the joints. Make sure the dadoes on the bottom line up properly.*

E. *Attach the drawer glides to the interior of the finished cabinet following the manufacturer's instructions.*

F. *Hang the cabinet door with concealed hinges. Adjust the door to sit precisely on the cabinet frame.*

Desktop Console

Designed to keep your desktop necessities organized and ready to use, this desktop console features four separate storage compartments. The middle section contains a covered pencil holder made from cove molding, while the two side compartments are pull-out drawers for notepads, stationery, or address books. A fourth compartment behind the pencil holder acts as a mail slot. The drawers are completely removable so you can access their contents without reaching all the way into the narrow compartments. Paint the project to complement its surroundings, and use decorative hinges and knobs on the lids and drawers.

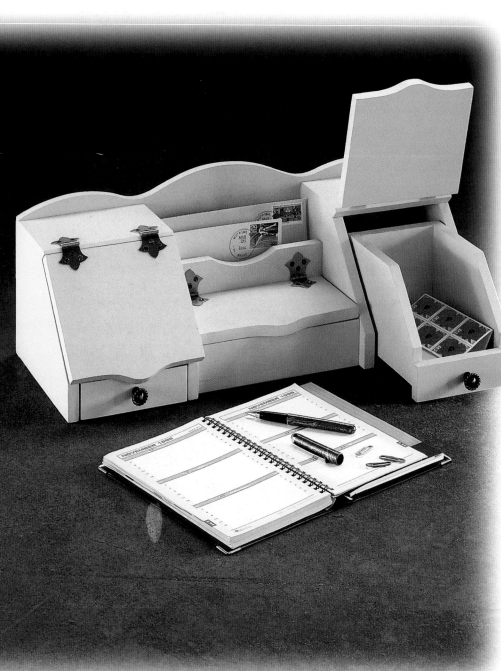

Decorative accents and efficient design replace your desktop clutter.

TOOLS & MATERIALS

- Circular saw
- Drill with bits
- Jig saw
- Finish sander
- Belt sander
- Compass
- Combination square
- Clamps
- Hammer
- Nail set

- (2) ½ × 8" × 8 ft. pine
- (1) ½ × 4" × 4 ft. pine
- (1) ½ × 1¾" × 3 ft. cove molding
- 1" wire brads
- Wood glue
- (2) ¾"-dia. brass knobs
- (6) 1⁵⁄₁₆ × 2¼" ornamental hinges
- Finishing materials

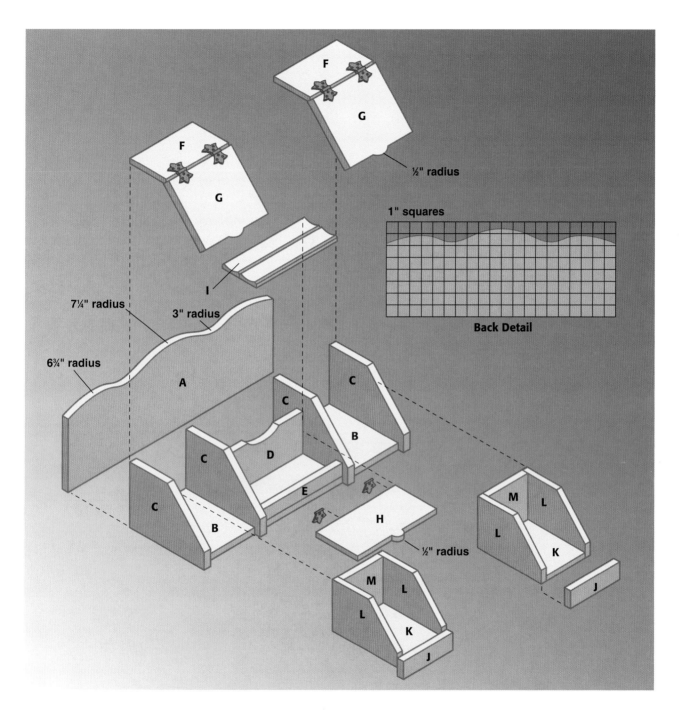

½" radius

1" squares

Back Detail

7¼" radius

3" radius

6¾" radius

½" radius

Key	Part	Dimension
A	(1) Back	½ × 7¼ × 20" pine
B	(1) Bottom	½ × 6½ × 19" pine
C	(4) Divider	½ × 5½ × 7" pine
D	(1) Letter holder	½ × 3½ × 8" pine
E	(1) Front	½ × 1½ × 8" pine
F	(2) Top	½ × 4 × 6" pine
G	(2) Lid	½ × 6 × 6" pine

Key	Part	Dimension
H	(1) Pencil cover	½ × 4½ × 7¾" pine
I	(2) Pencil holder	9⁄16 × 1¾ × 8" cove molding
J	(2) Drawer front	½ × 1½ × 4¾" pine
K	(2) Drawer bottom	½ × 3¾ × 6" pine
L	(4) Drawer side	½ × 4¼ × 6½" pine
M	(2) Drawer back	½ × 3¾ × 4¼" pine

Directions: Desktop Console

Step A: MAKE THE BACK & DIVIDERS.
1. Cut the back (A) to size. Draw a 1"-square grid pattern onto a sheet of sturdy paper, then copy the profile for the back, using the pattern on page 237 as a guide. Center the template over the back, and trace the shape.
2. Cut the back, using a jig saw. Sand the edges smooth.
3. Cut the letter holder (D) to size. Use a compass to draw a 3" radius curve, making sure the lowest point of the curve is ½" down from one long edge. The ends of the curve should fall 2¼" in from each end of the piece. Cut the curve with a jig saw. Sand the cut smooth.
4. Cut the dividers (C) to size. Designate one long edge of each divider as the top and one short edge as the back.
5. Use a pencil to mark the top edge, 3½" in from the back. Make another mark on the front edge, 1½" up from the bottom. Draw a straight line connecting the marks, and shade in the triangular section formed by the line.
6. Mark the cutting lines for the two dividers. To make the cutting lines for the notches, draw a straight line across two dividers, ½" up from the bottom edge. Start these cutting lines at the backs of the dividers, and end them ½" in from the front edges.
7. Shade the area between the bottom edge and the cutting line, and use a jig saw to cut out the shaded areas on the dividers. Sand all edges smooth.

Step B: ASSEMBLE THE FRAME.
1. Cut the bottom (B) and front (E) to size. Center the back against the long edge of the bottom. Drill pilot holes, apply glue, and drive evenly spaced 1" wire brads through the back panel and into the bottom. The back should extend ½" past the bottom.
2. Fasten the letter holder between the notched dividers, flush with the bottom edges. The rear face of the letter holder should be 2" in from the back edges.
3. Position the notched dividers and letter holder on the bottom. Make sure the dividers are butting flush against the bottom and back. The outside faces of the notched dividers should be 5" in from the ends of the bottom. Fasten the notched dividers with glue and 1" brads.
4. Position the front between the dividers, flush with the front edge of the bottom. Attach it with glue and 1" brads.
5. Apply glue to the ends of the bottom panel and the rear edges of the outside dividers, and butt them against each end of the bottom panel. Drive 1" wire brads through the end pieces and into the bottom panel.

Step C: MAKE THE TOPS, LIDS & PENCIL COVER.
1. Cut the tops, lids, and pencil cover to size. Designate a front and back on the lids and pencil cover, and draw a reference line across them, ½" in from the front edge.
2. Use a compass to draw a centered arc on each reference line: the tops of the arcs should face the front edges of the lids and pencil cover to create a small scallop, or handle, on the workpieces. Cut along the reference lines and arcs with a jig saw, and sand the edges smooth.

A. *Shade-in the waste areas on the dividers to avoid making mistakes when cutting out the profiles.*

B. *Assemble the frame, securing the pieces with glue and 1" brads.*

C. *Clamp a belt sander to your worksurface, and use it as a grinder to shape bevels into the front edges of the tops.*

3. On the tops, draw a reference line ½" in from the front edge. Clamp a belt sander with a medium-grit sanding belt to your worksurface, and make a bevel on the front edges, sanding from the top face down to the reference line.

4. Cut the pencil holders to size from ⅝₆" × 1¾" cove molding. Apply glue, and fasten the pencil holders between the front and letter holder.

Step D: MAKE THE DRAWER SIDES.

1. Cut the drawer fronts (J), drawer bottoms (K), drawer sides (L), and drawer backs (M) to size.

2. Position a drawer side on top of the bottom (B), with the front edge of the drawer side flush against the front edge of the divider. Trace the slanted profile of the divider onto the drawer side, then cut the drawer side to shape, and sand it smooth.

3. Using the finished drawer side as a tracing template, draw cutting lines onto the remaining drawer sides. Cut them to shape with a jig saw, and sand them smooth.

Step E: ASSEMBLE THE DRAWERS.

1. Position the drawer backs between the drawer sides with their bottom edges flush, and fasten the pieces together, using glue and 1" brads.

2. Test-fit the drawer bottoms to make sure the front edges are flush with the drawer sides. Fasten the drawer bottoms between the drawer sides, using glue and brads.

Step F: ATTACH DRAWER FRONTS & FINISH.

1. Attach the drawer fronts to the drawer sides and bottoms. Make sure the bottom edges overhang the bottom edges of the drawer sides by ½".

2. Test-fit the drawers between the ends. If necessary, sand the bottom edges of the drawer fronts so they are flush with the bottom edges of the bottom.

3. Use glue and brads to attach the tops (F) to the top edges of the dividers with the bevels on the front edges, facing the bottom of the project. Make sure the top edges butt directly against the back and are flush with the outside faces of the ends.

4. Use a file or belt sander to create a slight bevel on the top front edges of the lids. When combined with the larger bevels on the bottom faces, the small bevels allow the lids to swing open fully. Tape the lids in place, test-fitting the pieces to make sure the bevels mate. If necessary, sand the joints until they fit together.

5. Fill all the holes with wood putty. Sand all surfaces with medium (100- or 120-grit) sandpaper, then finish-sand with fine (150- or 180-grit) sandpaper. Prime and paint the desktop console—cover all the surfaces with enamel paint.

6. Fasten the lids to the tops, using ¹⁵⁄₁₆ × 2¼" brass ornamental hinges. Fasten the pencil cover to the divider in the same way. Attach ¾"-dia. decorative brass (screw-in-type) knobs to the drawer fronts, and insert the drawers between the ends.

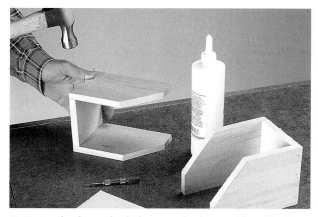

E. *Fasten the drawer backs between the drawer sides with glue and wire brads.*

D. *Mark the profiles of the divider onto the drawer sides. Cut and shape the drawer sides.*

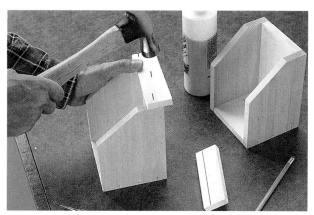

F. *Attach the drawer fronts to the front edges of the sides and bottoms so they overhang the bottoms by ½".*

Bookcase

An attractive bookcase adds just the right decorative and functional touch to a family room or den. And you don't need to shell out large amounts of cash for a high-end bookcase or settle for a cheap, throw-together particleboard unit—this sturdy bookcase looks great and will last for many years.

Four roomy shelf areas let you display and store everything from framed pictures to reference manuals. The decorative trim on the outside of the bookcase spices up the overall appearance of the project, while panel molding along the front edges of the shelves softens the corners and adds structural stability. With a few coats of enamel paint, this bookcase takes on a smooth, polished look.

Although the project is constructed mostly of plywood, the molding that fits around the top, bottom, and shelves allows the bookcase to fit in almost anywhere in the house. This bookcase is a great-looking, useful addition to just about any room.

A simple, functional bookcase on which to set your picture frames, books, and decorations; this project is as useful as it is attractive.

TOOLS & MATERIALS

- #6 × 2" wood screws
- 4d and 6d finish nails
- 16-ga. × 1" and 1¼" brads
- 16-ga. × ¾" wire nails
- ¾" birch veneer edge tape (25')
- Wood glue
- Finishing materials

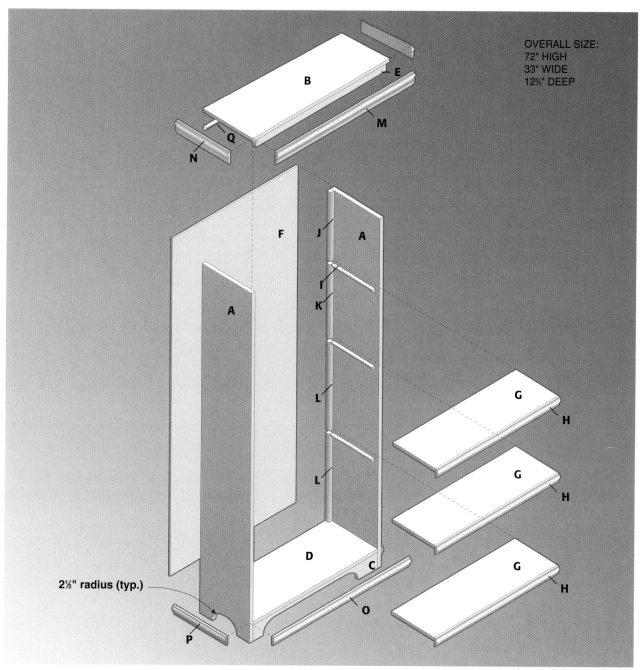

OVERALL SIZE:
72" HIGH
33" WIDE
12¾" DEEP

2½" radius (typ.)

Key	Part	Dimension
A	(2) Side	¾ × 12 × 71¼" plywood
B	(1) Top	¾ × 11¾ × 31½" plywood
C	(1) Front rail	¾ × 3¼ × 30" plywood
D	(1) Bottom	¾ × 11¾ × 30" plywood
E	(1) Top rail	¾ × 1½ × 30" plywood
F	(1) Back	¼ × 30 × 68¾" plywood
G	(3) Shelf	¾ × 10½ × 30" plywood
H	(3) Shelf nosing	¾ × 1⅝ × 30" panel molding
I	(6) Shelf cleat	¾ × ¾ × 9¾" cove molding

Key	Part	Dimension
J	(2) Back brace	¾ × ¾ × 14" quarter-round
K	(2) Back brace	¾ × ¾ × 15" quarter-round
L	(4) Back brace	¾ × ¾ × 18" quarter-round
M	(1) Top facing	¾ × 2⅝ × 33" chair-rail molding
N	(2) Top side molding	¾ × 2⅝ × 12¾" chair-rail molding
O	(1) Bottom facing	¾ × 1⅝ × 33" panel molding
P	(2) Bottom side molding	¾ × 1⅝ × 12¾" panel molding
Q	(1) Back brace	¾ × ¾ × 28½" quarter-round

Note: Measurements reflect the actual size of dimension lumber.

241

Directions: Bookcase

Step A: MAKE THE SIDES & FRONT RAIL.
1. Cut the sides (A) and front rail (C) to size from ¾"-thick plywood. Sand the parts smooth and clean the edges thoroughly.
2. Cut two strips of self-adhesive edge tape slightly longer than the long edge of the side piece. Attach the tape to one long edge of each side piece by pressing it onto the wood with a household iron set at a medium-low setting. The heat will activate the adhesive. Trim and sand the edges of the tape.
3. Designate a top and bottom to each side. Draw a cutting line across each side, 2½" up from the bottom edge.

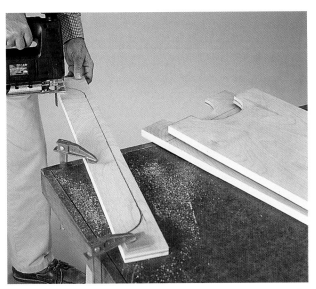

A. *Cut arches along the bottoms of the side panels and front rail to create the bookcase "feet."*

Draw marks on the bottom edges of the sides, 5½" in from the front and rear edges. Set a compass to draw a 2½"-radius arc, using the marks on the bottom edges as centerpoints. Set the point of the compass as close as possible to the bottom edges of the sides, and draw the arcs. Use a jig saw to cut the arch.
4. Repeat these steps to make the arch in the front rail, but place the point of the compass 4¾" in from each end of the front rail. Cut the front rail to shape with a jig saw.

Step B: BUILD THE CARCASE.
The top, bottom and sides of the bookcase form the basic cabinet—called the "carcase."
1. Cut the top (B), bottom (D) and top rail (E) to size. Sand the parts smooth.
2. Draw reference lines across the faces of the sides, 3¼" up from the bottom edges. Set the sides on edge, and position the bottom between them, just above the reference lines. Attach the bottom to the sides with glue and 2" wood screws, keeping the front edges flush. Drill ⁵⁄₆₄" pilot holes for the screws. Counterbore the holes ⅛" deep, using a ⅜" counterbore bit.
3. Set the sides upright, and position the front rail between the sides, flush with the side and bottom edges. Glue the rail edges. Then, clamp it to the bottom board. Drill ¹⁄₁₆" pilot holes, and secure the front rail with 6d finish nails driven through the sides, and 1¼" brads driven through the bottom. Set all nails with a nail set.
4. Use glue and 6d finish nails to attach the top to the top ends of the sides, keeping the side and front edges flush.
5. Fasten the top rail between the sides, flush with the front edges of the sides and top. Use glue and 6d finish nails to secure the top rail in place.

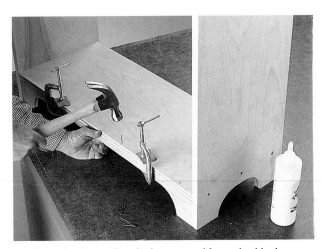

B. *Clamp the front rail to the bottom, and fasten it with glue, finish nails and brads.*

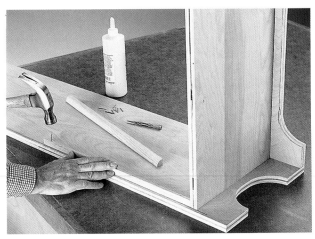

C. *Attach the back braces to the sides, creating a 1/4" recess for the back panel.*

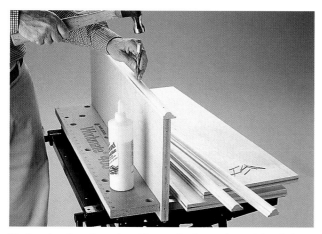

D. *Attach strips of panel molding to the front edges of the shelves.*

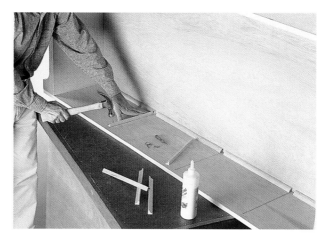

E. *Attach the shelf cleats with glue and brads.*

Step C: MAKE THE BACK.
1. Cut the back braces (J, K, L, Q) to length.
2. Set the carcase on its side. Starting at the bottom, use glue and 1¼" brads to fasten the back braces to the sides and top, ¼" in from the back edges. Use a ¾"-thick spacer to create gaps for the shelves between the strips. Install the top back brace (Q) flush with the back edge of the top. Place the carcase on its front edges.
3. Cut the back (F) to size.
4. Set the back in place so it rests on the back braces. Check for square by measuring diagonally from corner to corner across the back. When the measurements are the same, the carcase is square. Drive ¾" wire nails through the back and into the back braces. Do not glue the back in place.

Step D: MAKE THE SHELVES.
1. Cut the shelves (G) and shelf nosing (H) to size.
2. Drill 1/16" pilot holes through the nosing pieces. Use glue and 4d finish nails to attach the nosing to the shelves, keeping the top edges flush. Set the nails with a nail set.
3. Cut the shelf cleats (I) to length.
4. Use a combination square to draw reference lines perpendicular to the front edges of each side to help you position the shelf cleats. Start the lines at the top of the lower back braces (K, L), and extend them to within 1" of the front edges of the sides. Apply glue to the cleats, and position them on the reference lines. Attach the shelf cleats to the inside faces of the sides with 1" brads.
5. Apply glue to the top edges of the shelf cleats. Then, set the shelves onto the cleats. Drive 6d finish nails through the sides and into the ends of the shelves.
6. Drive ¾" wire nails through the back panel and into the rear edges of the shelves.

Step E: APPLY FINISHING TOUCHES.
1. Cut the top facing (M), top side molding (N), bottom facing (O) and bottom side molding (P) to length. Miter-cut both ends of the top facing and bottom facing and the front ends of the side moldings at a 45° angle so the molding pieces will fit together at the corners.
2. Fasten the top molding with glue and 4d finish nails, keeping the top edges flush with the top face of the top piece.
3. Attach the bottom facing, keeping the top edges flush with the top face of the bottom.
4. Draw reference lines on the sides to help you align the bottom side molding. The reference lines should be flush with the top of the bottom facing. Attach the bottom side molding.
5. Set all nails with a nail set, and fill the nail holes with wood putty. Finish-sand the project and apply the finish of your choice—we used primer and two coats of enamel paint.

F. *Using a combination square, draw lines on the sides, aligned with the top of the bottom facing.*

Nesting Office

Adesk and credenza are two principal furnishings needed in any home office. This nesting office pair features both components at full size. But because they fit together, they can be stored in about the same amount of space as a standard medium-size desk. Made of oak and oak plywood, both pieces are well constructed and pleasing to the eye.

The desk has a large writing surface, and the credenza is a versatile rolling storage cabinet with a hanging file box and shelves for storage of books, paper, and other materials. Flip-up tops let you use the credenza as an auxiliary writing or computer surface, while storing office supplies below.

The basic building blocks of a home office are designed to fit together in one small space.

TOOLS & MATERIALS

- Circular saw
- Drill with bits
- Jig saw
- Miter box with backsaw
- Finish sander
- Combination square
- Hammer
- Bar or pipe clamps
- Nail set
- Wood glue
- (3) 2 × 2" × 8 ft. oak
- (4) 1 × 4" × 8 ft. oak
- (2) 1 × 2" × 8 ft. oak
- (4) ¾" × 2 × 4 ft. oak plywood
- (1) ⅜ × 1¹⁄₁₆" × 6 ft. oak stop molding
- (2) ¾ × ¾" × 8 ft. oak cove molding
- Wood screws (#6 × 1" and 1⅝")
- 16-ga. × 1" brads
- (4) 1½ × 3" brass butt hinges
- (4) 2½" swivel casters
- (6) 1¼" brass corner braces with ⅝" brass wood screws
- (4) Brass lid supports
- (50 ft.) ¾" oak veneer edge tape
- ⅜"-dia. oak plugs
- Finishing materials

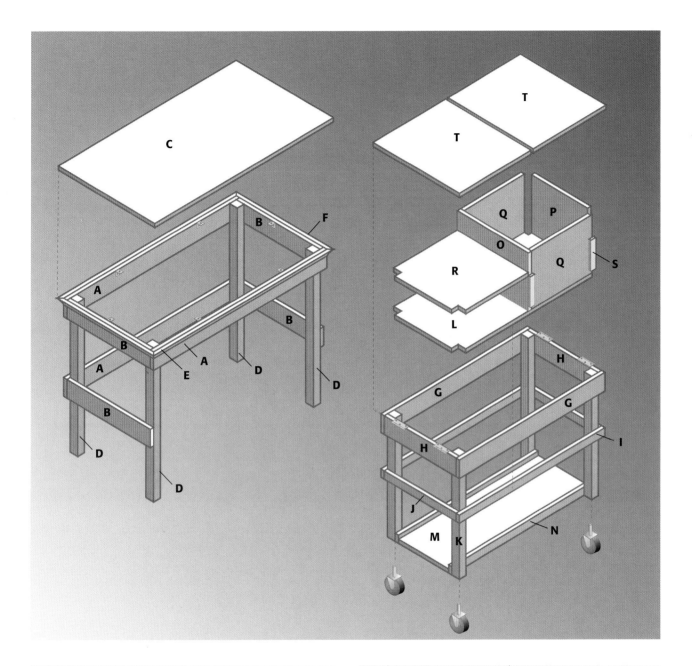

Key	Part	Dimension
A	(3) Desk side	¾ × 3½ × 38" oak
B	(4) Desk end	¾ × 3½ × 19" oak
C	(1) Desk top	¾ × 22 × 40" plywood
D	(4) Desk leg	1½ × 1½ × 29¼" oak
E	(2) Side molding	¾ × ¾ × 40" cove molding
F	(2) End molding	¾ × ¾ × 22" cove molding
G	(2) Credenza side	¾ × 3½ × 33" oak
H	(2) Credenza end	¾ × 3½ × 33" oak
I	(2) Middle rail	¾ × 1½ × 33" oak
J	(2) End rail	¾ × 1½ × 16" oak

Key	Part	Dimension
K	(4) Credenza leg	1½ × 1½ × 21¼" oak
L	(1) Middle shelf	¾ × 16 × 31½" plywood
M	(1) Bottom shelf	¾ × 11½ × 31½" plywood
N	(2) Bottom rail	¾ × 1½ × 31½" oak
O	(1) Divider	¾ × 11¼ × 16" plywood
P	(1) End panel	¾ × 11¼ × 13" plywood
Q	(2) Side panel	¾ × 11¼ × 13⅞" plywood
R	(1) Bin bottom	¾ × 15¼ × 16" plywood
S	(6) Stop	¾ × 1⁄16 × 7" stop molding
T	(2) Bin lid	¾ × 16⅜ × 11¼" plywood

Directions: Nesting Office

NOTE: For all screws used in this project, drill ³⁄₃₂" pilot holes. Counterbore the holes ¼" deep, using a ⅜" counterbore bit.

Step A: MAKE THE DESK-LEG PAIRS.
1. Cut the desk ends (B) and desk legs (D) to length, and sand the pieces smooth.
2. Lay the legs on a flat surface, arranged in pairs. Lay the desk ends across the legs to form the leg pair assemblies. One desk end should be flush with the tops of the legs, and the bottom of the other desk end should be 10½" up from the bottoms of the legs. Apply glue to the mating surfaces, then clamp the leg pair assemblies together. Check the assemblies with a square to make sure the legs are square to the end boards. Fasten the pieces together by driving 1⅝" wood screws through the desk ends and into the legs.

Step B: ASSEMBLE THE DESK BASE.
1. Cut the desk sides (A) to length and sand them smooth.
2. Drill a pair of pilot holes about 1½" in from each end of each desk side board. Before drilling the pilot holes, check the leg pairs to make sure the pilot holes will not run into the screws joining the end

boards and the legs. Apply glue to the mating ends of one side board, and clamp it in place so it spans between the leg pairs, flush with the tops of the legs and the outside faces of the desk ends. Check to make sure the leg pairs are square to the desk side. Drive 1⅝" wood screws through the pilot holes. Install the other top desk side, using the same method.
3. Use glue and 1⅝" wood screws to attach the lower side board to the legs so the top is flush with the tops of the end boards in the leg pairs. After the glue has set, insert glued oak plugs into all screw holes and sand the plugs flush with the surface.
4. Sand the entire desk base with medium-grit sandpaper to smooth the surfaces and dull any sharp edges.

Step C: ATTACH THE DESKTOP.
1. Cut the desktop (C) to size. Sand the edges smooth, and wipe them clean.
2. Cut strips of self-adhesive edge tape to fit the edges. Use a household iron set at low-to-medium heat to press the veneer onto the edges. After the adhesive cools, trim any excess tape with a utility knife. Sand the edges of the tape smooth, using fine-grit sandpaper.
3. Place the desktop on your worksurface with the top face down, and center the desk base on the desktop. The desktop should overhang the base by ¾" on

A. *Check with a combination square to make sure the desk legs are square to the ends.*

B. *Glue oak plugs into the screw holes to cover the screws.*

C. *Fasten the desktop to the desk base with brass corner braces.*

all sides. Clamp the base in place, and arrange 1¼" brass corner braces along the inside edges of the desk side and end boards. Use two braces on each side and one at each end. Drill pilot holes, and drive ⅜" brass wood screws to attach the desktop.

Step D: ATTACH THE DESK MOLDING.
Fit the side and end molding pieces underneath the desktop, and fasten them to the desk sides and ends.
1. Cut the side molding (E) and end molding (F) pieces to fit the desk dimensions, miter-cutting the ends at a 45° angle.
2. Drill ⅟₁₆" pilot holes through the molding pieces, and position them against the bottom of the desktop. Apply glue to the molding, including the mitered ends, and attach the pieces with 1" brads.

Step E: MAKE THE CREDENZA BASE.
The credenza base is similar to the desk base. Build the leg pairs first, then join them together with long side boards. Remember to check the frame parts for square before you fasten them.
1. Cut the credenza sides (G), credenza ends (H), middle rails (I), end rails (J), and credenza legs (K) to length.
2. Arrange the legs in pairs with the end rails and credenza ends positioned across them. The credenza

ends should be flush with the outside edges and tops of the legs. The end rails should be flush with the outside edges of the legs, with the bottom edges of the rails 12" down from the tops of the legs. Apply glue to the mating surfaces, and clamp the parts together. Make sure the assemblies are square, then drive 1⅝" wood screws through the ends and rails, and into the legs.
3. Set the leg pairs on one side edge, spacing them about 30" apart. Position a credenza side so its top edge is flush with the tops of the credenza ends. The ends of the side board should be flush with the outside faces of the credenza ends. Fasten the side piece with glue, and drive 1⅝" wood screws through the side and into the legs.
4. Attach the middle rail, flush with the end rails in

TIP:

Plain file boxes can be easily converted to hanging file boxes by installing a self-standing metal hanger system. Sold at office supply stores, the thin metal standards and support rods are custom-cut to fit the box, then assembled and set in place. The metal tabs on the hanging folders fit over the metal support rods.

D. *Install strips of oak cove molding along the underside of the desktop.*

E. *Attach the credenza ends and end rails to the legs with glue and wood screws.*

the leg assemblies, using the same methods. Attach the other credenza side and middle rail to complete the base.

Step F: MAKE & INSTALL THE BOTTOM CREDENZA SHELF.
1. Cut the bottom shelf (M) and bottom rails (N) to size. Apply self-adhesive edge tape to both short edges of the bottom shelf.
2. Position a bottom rail against each long edge of the bottom shelf. Make sure the ends are flush and the bottom edges of the rails are flush with the bottom face of the shelf. Fasten the parts with glue, and drive 1⅝" wood screws through the bottom rails and into the edges of the bottom shelf.
3. Position the bottom shelf between the credenza legs so the bottom edges are flush. Drive 1⅝" wood screws through the bottom rails and into the legs.

Step G: MAKE & INSTALL THE MIDDLE CREDENZA SHELF.
1. Cut the middle shelf (L) to size and use a jig saw to cut a 1½ × 1½" notch in each corner of the middle shelf so it will fit between the credenza legs.
2. To attach the middle shelf between the middle rails and end rails, apply glue to the inside edges of the rails, and slide the shelf into position. The shelf

should be flush with the bottom edges of the rails. Drive 1⅝" wood screws through the middle and end rails, and into the middle shelf.

Step H: MAKE THE CREDENZA BINS.
The credenza bins include a file box for hanging file folders and a supply storage box. Each bin has a flip-up lid.
1. Cut the divider (O), end panel (P), side panels (Q), and bin bottom (R) to size.
2. Cut 1½ × 1½" notches in both corners at one end of the bin bottom so it will fit between the legs.
3. Position the side panels on top of the middle shelf so their outside edges are flush against the legs. Apply glue and drive 1" wood screws through the side panels and into the credenza sides and middle rails.
4. Position the end panel between the legs, with its bottom edge flush against the middle shelf. Apply glue and drive 1" wood screws through the end panel and into the credenza end and end rail.
5. Slide the divider into place so it butts against the inside edges of the side panels and is flush with the tops of the side panels. Fasten the divider with glue, and drive 1⅝" wood screws through the divider and into the edges of the side panels.

F. *Fasten the bottom shelf by driving wood screws through the bottom rails and into the legs.*

G. *Cut notches at each corner of the middle shelf so it will fit between the credenza legs.*

6. From the outside of the credenza, drill evenly spaced pilot holes for the bin bottom in the credenza sides and end, ⅜" up from the bottom edges of the boards. Apply glue to the edges of the bin bottom and slip it into place, flush with the bottom edges of the credenza sides and ends. Drive 1⅜" wood screws through the sides and ends and into the edges of the bin bottom.

Step I: INSTALL STOP MOLDING & APPLY THE FINISHING TOUCHES.

1. Cut the stops (S) to length and drill ¹⁄₁₆" pilot holes through the stop pieces. Position the stops to conceal the joints and the edges of the panels that make up the large bin. Use glue and 1" brads to attach the stops.
2. Cut the lids (T) to size from a single plywood panel. Apply edge tape to all of the edges. Do not attach the lids until after the finish has been applied.
3. Insert glued oak plugs into all visible screw holes in the desk and credenza. Sand the plugs flush with the surface. Set all nails with a nail set, and fill the nail holes with wood putty.
4. Finish-sand both furnishings with 180- or 220-grit sandpaper, and then apply the finish of your choice. You may find it easier to finish the desk if you re-

move the desktop first. It is important that you finish the underside of the desk as well as the top. We used only a clear topcoat for a light, contemporary look. You may prefer to use a light or medium wood stain first.
5. When the finish has dried, reattach the desktop. Fasten 1½ × 3" brass butt hinges to the bottom faces of the credenza lids, 2¼" in from the side edges. The backs of the hinge barrels should be flush with the back edges of the lids when closed. Attach the bin lids to the credenza by fastening the hinges to the credenza ends. Attach sliding lid supports to the lids and inside faces of the credenza sides to hold the lids open for access to the bins.
6. Attach a 2½" swivel caster to the bottom end of each credenza leg.

H. *Glue the bin bottom between the credenza sides, flush with their bottom edges, and secure it with screws.*

I. *Attach strips of oak molding to cover the exposed plywood edges on the outside of the credenza.*

FRAMED-IN STORAGE

The beauty of framed-in storage projects is that they generally make use of spaces that are otherwise unused. Framed-in projects minimize wasted space because they're custom-built for their areas. And they can make ingenious use of irregular spaces, such as the area under a stairway, or in a short attic kneewall.

Unlike the other projects in this book, most of which are moveable, these projects are built permanently into place. For this reason, it's important to carefully plan their placement. See page 7 for helpful planning suggestions. Also, carefully consider the impact the project makes on the style and décor of the room. When possible, build these projects with moldings that match the style of the room's woodwork, helping them to blend in.

Some framed-in projects require cutting into existing walls. Make sure you know the location of existing plumbing and electrical lines or other mechanicals before you cut into any wall, and always wear the proper safety equipment when operating power tools.

IN THIS SECTION:

An attractive and functional built-in may take up as little as 6" of floor space. This ultra-shallow hutch unit is perfect to display pottery, china, and glassware, yet is barely deeper than an ornate picture frame.

The smooth curves of this built-in shelving and matching floating floor, combined with the rich colors of the terracotta red and slate blue cabinets, transform an unremarkable rectangular room into a functional work of art. Alternating open storage with closed cabinet space leaves room to display books, plants, pottery, woodcarvings, and artwork.

Built-in book shelves and cabinets maintain clean architectural lines in this modern office. Built-in features make it possible for small spaces to serve big functions.

This striking architectural design is enhanced by a split-level, framed-in bookcase that spans from wall to wall and ascends from floor to vaulted-ceiling—conforming precisely to the available space.

Framed-in cabinets and bookcases that wrap under and around windows can make the best use of available wall space. Putting shelving under a window not only utilizes this often-neglected area, but it creates a sunlit platform to showcase other items.

Roll-out storage units designed to fit the space create wonderful storage for seasonal clothing.

A permanent ladder structure serves as a bookshelf most of the time—but provides access to a loft storage area when needed.

This built-in shelving with low-voltage lighting and glass shelves creates an artistic focal point in a small sitting room.

Two display shelves *flanked by vertical mini-pantries create a cozy eating nook with a lowered ceiling that creates a sense of enclosure. The warmth of the sheltered space is accentuated by the indirect display lighting above the bench seating, and the warm amber lighting suspended over the table.*

The staggered layout *of these built-in shelves, echoing the rhythm of the stairway, creates a striking backdrop to display favorite books and objects, and provides extra storage where there is usually just unused wall space.*

Building a Closet

Closets are undoubtedly one of the most frequently used storage areas. Closets are used every day to store a wide variety of items, from canned foods to sporting goods. Yet, many people feel they have a lack of closet space because their existing closets are overflowing with items. If you have the space, building a new closet could be the solution to your storage problems.

The location and direction of the wall studs and ceiling joists are important to consider when planning the dimensions for your new closet. Whenever possible, position the walls of your closet so they can be anchored to ceiling joists and wall studs. Always maintain a minimum closet depth of 30".

Install all needed electrical and plumbing lines in the walls of the closet before hanging the wallboard. Make sure you comply with local building codes when building a closet. Many building codes require a permanent light fixture in closets.

The plan shown here presumes a room with 8-foot ceilings and a closet with a 32" door. If you alter the dimensions, then the sizes of the pieces will also change. Choose the style and size of the door for your closet before you begin the framing. The type of door you choose will determine the size of the rough opening needed for it.

After finishing the closet, install a closet rod or organizer to minimize wasted space. See page 198 for a good example of a closet organizer.

Use the double-plate design to install this closet anywhere, without having to install blocking above a finished ceiling.

TOOLS & MATERIALS

- Stud finder
- Framing square
- Circular saw
- Screw gun or drill with bits
- Plumb bob
- Chalk line
- Hammer
- Wallboard knives
- Wallboard lifter
- Level
- Tape measure
- Ladder
- Hand saw

- Shims
- Corner bead
- Nail set
- (17) 2 × 4" × 8 ft. pine studs
- 10d and 16d common nails
- 8d casing nails
- 1¼" wallboard nails or screws
- Wallboard tape
- Wallboard compound
- (6) ½" × 4 × 8 ft. wallboard
- 32" × 80" Prehung interior door kit
- Finishing materials

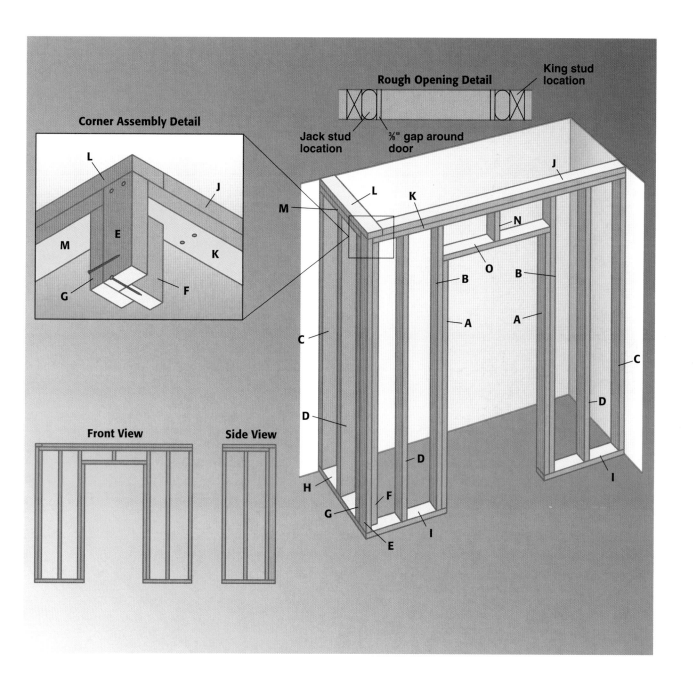

Corner Assembly Detail

Rough Opening Detail

King stud location

Jack stud location

⅜" gap around door

Front View

Side View

Key	Part	Dimension
A	(2) Jack stud	1½ × 3½ × 83½"
B	(2) King stud	1½ × 3½ × 91½"
C	(2) End stud	1½ × 3½ × 91½"
D	(3) Intermediate stud	1½ × 3½ × 91½"
E	(1) Outside corner stud	1½ × 3½ × 93"
F	(1) Inside corner stud	1½ × 3½ × 91½"
G	(1) Corner stud	1½ × 3½ × 91½"
H	(1) Side wall sole plate	1½ × 3½ × 31½"

Key	Part	Dimension
I	(2) Front wall sole plate	1½ × 3½ × 30"
J	(1) Upper top plate, front wall	1½ × 3½ × 90½"
K	(1) Lower top plate, front wall	1½ × 3½ × 92½"
L	(1) Upper top plate, side wall	1½ × 3½ × 35"
M	(1) Lower top plate, side wall	1½ × 3½ × 31½"
N	(1) Cripple stud	1½ × 3½ × 6½"
O	(1) Header	1½ × 3½ × 37"

Directions: Building a Closet

Step A: LOCATE THE WALL STUDS & CEILING JOISTS.
Use a stud finder to locate the wall studs and ceiling joists in the planned closet location. Locate the edges of each framing member and mark the direction of the ceiling joists with a pencil.

Step B: LAY OUT THE TOP PLATE LOCATIONS.
Whenever possible, adjust the dimensions of the closet to line up with the ceiling joists and wall studs. The double top plate construction makes it possible to build the closet even if the top plates for one of the walls cannot be attached to a ceiling joist, but the end studs for each wall must be positioned so they can be fastened to the studs or top and sole plates in the existing walls.
1. Using a tape measure and a pencil, measure out from the back and side walls and make reference marks indicating the locations of the new top plates of the closet.
2. Use a framing square to make sure the reference marks are straight and perpendicular to the back wall. Snap chalk lines to join the reference marks and check the chalk lines with the framing square to ensure the lines are still straight and perpendicular with the existing walls.

Step C: INSTALL THE TOP PLATES.
If the top plates of both new walls can be anchored to the ceiling joists, install each of the four top plates separately, starting with the upper top plate of the side wall.
1. Measure and cut the upper and lower top plates for the side wall of the closet with a circular saw. The lower top plate should be 3½" shorter than the upper top plate to allow space for the corner construction. Position the upper top plate of the side wall flush with the chalk lines and drive 16d nails through the top plate into the ceiling joists.
2. Attach the lower top plate to the upper top plate with 16d nails, making sure the side edges of the two plates are flush and the spacing is adequate for the corner construction.
3. Cut the upper and lower top plates for the front wall of the closet to length with a circular saw. Make sure the lower top plate is 2" longer than the upper top plate to allow space for the corner construction. Position the upper top plate of the front wall flush with the chalk lines and facenail it to the ceiling joists with 16d nails.
4. Position the lower top plate against the upper top plate so the side edges are flush and the spacing is adequate for the corner construction. Facenail the lower top plate to the upper top plate with 10d nails.

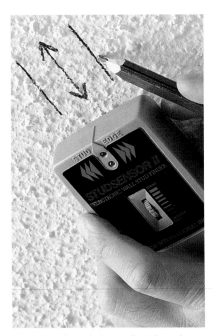

A. *Locate the existing wall studs and ceiling joists. Mark the direction and edges of each joist with a pencil.*

B. *Check the chalk line with a framing square to ensure the layout is correctly placed.*

C. *Install the top plates with 16d nails driven into the ceiling joists.*

If the top plates for one of the new walls of the closet cannot be anchored to a ceiling joist, start the top plate installation with the plates that can be anchored.

1. Measure and cut the upper and lower top plates for the wall that can be anchored to the ceiling joists. Position the upper top plate flush with the chalk lines and drive 16d nails through the top plate into the ceiling joists.

2. Attach the lower top plate to the upper top plate with 16d nails, making sure the side edges of the two plates are flush, and the ends are spaced properly for the corner construction.

3. Measure and cut the top plates for the remaining wall to length. Then facenail the two plates together with 10d nails, making sure the side edges are flush and the ends are properly spaced for the corner construction.

4. Position the top plate assembly on the chalk line layout and drive 16d nails through the lower top plate of the front wall into the upper top plate of the side wall. Attach the other end of the top plates by toenailing 16d nails through the top plate assembly, into the top plate of the existing wall.

Step D: LAY OUT THE ROUGH OPENING & SOLE PLATES.
1. Using a tape measure and a pencil, measure and

mark the layout for the framing members of the rough opening of the door on the lower top plate of the front wall. The width of the rough opening should equal the width of the door frame plus ⅜" on each side. Make marks indicating the jack and king stud locations. See the drawing on page 257 for an example of the rough opening layout.

2. Determine the position of the sole plates with multiple plumb bob readings. Hang a plumb bob from the outside edges of each end of the top plate assemblies for both new walls. The tip of the plumb bob should nearly touch the floor. When it is completely motionless, mark the plumb bob's position on the floor with a pencil.

3. Take additional plumb bob readings from the door-side mark of both jack studs to indicate the end of each bottom plate for the front wall.

4. Snap chalk lines on the floor, marking the locations for the sole plates. Then use a right angle and a pencil to square off the ends of the markings for the sole plates of the front wall, indicating the beginning of the rough opening for the door.

Step E: INSTALL THE SOLE PLATES.
Measure and cut the sole plates to length. Following the chalk lines snapped on the floor, install the sole plates with 10d nails driven through the sole plates

D. *Take multiple plumb bob readings to determine the locations of the sole plates.*

E. *Install the sole plates with 10d nails driven every 16".*

F. *Toenail the end and intermediate studs with 8d nails driven into the lower top plates and the sole plates.*

at 16" intervals. Make sure the plates are flush with the chalk lines.

Step F: INSTALL THE END & INTERMEDIATE STUDS.

1. Measure and cut the end studs to length.
2. Toenail the end studs to the top and sole plates with 10d nails. Then facenail the end studs to the existing wall studs with 16d nails.
3. Measure and cut the intermediate studs to length individually, working from the existing walls toward the new corner. Install the studs at intervals no greater than 24" so the wallboard will have proper backing support. Toenail the studs to the lower top plates and sole plates with 10d nails.

Step G: INSTALL THE CORNER ASSEMBLY.

Refer to the Corner Assembly Detail on page 257 for the exact placement of the studs and the nailing method of the corner assembly.
1. Measure and cut the three studs of the corner assembly to length.
2. Toenail and facenail each stud to the top and sole plates with 8d nails. Then drive 10d nails through the surface of each stud as shown in the Corner Detail.

Step H: INSTALL THE KING STUDS & HEADER.

1. Measure, cut, and toenail the king studs with 10d nails on the king stud markings of the lower top plate and 1½" from the end of each sole plate.
2. Use a combination square and a pencil to mark the height of the jack stud on each king stud. The height of a jack stud for a standard door is 83½", or ½" taller than the door.
3. Cut the header to fit snugly between the king studs and endnail it to the king studs so the bottom edge is flush with the reference lines indicating the height of the jack studs.

Step I: INSTALL THE JACK & CRIPPLE STUDS.

1. Measure, cut, and position the jack studs against the inside surfaces of the king studs, making sure the edges are flush. Endnail the jack studs in place, driving 10d nails through the header, into the jack studs. Then facenail the jack studs to the king studs.
2. Measure and cut a cripple stud to install above the header, centered in the rough opening.
3. Toenail the cripple stud to the lower top plate, and drive 10d nails through the bottom of the header into the cripple stud.

G. *Toenail the corner stud assembly in place with 10d nails. Follow the Corner Detail drawing on page 257 for the exact placement of the studs.*

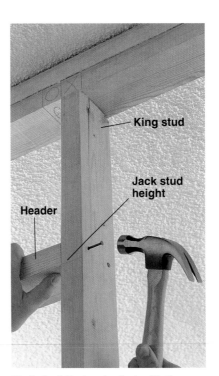

King stud

Jack stud height

Header

H. *Endnail the header flush with the reference marks indicating the height of the jack studs.*

I. *Drive 10d nails through the top of the header into the ends of the jack studs.*

Step J: PLAN THE DOOR WALLBOARD PLACEMENT.
Plan the layout of the wallboard panels, avoiding joints that fall at the corners of the door opening. Joints at these corners often crack and cause bulges that interfere with door trim installation. Unless the panels span the entire wall, install them vertically to avoid butt joints that are difficult to finish.

Step K: HANG THE WALLBOARD.
1. Install any electrical wiring or mechanical lines in the walls before you begin to hang the wallboard.
2. Hang wallboard on the interior and exterior of the closet, beginning with the interior. Use a wallboard lifter to raise the panels tight against the ceiling. Measure and cut each panel to size, working from one end of the closet to the other. Plumb the first panel with a level, making sure the side edges fall on the center of a stud and are flush with the existing wall. Attach each panel with 1¼" wallboard screws driven every 10" into the studs.

Step L: FINISH THE WALLBOARD JOINTS.
1. Apply a thin layer of wallboard compound over the joints with a 4" or 6" wallboard knife. Press wallboard tape into the compound immediately, centering the tape on the joint. Wipe away any excess compound and smooth the joint with a 6" knife. Let the compound dry overnight.
2. Apply a thin finish coat of compound with a 10" wallboard knife. Allow the second coat to dry and shrink overnight.
3. Apply the last coat and let it harden slightly before sanding the joints smooth.
4. To finish inside corners, fold a piece of wallboard tape in half and apply a thin layer of wallboard compound to both sides of the corner with a 4" knife. Position the end of the folded tape strip at the top of the joint and press the tape into the compound with the knife. Smooth both sides of the corner, and finish the joint with three layers of compound.

Step M: INSTALL THE CORNER BEAD.
1. Position the corner bead on the outside corner. Use a level to adjust the bead so the corner is plumb and attach it with 1¼" wallboard nails or screws spaced at 8" intervals.
2. Cover the corner bead with three coats of wallboard compound, using a 6" or 10" wallboard knife.

J. *Plan the wallboard placement so that there are no joints at the corners of the door opening.*

K. *Install the panels using a screwgun and 1¼" wallboard screws, spacing the screws every 10".*

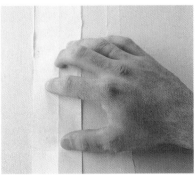

L. *Press the wallboard tape into the compound and smooth out the tape with a 6" wallboard knife.*

Let each coat dry and shrink overnight before applying the next coat. Sand the final coat smooth.

Step N: INSTALL THE PREHUNG INTERIOR DOOR.
1. Slide the door unit into the framed opening and position it so the edges of the jambs are flush with the wall surface and the hinge-side jamb is plumb.
2. Drive pairs of wooden shims from opposite directions into the space between the framing members and the hinge-side jamb, spacing the shims every 12". Make sure the jamb is plumb and does not bow. Then drive 8d casing nails through the jamb and shims into the jack stud.
3. Drive pairs of shims spaced every 12" into the spaces between the framing members and the latch-side jamb and top jamb. Close the door and adjust the shims so the spaces between the door edges and the jambs are ⅛" wide. Then drive 8d casing nails through the jambs and shims into the studs.
4. Cut the shims flush with the wall surface using a handsaw. Finish the door and install the lockset as directed by the manufacturer.

Step O: INSTALL THE DOOR CASING.
1. Mark reveal lines ⅛" from the edge of each jamb.
2. Cut the head casing to length and mark the centerpoints of the head casing and the head jamb.
3. Align the casing with the head jamb reveal line, matching the centerpoints so the casing extends evenly beyond both side jambs. Drill pilot holes and drive 8d finish nails through the casing at the stud and jamb locations.
4. Hold the side casings against the head casing, and mark them for cutting. Cut the casings to fit.
5. Align the side casings with the jamb reveal lines and nail them to the jambs and framing members with 8d finish nails.
6. Set the nails using a nail set, and fill the holes with wood putty. Finish the casings as desired.

M. *Install the corner bead with nails or screws driven every 8".*

N. *Drive shims between the jamb and the jack stud, spaced every 12".*

O. *Install the door casings using 8d finish nails driven through pilot holes into the wall framing.*

Option: Framing Openings for Sliding & Folding Doors

The same basic framing techniques are used, whether you're planning to install a bypass, bifold, pocket, or pre-hung interior door. The different door styles require different frame openings. You may need to frame an opening 2 to 3 times wider than the opening for a standard pre-hung door. Purchase the doors and hardware in advance, and consult the hardware manufacturer's instructions for the exact dimensions of the rough opening for the type of door you select.

Most bi-fold doors are designed to fit in an 80"-high finished opening. Wood bi-fold doors have the advantage of allowing you to trim the doors if you prefer a slightly shorter opening.

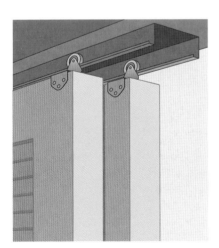

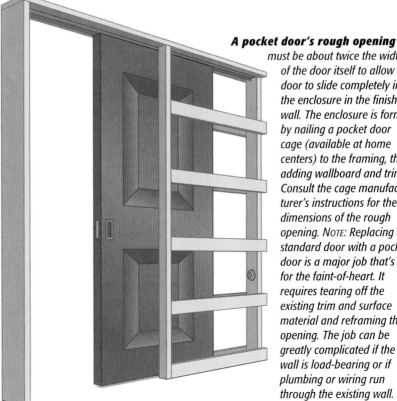

Standard bypass-door openings are 4, 5, 6, or 8 ft. The finished width should be 1" narrower than the combined width of the doors to provide a 1" overlap when the doors are closed. For long closets that require three or more doors, subtract another 1" from the width of the finished opening for each door. Check the hardware installation instructions for the required height of the opening.

A pocket door's rough opening must be about twice the width of the door itself to allow the door to slide completely into the enclosure in the finished wall. The enclosure is formed by nailing a pocket door cage (available at home centers) to the framing, then adding wallboard and trim. Consult the cage manufacturer's instructions for the dimensions of the rough opening. NOTE: Replacing a standard door with a pocket door is a major job that's not for the faint-of-heart. It requires tearing off the existing trim and surface material and reframing the opening. The job can be greatly complicated if the wall is load-bearing or if plumbing or wiring run through the existing wall.

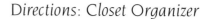

Closet Organizer

One of the best ways to maximize the capacity of your closet is to install an organizer that is tailored to your specific storage needs. This closet organizer was designed with a bedroom closet in mind, but it could be adapted for a pantry or entryway closet.

With a custom-built central shelf unit, items such as shoes, blankets, and sweaters stay organized. The two upper shelves are perfect for accessory items or seasonal clothing.

Best of all, you can build this organizer for a 5-foot closet for the cost of a single sheet of plywood, a clothes pole, and a few feet of 1 × 3 lumber.

Directions: Closet Organizer

Step A: CUT & INSTALL WALL SUPPORTS.
1. Cut the shelf supports for the two upper shelves (D, E) to fit the dimensions of the closet.
2. Attach the supports to the wall so the top edges are 84" and 76" above the floor. Anchor the supports with 8d finish nails driven into wall studs.

Step B: ASSEMBLE THE CENTRAL SHELVING UNIT.
1. Measure and cut the shelf sides (A) and shelves (B) to size.
2. Assemble the central shelf unit, using 6d finish nails. Space the shelves according to the height of the items you will store, but leave the top of the unit open.
3. Position the central shelf unit in the middle of the closet and use a pencil to mark notches at the top of each side to fit around the lower support.

Make efficient use of your closet space with this easy-to-build closet organizer.

TOOLS & MATERIALS

- Hammer
- Tape measure
- Framing square
- Circular saw
- Screwdriver
- Jig saw
- Level
- 6d, 8d finish nails

- ¾" × 4 × 8 ft. finish-grade plywood
- 1¼"-dia. × 6 ft. clothes pole
- (2) 1 × 3" × 8 ft. pine
- (1) 1 × 3" × 6 ft. pine
- Clothes-pole brackets
- Finish materials

4. Cut away the notched area with a jig saw, and place the shelf against the back wall of the closet.

Step C: INSTALL THE UPPER SHELVES & CLOTHES POLE.

1. Measure and cut the upper shelves (C) to size.

2. Position one upper shelf on the lower shelf supports and the top of the central shelf unit. Attach it with 6d finish nails driven into the wall supports and the central shelf sides.

3. Lay the remaining upper shelf on the top shelf supports and attach it with 6d finish nails.

4. Attach pole brackets to the shelf unit, 11" from the rear wall and 3" below the upper shelf. Attach the opposing brackets to the walls. Make sure the brackets are attached to a stud in the closet wall, or use a wall anchor to attach it to the wallboard.

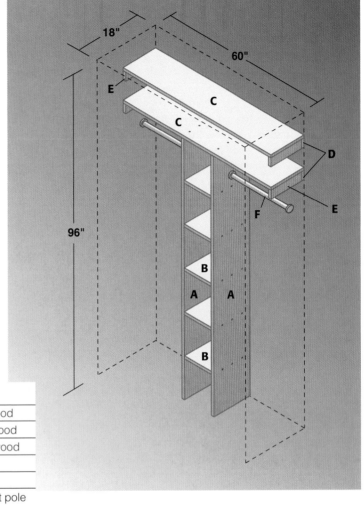

Key	Part	Dimension
A	(2) Central shelf side	¾ × 11⅞ × 76" plywood
B	(5) Shelf	¾ ×11⅞ × 11⅞" plywood
C	(2) Upper shelf	¾ × 11⅞" × 5 ft. plywood
D	(2) Back wall support	¾ × 2½" × 5 ft. pine
E	(4) End wall support	¾ × 2½ × 20" pine
F	(2) Clothes pole	1¼"-dia. × 6 ft. closet pole

A. *Drive 8d finish nails through the supports into the wall studs.*

B. *Assemble the central shelving unit, leaving the top open.*

C. *Install the upper shelves with 6d finish nails.*

Adjustable Closet System

An adjustable closet system puts clothes and accessories within reach for people of all sizes and abilities.

Build your own closet system to attain accessibility features like roll-under space, as well as adjustable shelves and rods. Add closet accessories, such as hooks, additional rods or shelves, pull-out drawers, baskets, slide-out belt and shoe racks, and fold-down pants racks to customize your system.

The closet organizer shown here can be adapted to fit almost any closet. It has a simple plywood cabinet with three adjustable shelves and space above and below for additional storage and easy access.

Use finish-grade plywood for the cabinet and support piece. Then paint, stain, or protect the wood with a clear finish. Solid wood trim covers the plywood edges and lends strength to the shelves. For this, you can use clear pine, which has few knots, or a hardwood, such as aspen, oak, or maple.

The shelves shown in this project are 11" deep. You may want to make them deeper. Just keep in mind that shelves longer than 36" may require additional support to prevent sagging.

Build a complete closet system from one sheet of plywood.

TOOLS & MATERIALS

- Measuring tape
- Circular saw
- Straightedge cutting guide
- Drill
- Router w/straight bit
- Hacksaw
- Framing square
- Nail set
- Studfinder
- Level
- ¾" × 4 × 8 ft. finish-grade plywood
- ¾" × 4 × 4 ft. finish-grade plywood
- 1/2" × 4 × 8 ft. finish-grade plywood
- (2) 10-ft.-long 1 × 2 trim
- (1) 8-ft.-long 1 × 2 trim
- (1) 8-ft.-long 1 × 1 trim
- ⅝" screws
- 2½" trim-head screws
- 2" coarse-thread drywall screws
- 6d finish nails
- Wood glue
- Wood finishing materials
- 1¼"-dia. × 6 ft. closet rod
- Metal shelf standards w/shelf clips & closet rod hangers

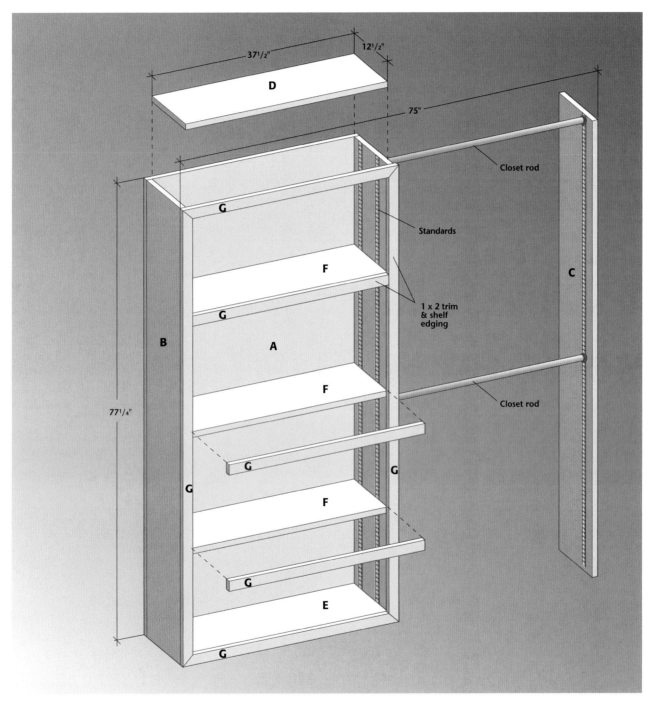

Key	Part	Dimension
A	(1) Cabinet back	½ × 37½ × 77¼" plywood
B	(2) Cabinet sides	½ × 11⅞ × 77¼" plywood
C	(1) Side support	½ × 11⅞ × 77¼" plywood
D	(1) Cabinet top	½ × 11⅞ × 36" plywood
E	(1) Cabinet bottom	½ × 11⅞ × 36" plywood
F	(3) Shelves	½ × 11⅞ × 35⅞" plywood
G	(7) Trim	1 × 2* pine

*Cut to fit

This project is tailored to fit a 75" closet. Adjust the dimensions to fit your closet space.

Directions: Adjustable Closet System

Step A: Cut the plywood pieces

1. From a 4 × 8-ft. sheet of ¾" plywood, cut the two cabinet sides, the side support, and the cabinet top and bottom. Use a table saw or a circular saw with a straightedge guide, and measure carefully so the cuts are straight and the pieces uniform. The saw will remove ⅛" of material with each cut, so the sheet can be ripped into four 11⅞"-wide pieces. Cut the cabinet sides and side support at 11⅞ × 77¼", and cut the cabinet top and bottom at 11⅞ × 36".

2. From a 4 × 4-ft. sheet of ¾" plywood, cut the three shelves at 11⅞ × 35⅞".

3. Cut the cabinet back at 37½ × 77¼", using a 4 × 8-ft. sheet of ½" plywood.

Step B: Install the shelf standards

1. Mark the locations of the grooves that will receive the metal shelf standards for the cabinet shelves. On the inside faces of the cabinet sides, make a mark 1" from the side edges. These marks represent the outside edges of the standards. You can make these standards as long as you wish: they can run the full length of the sides or stop short of the ends.

2. Mark the grooves for the closet rod standards on the outside face of the right cabinet side piece and the inside face of the side support. Make marks for one standard on each piece, 2" from the front edge. If you want the option of installing shelves on this side of the system, you can install an additional standard on each piece, 2" from the rear edge.

3. Using a router fitted with a straight bit that matches the width of the standards, cut the groove, using a straightedge guide to ensure straight cuts. The depth of the grooves should match the thickness of the standards.

4. Cut the standards to length, as needed, using a hacksaw. Set the cabinet sides together with their ends aligned. Lay the standards into the grooves and use a framing square to make sure all the standard slots are aligned, so the shelves will be level. Fasten the standards to the sides with the included nails or ⅜" screws.

Step C: Assemble the cabinet

1. Using wood glue and 2½" trim-head screws, fasten the cabinet top and bottom pieces between the ends of the cabinet sides. Make sure the outside faces of the top and bottom are flush with the ends of the sides.

2. Before the glue dries, fasten the back panel to the cabinet, using 2" coarse-thread drywall screws driven

A. Cut the plywood pieces using a straightedge cutting guide.

B. Rout the dado grooves. Then use a framing square (inset) to align the shelf standards.

C. Assemble the cabinet sides, top, and bottom, then add the plywood back.

every 12". As you work, make sure the cabinet is flush with the edges of the back panel—this will keep the cabinet square. Let the glue dry.

Step D: ADD THE TRIM
1. Cut the 1 × 2 trim to fit around the cabinet, using 45° miter joints at the corners. Test-fit the pieces as you work. Position the top edge of the upper horizontal trim piece flush with the top of the cabinet. Position the top edge of the lower horizontal trim flush with the top of the cabinet bottom. Position the outside edges of the side trim flush with the cabinet sides. Fasten the trim to the front cabinet edges with wood glue and 6d finish nails. If necessary, drill pilot holes for the nails to prevent the trim from splitting. Use a nail set to drive the nail heads slightly below the surface.
2. Cut the 1 × 1 trim piece at 77¼" and fasten it to the front edge of the side support with glue and finish nails. Make sure the outside edge of the trim is flush with the outside face of the side support.
3. Cut the 1 × 2 shelf trim at 34⅜". Fasten each piece to the front edge of a shelf so the ends of the trim are ¾" from the shelf ends and the top edges are flush.
4. If desired, sand and finish wood pieces.

Step E: INSTALL THE CABINET & SHELVES
1. Use a studfinder (page 258) to locate and mark the wall studs in the areas where you'll install the cabinet and side support. Make light pencil marks at both edges of each stud, marking above the area that will be covered by the cabinet and side support.
2. Position the cabinet in the closet corner, using temporary blocks to prop it up 6" above the floor.
3. Fasten the cabinet in place, driving 2½" trim-head screws through the side and back pieces and into the wall studs. Space the screws about 16" apart.
4. Install the shelves using clips set into the standards.

Step F: INSTALL THE SIDE SUPPORT & CLOSET RODS
1. Measure over and align the top of the cabinet. Then mark the cabinet height onto the opposing closet wall.
2. Position the side support against the wall so its top end is on the height mark and its rear edge is ½" from the back wall. Fasten the support to the wall studs with 2½" trim-head screws.
3. Insert closet rod hangers into the standards on the outside of the cabinet and the side support.
4. Measure between the hangers, cut the rods to fit, and install them.

D. *Install trim along the front edges of the cabinet, shelves, and side support, then use a nail punch to set the nails.*

E. *Mount the cabinet to the closet wall so its bottom edge is 6" above the floor.*

F. *Install the side support at the cabinet height, then cut the closet rods to fit.*

269

Floor-to-ceiling Shelves

Floor-to-ceiling shelves are sturdier and make better use of space than freestanding bookcases. When finished and trimmed to match the surrounding room, floor-to-ceiling shelves turn an ordinary room into an inviting den or library.

Made of finish-grade oak plywood and a solid oak face frame, this project has the look and feel of an expensive, solid oak shelf unit—but at a fraction of the cost. The plywood panels are supported and strengthened by an internal framework of 2 × 4 stud lumber.

When installing floor-to-ceiling shelves in a corner, as shown, add ½" plywood spacers to the support studs that adjoin the wall. Spacers ensure that face frame stiles of equal width can be installed at both shelf ends.

This fully adjustable shelving unit creates an elegant built-in look.

TOOLS & MATERIALS

- Tape measure
- Level
- Framing square
- Plumb bob
- Hammer
- Circular saw
- Router with ¼", ¾" straight bits
- Wood glue
- (2) 1 × 2" × 8 ft. oak
- (4) 1 × 4" × 8 ft. oak
- (1) 1 × 3" × 8 ft. oak
- (12) 2 × 4" × 8 ft. oak
- (2) ½" × 4 × 8 ft. oak plywood
- (1) ½" × 2 × 4 ft. oak plywood
- Shims
- Utility screws (1¾", 2", 3")
- Finish nails (1½")
- Metal shelf standards and clips
- Finishing materials

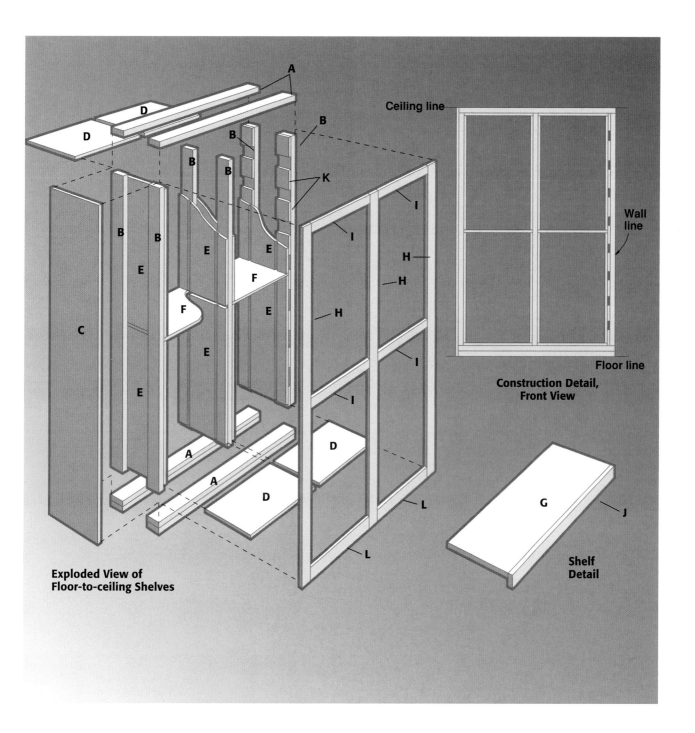

**Exploded View of
Floor-to-ceiling Shelves**

**Construction Detail,
Front View**

Ceiling line

Wall
line

Floor line

**Shelf
Detail**

Key	Part	Dimension
A	(6) Top and sole plate	1½ × 3½ × 59½" pine
B	(6) Support stud	1½ × 3½ × 91½" pine
C	(1) End panel	½ × 95¾ × 13" oak plywood
D	(4) Top, bottom panel	½ × 27¼ × 13" oak plywood
E	(8) Upper, lower riser	½ × 44⅞ × 13" oak plywood
F	(2) Permanent shelf	¾ × 27¼ × 13" oak plywood

Key	Part	Dimension
G	(6) Adjustable shelf	¾ × 26⅛ × 13" oak plywood
H	(3) Stile	¾ × 3½ × * oak
I	(4) Top, middle rail	¾ × 2½ × 16⅛" oak
J	(6) Shelf edging	¾ × 1½ × 26⅛" oak
K	(16) Spacer	½ × 3½ × 6" oak
L	(2) Bottom rail	¾ × 3½ × 16⅛" oak

*Cut to fit

271

Directions: *Floor-to-ceiling Shelves*

Step A: MAKE & INSTALL THE TOP PLATES.

1. Mark the location for two parallel 2 × 4 top plates on the ceiling, using a framing square as a guide. The front edge of the outer plate should be 13" from the wall; the inner plate should be flush against the wall.

2. Mark the location of the ceiling joists. If necessary, install blocking between the joists to provide a surface for anchoring the top plates.

3. Cut two 2 × 4 top plates to length with a circular saw. Position each plate and check to make sure it is level, using shims if necessary.

4. Attach the plates to the ceiling with 3" screws driven into the joists or blocking.

Step B: INSTALL THE SOLE PLATES & SUPPORT STUDS.

1. Cut four 2 × 4 sole plates to length and screw them together to form two double-sole plates.

2. Suspend a plumb bob from the outside corners of the top plates to align the sole plates, then shim them to level, if needed, and anchor the plates by driving 3" screws toenail-style into the floor.

3. Cut six support studs (B) to length. Position a stud between each end of the top plates and sole plates.

Attach the studs with 3" screws driven toenail-style into the top and sole plates.

4. Install two support studs midway between the end support studs. Attach them to the bottom plate first, using 3" screws driven toenail-style. Then use a level to make sure the studs are plumb, and attach them to the top plates with 3" screws.

5. Where the shelves fit into a corner, use 2" screws to attach ½" plywood spacers on the inside faces of the support studs, spaced every 4". Do not extend the spacers past the front face of the support studs.

Step C: INSTALL END PANEL & TOP & BOTTOM PANELS.

1. Measure and cut the end panel (C) to floor-to-ceiling height. Attach the panel to the support studs so the front edges are flush, using 1¾" screws driven through the studs and into the end panel.

2. Measure and cut four top and bottom panels (D) to fit between the support studs. Attach the panels to the top and sole plates using 1½" finish nails.

Step D: MAKE & INSTALL SHELVES & RISERS.

1. Measure and cut four lower risers (E) to size with a circular saw. Lay out and cut dadoes for metal shelf standards as instructed on page 39.

A. *Position each plate, check to make sure they are level, and attach them to the ceiling with 3" screws driven into the joists or blocking.*

B. *Use a plumb bob suspended from the outside corners of the top plates to align the sole plates. Anchor the plates with 3" screws driven toenail-style into the floor.*

C. *Attach the plywood top and bottom panels to the top and sole plates using 1½" finish nails.*

2. Install the lower risers on each side of the support studs so the front edges are flush with the edges of the studs. Attach the risers with 1½" finish nails. For a riser that adjoins a wall, drive the nails through the riser at the spacer locations.

3. Measure and cut permanent shelves (F), to fit between the support studs, just above the lower risers. Position the shelves on the risers and attach them by driving 1½" finish nails through the shelves into the risers.

4. Measure and cut upper risers (E) to fit between the permanent shelves and the top panels. Repeat the process of cutting dadoes for shelf standards outlined on page 39. Attach the risers to the studs with 1½" nails.

Step E: INSTALL THE STILES & RAILS & APPLY A FINISH.
1. Measure and cut the stiles (H) to reach from floor to ceiling along the front edges of the exposed support studs. Drill pilot holes and attach the stiles to the support studs so they are flush with the risers, using glue and 1½" finish nails driven at 8" intervals.
2. Measure and cut the top rails (I) to fit between the stiles. Drill pilot holes and attach the rails to the top plate and top panels, using glue and 1½" finish nails.

3. Measure and cut the middle rails (I) to fit between the stiles. Drill pilot holes, and attach the rails to the permanent shelves using glue and 1½" finish nails.
4. Measure and cut the bottom rails (L) to fit between the stiles. Drill pilot holes, and attach the rails to the sole plates and bottom panels using glue and 1½" finish nails. The top edge of the rails should be flush with the top surface of the bottom panels.
5. Set all the nails with a nail set and fill the nail holes with putty. Then sand and finish the wood surfaces as desired.

Step F: INSTALL ADJUSTABLE SHELVES & TRIM MOLDINGS.
1. Measure, cut, and install the metal shelf standards in the dado grooves using the hardware provided by the manufacturer.
2. Measure and cut adjustable shelves (G) ⅛" shorter than the distance between the metal standards using a circular saw and a straightedge guide.
3. Cut shelf edging, and attach it with glue and 1½" finish nails. Sand and finish the shelves.
4. Insert shelf clips into the metal shelf standards and install the adjustable shelves at desired heights.
5. Cover the gaps between the project walls and floor with molding that has been finished to match.

D. *Install the lower risers on each side of the 2 × 4 support studs with 1½" finish nails.*

E. *Measure and cut the 1 × 3 top rails to fit between the stiles. Then drill pilot holes and attach the rails to the top plate and top panels.*

F. *Insert shelf clips into the metal shelf standards and install the adjustable shelves.*

Understairs Work Center

The irregular space beneath a staircase can be used for a variety of creative storage projects. However, because the dimensions and angles of understairs areas vary widely, finding stock cabinetry that fits the space is difficult. The design shown here can be built to fit almost any area.

The understairs work center, in its simplest form, is a pair of basic cabinets that support a countertop. The basic cabinets are built to a standard height, depending on the use. You can adapt the size of the understairs work center by shortening or lengthening the countertop and connecting shelf. A small cabinet and upper shelves are added to fill the remaining space. The depth of the countertop also can be adjusted to match the width of your staircase.

Most understairs projects require that you make many angled cuts, but in the project shown here, you will need to make only a few miters and bevels. Beveled cuts can be made with a circular saw, but a table saw or power miter saw is preferable.

Put the area under your stairs to good use with this versatile work center.

TOOLS & MATERIALS

- Tape measure
- T-bevel
- Level
- Circular saw
- Drill with bits
- Hammer
- Router with bits
- Bar clamps
- Miter saw
- (1) ¾" × 4 × 4 ft. oak plywood
- (3) ¾" × 4 × 8 ft. oak plywood
- (2) ½" × 4 × 8 ft. oak plywood
- (1) ¼" × 4 × 8 ft. oak plywood
- (2) 1 × 3" × 8 ft. oak
- (1) 1 × 3" × 12 ft. oak
- (4) 1 × 2" × 8 ft. oak
- (1) ¼ × ¾" × 8 ft. oak screen molding
- Shims
- Finish nails (1", 1¼", 1½")
- Utility screws (1", 1¼", 2½")
- 1" wire nails
- Trim molding
- Finish materials
- Door and drawer hardware
- Wood glue

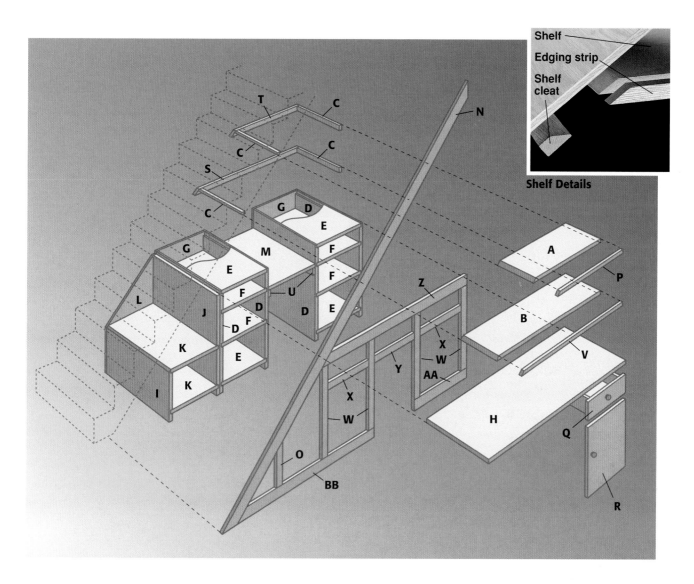

Shelf Details

Key	Part	Dimension
A	(1) Top shelf	¾ × 28 × 18" oak plywood
B	(1) Lower shelf	¾ × 42 × 18" oak plywood
C	(4) Side shelf cleat	¾ × 1½" × 1 ft. oak
D	(4) Cabinet sides	¾ × 35½ × 2 ft. oak plywood
E	(4) Cabinet base, top	¾ × 24 × 19¼" oak plywood
F	(4) Cabinet shelf	¾ × 24 × 19¼" oak plywood
G	(2) Cabinet back	¼ × 20 × 35" oak plywood
H	(1) Countertop	¾ × 32 × 64" oak plywood
I	(1) Small cabinet side	¾ × 18" × 2 ft. oak plywood
J	(1) Small cabinet side	¾ × 18 × 34½" oak plywood
K	(2) Sm. cab. bottom, top	¾ × 19¼ × 2 ft. oak plywood
L	(1) Small cabinet back	¼ × 20 × 34" oak plywood
M	(1) Connecting shelf	¾ × 27⅞ × 2 ft. oak plywood
N	(1) Diagonal rail	¾ × 2½ × * oak
O	(1) Short face frame stile	¾ × 1½ × * oak

Key	Part	Dimension
P	(1) Short shelf edge strip	¼ × ¾ × 25" oak screen molding
Q	Drawer	See page 30
R	Cabinet door	See page 40
S	(1) Middle shelf cleat	¾ × 1½ × 42" oak
T	(1) Upper shelf cleat	¾ × 1½ × 28" oak
U	(2) Lower shelf cleat	¾ × 1½ × 27⅞" oak plywood
V	(1) Long shelf edge strip	¼ × ¾ × 42" oak screen molding
W	(4) Face frame stile	¾ × 1½ × 31¼" oak
X	(2) Face frame rail	¾ × 1½ × 18½" oak
Y	(1) Face frame rail	¾ × 1½ × 2 ft. oak
Z	(1) Countertop face rail	¾ × 2½ × * oak
AA	(1) Short base rail	¾ × 2½ × 21½ oak
BB	(1) Long base rail	¾ × 2½ × * oak

*Cut to fit

275

Directions: Understairs Work Center

Step A: DUPLICATE THE SLOPE OF THE STAIRS.
1. Duplicate the slope of your stairs using a T-bevel and a level. Set one arm of the T-bevel against the back wall, then align the other arm with the stairs. Use the level to ensure the angle is measured properly against a level surface.
2. Transfer the angle directly to your saw to make mitered and beveled cuts throughout the project.

Step B: COVER THE UNDERSIDE & INSTALL UPPER CLEATS.
Cover the underside of the stairs before you build your work center. Panels of ½" plywood attached to the stringers of the staircase create an understairs cover that can be used to anchor the shelf cleats. If you plan to add electrical or plumbing lines, hire a professional or do the work yourself before beginning the work center installation.

Step C: INSTALL THE UPPER SHELVES.
1. Mark the location for the shelf cleats on the walls and understairs cover, using a pencil and a level as a guide. Allow at least 12" of clearance between the countertop and the bottom shelf.

2. Measure and cut 1 × 2 shelf cleats (C, S, T) to fit along the reference lines on the walls and the understairs cover.
3. Bevel the cleats that will be attached to the understairs cover to match the stair slope. Attach the cleats with 2½" utility screws.
4. Measure and cut two ¾" plywood shelves (A, B) to size. Attach a ¾" hardwood strip (P, V) to each shelf edge with glue and finish nails (see Shelf Details page 275).
5. Set the shelves on the cleats and attach them with 1½" finish nails driven through pilot holes.

Step D: BUILD THE CABINET FRAMES.
1. Measure and cut the side panels (D), top and bottom panels (E), and shelves (F) for the main cabinets.
2. Use a router and straightedge guide (page 19) to cut rabbet grooves for the top panels and dado grooves for the bottom panels and shelves (see Cabinet Details, page 277, for the precise measurements and locations of the grooves).
3. Clamp and glue the cabinet sides to the top and bottom panels and shelves to form rabbet and dado joints.

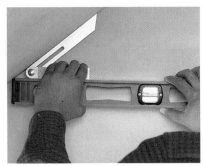

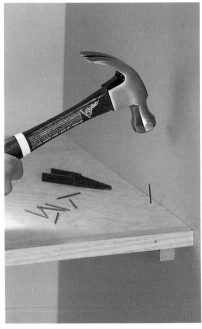

A. *Duplicate the slope of the staircase with a T-bevel and a level and transfer the angle directly to a power miter saw or a miter box with a hand saw.*

B. *Use a 2 × 4 and some scrap wood to hold the understairs cover in place while you install it.*

C. *Attach the shelves to the cleats with 1½" finish nails driven through pilot holes.*

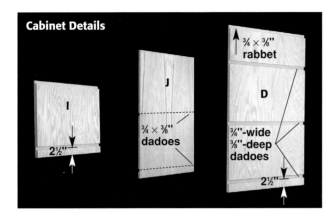

Cabinet Details

I

J

³⁄₄ × ³⁄₈"
rabbet

D

³⁄₄ × ³⁄₈"
dadoes

³⁄₄"-**wide**
³⁄₈"-**deep**
dadoes

2½"

2½"

4. If you plan to use center-mounted drawer slides, attach the slide tracks before you assemble the cabinet.

Step E: REINFORCE THE JOINTS & CUT THE BACK PANELS.
1. Reinforce each cabinet joint with 2" finish nails driven at 4" intervals.
2. Cut a ¼" plywood back panel (G) for each main cabinet. Position each back panel onto the cabinet frames so the edges of the panels are flush with the cabinets on all sides. Attach the back panels to the cabinet side, base, and top panels using 1" wire nails.

Step F: INSTALL THE CABINETS.
1. Position one cabinet so the corner of the top panel is pressed against the understairs cover and the front face is flush with the edge of the stairway.
2. Shim under the cabinet to level it if needed. Then attach the cabinet by toenailing 2" finish nails through the side panels and into the floor. If you have a masonry floor, attach the cabinet with construction adhesive.
3. Position the second cabinet ¾" away from the side wall, so the front face is aligned with the first cabinet.
4. Check the second cabinet with a level and shim under it if needed.
5. Insert ¾" spacers between the second cabinet and the side wall, and anchor the cabinet to the wall with 2½" utility screws driven into the framing members.

Step G: MAKE & INSTALL THE CONNECTING SHELF.
1. Cut the lower shelf cleats (U) to size from ¾" plywood. The lower shelf cleats hold up the connecting shelf (M) that fits between the main cabinets.
2. Mark level lines on the inner cabinet sides at the desired height for the shelf, and attach the shelf

D. *Glue and clamp the cabinet frames together, making sure the front edges of the pieces are flush.*

E. *Reinforce each joint with 2" finish nails.*

F. *Check to ensure the cabinet is level. Attach it to the floor with 2" finish nails.*

cleats to the cabinet sides with 1¼" screws driven through counterbored pilot holes.

3. Measure and cut a ¾" plywood connecting shelf (M) to fit between the cabinets. If you plan to install a drawer using a center-mounted drawer slide, attach the slide track to the shelf before you attach the shelf to the cleats.

4. Attach the shelf to the cleats with 1¼" finish nails.

Step H: INSTALL THE COUNTERTOP PANEL.
1. Measure and cut the plywood countertop panel (H) that extends all the way to the back wall, with one side flush against the understairs cover.
2. Attach the countertop to the panels of the cabinets by driving 1½" finish nails down through the countertop.
3. Install any special countertop finishing material, like ceramic tile or plastic laminate. Obtain installation instructions and follow them carefully if you have not installed tile or laminate before.

Step I: BUILD & INSTALL THE SMALL CABINET.
1. Build a small cabinet the same width and depth as

the main cabinets (Steps D and E). Adjust the height of the side panels to follow the stair slope (see drawing, page 275).
2. Cut a ¼" plywood back panel (L), so the top edge is sloped at the same angle as the stairs.
3. Attach the back panel to the cabinet with 1" wire nails.
4. Position the small cabinet so the taller side panel is flush against the main cabinet. Align the face of the small cabinet with the face of the main cabinet. Check the cabinet with a level, shimming under it if necessary.
5. Connect the cabinets by drilling pilot holes, and driving 1¼" screws through the side panels.
6. If the corner near the bottom of the steps is open, attach nailing strips to the understairs cover and cabinet side panel. Then cut a ½" plywood panel to fit the space, and attach it to the nailing strips with 1" utility screws.

Step J: INSTALL BOTTOM, DIAGONAL & COUNTERTOP RAILS.
1. Measure and cut 1 x 3 bottom rails (AA, BB) for the cabinets, then cut a long, diagonal rail (N) to fit

G. *Attach the cleats for the connecting shelf with 1¼" screws driven through pilot holes.*

H. *Install the countertop panel with 1½" finish nails driven through the countertop, into the cabinet sides.*

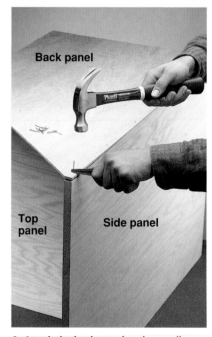

Back panel

Top panel

Side panel

I. *Attach the back panel to the smaller cabinet with 1" wire nails.*

along the edge of the understairs cover. Miter the ends of the diagonal rail to fit against the floor and the side wall, and miter the longer bottom rail to form a clean joint with the diagonal rail.

2. Test-fit the rails, then attach them with glue and 2" finish nails driven through pilot holes.

3. Measure and cut the countertop face rail (Z) to length. Miter the end of the countertop rail that joins the long, diagonal rail.

4. Attach the countertop rail flush with the counter-top surface, using glue and 2" finish nails driven through pilot holes.

Step K: INSTALL THE FACE FRAME & FINISH THE PROJECT.
1. Cut the face frame stiles (O, W) to length for the front edges of the cabinets. Attach the stiles, flush with the edges of the cabinet sides, using glue and 2" nails driven through pilot holes.

2. Measure and cut 1 × 2 rails (X, Y) to fit between the stiles so they cover the cabinet shelf edges and are flush with the shelf tops. Attach the rails, using glue and 2" finish nails driven through pilot holes.

3. Cut base-shoe trim molding to cover gaps along

wall and floor surfaces, mitering the corners. Attach the molding, using 1" finish nails.

4. Fill any screw heads with wood putty and sand the understairs center smooth. Then apply the finish of your choice.

Step L: BUILD & INSTALL DOORS AND DRAWERS.
1. Attach slide tracks, if you're using side-mounted drawer slides, according to the manufacturer's directions.

2. Build, finish, and install overlay drawers (page 31) and drawer hardware.

3. Purchase or build and finish cabinet doors (page 40). Hang the doors using ⅜" semi-concealed hinges.

J. *Attach the countertop rail with 2" finish nails driven through pilot holes.*

K. *Measure and cut the stiles to size. Attach them with 2" finish nails, making sure the ends are flush with the bottom and countertop rails.*

L. *Hang the doors with ⅜" semi-concealed hinges. See page 40 for more information.*

Recessed Kneewall Shelves

A kneewall is a short wall that meets the slope of the roofline in an upstairs room. By cutting a hole in a kneewall and installing a recessed cabinet, you can turn the wasted space behind it into a useful storage area.

Because the cabinet frame of a kneewall cabinet is not visible, it can be built using ordinary plywood and simple butt joints. The face frame and drawer faces, however, should be built with hardwood, and finished carefully. Before beginning work, check the spacing of studs and the location of electrical or plumbing lines behind your kneewall. Your kneewall may have a removable access panel, which makes it easy to check behind the wall.

This project fits in a space that is 30" wide—the standard width of two adjacent stud cavities with a center stud removed. You can adjust the width of the cabinet to fit your wall stud spacing, but regardless of size, be sure to leave a few inches of space between the back of the cabinet and the rafters.

Put wasted kneewall space to use with a simple shelving unit built directly into the wall.

TOOLS & MATERIALS

- Level
- Circular saw
- Jig saw
- Flat pry bar
- Reciprocating saw
- Drill
- Tape measure
- Bar clamps
- Hammer
- Nail set
- (1) ¾" × 4 × 8 ft. oak plywood
- (1) ¼" × 4 × 4 ft. oak plywood
- (1) 2 × 4" × 8 ft. pine
- (1) 1 × 2" × 6 ft. oak
- (1) 1 × 4" × 6 ft. oak
- Utility screws (2", 3")
- Wire nails
- Finish nails (1½", 3")
- Wood glue
- Finishing materials

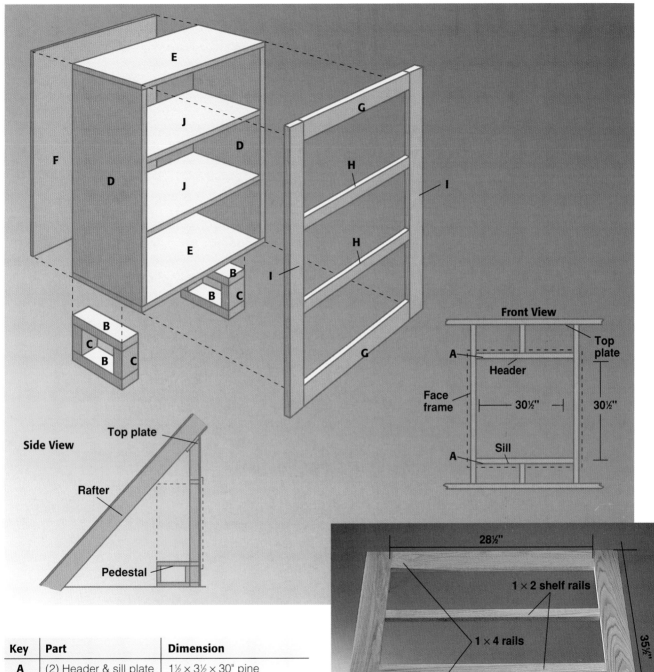

Side View

Top plate

Rafter

Pedestal

Front View

A

Header

Face frame

A

Sill

Top plate

30½"

30½"

Key	Part	Dimension
A	(2) Header & sill plate	1½ × 3½ × 30" pine
B	(4) Pedestal rail	1½ × 3½ × 15*" pine
C	(4) Pedestal stile	1½ × 3½ × 11*" pine
D	(2) Side	¾ × 28½ × 19" oak plywood
E	(2) Top and bottom	¾ × 30 × 19" oak plywood
F	(1) Back panel	¼ × 30 × 30" oak plywood
G	(2) Face rail	¾ × 3½ × 28½" oak
H	(2) Shelf rail	¾ × 1½ × 28½" oak
I	(2) Face stile	¾ × 3½ × 35½" oak
J	(2) Shelf	¾ × 19 × 28½" oak

*Cut to fit

28½"

1 × 2 shelf rails

1 × 4 rails

8½ × 28½" opening

35½"

1 × 4 stiles

Build the outer face frame with 1 × 4 hardwood. The outer frame will cover the rough edges of the wall opening. The shelf rails are made from 1 × 2 hardwood.

Directions: Recessed Kneewall Shelves

Step A: FRAME THE ROUGH OPENING.

1. Locate the wall studs where the cabinet will be installed, and mark the cutout line on the wall using a level as a guide. The sides of the cutout should follow the edges of the wall studs and the bottom should be at least 3" above the baseboard. The cutout should also be 3¼" taller than the overall height of the cabinet to allow space for framing.

2. Remove the wall material using a circular saw. Finish each corner cut with a jig saw. Cut away the center stud at the top and bottom of the opening, using a reciprocating saw.

3. Measure and cut a 2 × 4 header and sill plate (A) to fit snugly between the side studs. Position each plate in the opening and check them for level, shimming under them if necessary. Attach the header and sill plate to the surrounding studs, using 3" utility screws.

Step B: MAKE & INSTALL THE PEDESTALS.

1. Measure the distance behind the opening from the floor to the top of the sill, and build two 2 × 4 pedestals to this height with glue and 3" screws.

2. Set the pedestals on the floor inside the wall opening, even with the sides of the framed opening. Check to make sure the pedestals are level, shimming under them if necessary. Attach the pedestals to the floor, using 3" screws.

Step C: BUILD THE CABINET FRAME.

All cuts should be carefully marked and cut using a circular saw with a straightedge guide.

1. Measure the width and height of the rough opening and cut the sides (D) 2" shorter than the height. Cut the top and bottom (E) ½" narrower than the width of the rough opening. Then cut the shelves (J) 1½" narrower than the opening width.

2. Clamp and glue the shelves and the top and bottom panels to the side panels, reinforcing each joint with 2" utility screws.

A. *Position a 2 × 4 header and sill in the opening and check for level, shimming if necessary. Attach the header and sill to the surrounding studs, using 3" screws.*

B. *Set the pedestals inside the wall opening, even with the sides of the framed opening. Make sure they are level, and attach them to the floor.*

C. *Clamp and glue the top and bottom panels to the side panels, then reinforce the joints with 2" screws.*

3. Measure and cut a ¼" plywood panel to cover the back of the cabinet.

4. Attach the back panel with wire nails driven through the back and into the cabinet panels. To allow for expansion and contraction of the wood, do not use glue on this joint.

Step D: BUILD & INSTALL THE FACE FRAME.

1. Measure the width and height of the inside edges of the cabinet.

2. Cut the rails (H, G) and stiles (I) to size. The stiles should equal the height measured plus 7", and the rails should equal the width measured.

3. Clamp and glue the face frame together, and toe-nail each joint with 3" finish nails driven into pilot holes, through the rails and into the stiles.

4. Apply glue to the edges of the cabinet and position the face frame over the cabinet so the inside edges of the frame are flush with the cabinet edges.

5. Attach the face frame by drilling pilot holes and driving 1½" finish nails into the cabinet every 8". Use a nail set to countersink the nail heads.

Step E: INSTALL THE CABINET.

1. Slide the cabinet into the opening so it rests on the pedestals and so the face frame is flush against the wall.

2. Anchor the cabinet by drilling pilot holes and driving 3" finish nails through the face frame and into the wall framing members.

3. Sand and finish the cabinet frame and shelves.

D. *Glue the frame in place and attach it by drilling pilot holes and driving 1½" finish nails into the cabinet every 8". Use a nail set to countersink the nail heads.*

E. *Anchor the cabinet by drilling pilot holes and driving 3" finish nails through the face frame and into the wall framing members.*

Resources

Materials Contributer

California Closets
For a complimentary in-home consultation call 800.274.6754 or visit
www.calclosets.com

The Company Store
800-323-8000
www.the companystore.com

The Container Store
888-CONTAIN (888-266-8246)
www.thecontainerstore.com

elfa ® International (manufacturing)
elfa ® North America (distribution)
800-384-3532
www.elfa.com

**Gladiator GarageWorks/
Whirlpool Corporation**
866-342-4089
www.gladiatorgw.com

IKEA Home Furnishings
610-834-0180
www.ikea-usa.com

Jewelsleeve
800-863-3312
www.jewelsleeve.com

Kraftmaid Cabinetry, Inc.
800-571-1990
www.kraftmaid.com

Mill's Pride
800-274-6754
Mill's Pride cabinets are available exclusively at Home Depot
www.millspride.com

The Museum of Useful Things (The MUT)
800-515-2707
www.themut.com

ORG. by Windquest Companies
616-399-3311
www.windquestco.com

Plain and Fancy Custom Cabinetry
800-447-9006
www.plainfancycabinets.com

Rubbermaid
888-895-2110
www.rubbermaid.com

SieMatic
888-316-2665
www.siematic.com

Stacks and Stacks
866-376-6856
www.stacksandstacks.com

storeWALL
414-224-0878
www.storewall.com

Photography Contributers

key t=top, b=bottom, l=left, r=right.

pp. 4-5: © 2005 California Closet Co., Inc. All Rights Reserved.

pp 44-45: Photo Courtesy of Gladiator Garageworks/Whirlpool Corporation.

p. 46: (t) Photo courtesy of IKEA.

p. 47: (t) Photo courtesy of Rubbermaid; (bl) photo courtesy of Stacks and Stacks; (br) photo courtesy of Plain and Fancy Custom Cabinetry.

p. 48: (t) Photo courtesy of Rubbermaid; (bl, br) © 2005 California Closet Co. Inc. All Rights Reserved.

p. 49: (t) Photo courtesy of ORG by Windquest Co.; (b) © Jessie Walker.

p. 90-91: © Tony Giammarino/Giammarino & Dworkin.

p. 92: (t) Andrea Rugg for Locus Architecture; (b) Alamy/Elizabeth Whitting and Associates.

p. 93: (tl) © Brian Vanden Brink for Scholtz and Barclay Architects; (tr) © The Interior Archive/Andrew Wood; (b) Photo courtesy of Room and Board.

p. 94: Photo courtesy of The Container Store.

p. 95: (t) © Alamy/Elizabeth Whitting and Associates; (bl) Photo courtesy of The Container Store; (br) Photo courtesy of the Museum of Useful Things.

p. 134: © Alamy/Elizabeth Whitting and Associates.

p. 135: (top left) Photo courtesy of Plain and Fancy Custom Cabinetry; (tr) Alamy/Alberto Piovano; (b) Photo courtesy of The SieMatic Corporation.

p. 136: (tl, b) Photos courtesy of Plain and Fancy Custom Cabinetry; (tr) Photo courtesy of Mill's Pride.

p. 137: (t, br) © 2005 California Closet Co., Inc. All Rights Reserved; (bl) © Alamy/Jefferson Smith.

pp. 164-165: The Interior Archive/Tim Beddow.

p. 168: (t) Photo courtesy of IKEA; (b) Photo courtesy of jewelsleeve.

p. 169: (t) Photo courtesy of elfa® North America; (b) Photo courtesy of IKEA.

p. 170: (t) Photo courtesy of elfa® North America; (b) Photo courtesy of The Company Store.

p. 171: (t, br) Photos courtesy of Stacks and Stacks; (bl) Photo courtesy of Loft it/Tivan Inc.

p. 196-197: Photo courtesy of IKEA.

p. 198: (t) Photo courtesy of elfa® North America; (b) Photo courtesy of IKEA.

p. 199: (t) Photo courtesy of IKEA; (b) © Brian Vanden Brink.

p. 200 (t) Photo courtesy of The Company Store, (bl, br) Photos courtesy of Stacks and Stacks.

p. 201: (all) Photos courtey of Stacks and Stacks.

pp. 222-223: © Andrea Rugg for Newland Architecture.

p. 224: (t) Photo courtesy of KraftMaid Cabinetry, Inc.; (b) Photo courtesy of IKEA.

p. 225: (t) Photo courtesy of The SieMatic Corporation; (b) Photo courtesy of Room and Board.

p. 226: © Alamy/Beateworks, Inc.

p. 227: (t) © 2005 California Closet Co. Inc. All Rights Reserved; (bl) Photo courtesy of IKEA; (br) Photo courtesy of storeWALL.

pp. 250-251: © Andrea Rugg for Tea 2 Architects.

p. 252: (tl) © Alamy/Elizabeth Whitting and Associates.; (tr) © The Interior Archive/Tim Beddow; (b) © Brian Vanden Brink for Bootabay Homebuilders.

p. 253: (t)The Interior Archive/Fritz Von Der Schulenburg; (b) © Alamy/Beateworks, Inc.

p. 254: (tl) © Davidduncanlivingston.com; (tr) © Alamy/Elizabeth Whitting and Associates; (b) The Interior Archive

p. 255; (t) © Karen Melvin for Sylvestre Construction; (b) © Alamy/Elizabeth Whitting and Associates.

INDEX

Also from

CREATIVE PUBLISHING INTERNATIONAL

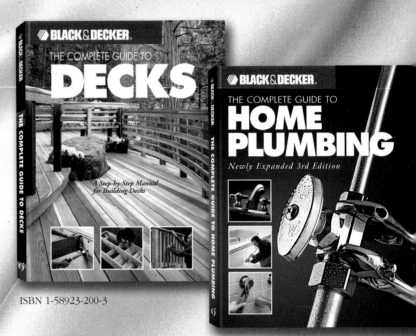

ISBN 1-58923-200-3

ISBN 1-58923-201-1

ISBN 1-58923-045-0

ISBN 0-86573-577-8

CREATIVE PUBLISHING INTERNATIONAL

18705 LAKE DRIVE EAST
CHANHASSEN, MN 55317

WWW.CREATIVEPUB.COM